About the Author

Richard P. Trenbeth entered the membership field just as it started to take its modern form, accomplishing a few "world's firsts" on the way.

He is the fund-raising and marketing executive who created the first truly professional museum development department in the world. It was at The Art Institute of Chicago. During the 15 years he directed the Institute's fund-raising and membership programs, Mr. Trenbeth pioneered in direct marketing techniques that enabled the Institute to develop the largest membership of any art museum in the world. Fed by that membership, a highly successful annual giving program was established, and capital gifts, bequests and the endowment reached new highs. This made possible tremendous development of the Institute's collections, programs and physical plant.

From the Institute, Mr. Trenbeth moved into computer-letter marketing as vice president of a commercial firm. He also expanded his consulting practice. Then he returned to nonprofit work as director of development for the Chicago Symphony Orchestra, where he established the highly successful and innovative Chicago Symphony Society. Five years later, he became a full-time consultant in membership, fund raising and mail marketing, now based in Aptos, California.

Mr. Trenbeth helped found the Chicago Chapter of the National Society of Fund-Raising Executives and served as its president. He helped found the Chicago Association of Direct Marketing and also was president of that group. His development career began at his alma mater, Northwestern University. He is a member of Phi Beta Kappa and has received many professional and civic honors.

The MEMBERSHIP MYSTIQUE

By RICHARD P. TRENBETH

HOW TO CREATE **INCOME** AND **INFLUENCE** WITH **MEMBERSHIP PROGRAMS**

FUND-RAISING INSTITUTE

For Joan

Library of Congress Catalog Card Number: 85-70785

ISBN 0-930807-01-4

CONTENTS

Foreword

"I wouldn't belong to any club that would have me as a member."
— GROUCHO MARX

Groucho Marx's touchingly wry view of membership apparently is not shared by many Americans. We are a nation of joiners. With more than 800,000 known voluntary organizations and probably several hundred thousand more branches and less formal groups, we have a wide variety of choices of affiliations. It's highly likely that about 100 million Americans belong to at least one organization; some true "joiners" may belong to 10 or more.

By almost any measure, the number of memberships in the United States undoubtedly exceeds the population of the country.

Yet even with this almost universal desire to belong to something and despite the availability of so many organizations to belong to, there is good reason to believe that many opportunities for membership have been inadequately marketed. Many existing membership groups fall short of their potential, because they have never made their services known to countless people whose needs and interests could be met through joining. And far too many organizations promoting desirable causes and objectives somehow have failed to spot an opportunity. They have failed to perceive how the creation of a membership group within the organization would enlist the support and raise the money they need to accomplish their objectives — bringing satisfaction to the joiner and power and profit to the organization itself.

I should mention that this book is a kind of confession of a born-again membership freak. In my school days I belonged to every organization in sight. Then I totally lost the faith when I became a university development officer and started to view required alumni-association dues as one of the worst deterrents to more generous, habitual giving. It was only after I entered the museum field and inherited a large, but static and underused, membership group that I began to see the light. I began to perceive the incredible potential of a large and enthusiastic membership. Just about any type of organization can benefit from a sound membership program, if that program is correctly understood by the group's management and governing board. For some organizations with wide appeal and a willingness to invest in adequate promotion, membership can revolutionize the group's effectiveness and impact.

Much of what needs to be done to achieve an effective membership program is just plain common sense. Yet because of apathy and by clinging to old customs, many very fine and otherwise enlightened organizations continue to lose substantial potential income and influence through neglect of their membership groups. In the fund-raising field, with potential capital gifts and all of the possibilities of bequests and other forms of planned giving, an intelligently promoted and cultivated membership is often the greatest asset an organization can have.

In this book, I'll use many examples from museums and other cultural organizations; let me explain why. These groups not only pioneered in membership programs and promotion but also continue to be among the most innovative and professional users of the membership mystique. What they have been doing so well can be adapted to the needs of many other types of organizations: education, health, welfare, hospitals, civic improvement, professional advancement, recreation, etc. Most of the strongest new membership organizations in a wide variety of fields have patterned their programs after those of museums or after such pioneers as the National Geographic Society. The only mystery is why so many have waited so long.

I plead guilty to having spent much of my professional life working with institutions in the Chicago area and especially with cultural organizations. There are few better examples to follow anywhere. Among the earliest and strongest "minimum-gift" clubs are The John Evans Club of Northwestern University and the Anchor-Cross Society at Rush-Presbyterian-St. Lukes Medical Center. The Chicago Symphony Society is probably the first organization of its type ever established by a major symphony orchestra.

Most of the text and examples you II read here offer practical, step-by-step guides you can follow in planning your own membership program. But the early chapters of this book also present some history and rationale. These will help you think through your own objectives, plan ways to accomplish them, and probably most important of all, devise tactics to use in selling your board on taking the necessary steps toward a more successful membership program.

This is a book that teaches by example and experience. It shows executives of nonprofit organizations, professional and trade associations, and just about every group formed to provide a service, how they can apply certain principles of self-study, planning, and marketing to grow in income and influence. The emphasis in these pages is on the marketing aspects of membership for fund-raising purposes. But most of the principles have been applied successfully for the promotion of membership in many other types of organizations throughout the world.

This may well be the only book that views membership as a ''commodity'' — one that's richly deserving of the same investment of time and money that normally goes into the marketing of goods and services in ordinary commerce. In terms of human satisfaction and accomplishment of high aims for the common good, membership could well be the most important single commodity in America. For those whose vocations or avocations are based on a desire to experience for themselves, and to share with others, a life that's rich in fulfillment, this book will be a helpful guide.

I gratefully acknowledge the assistance of many talented writers, graphic designers and printing craftsmen, list and mailing service executives, membership directors and their dedicated staffs who produce the best membership programs in the world. Special thanks are expressed to Louise Biga, Samuel E. Brown, Earle Ludgin, Craig Peterson, Park Phipps, and to my wife, Joan Harrington-Trenbeth, as well as to William F. Balthaser and his colleagues at the Fund-Raising Institute.

In addition, I want to recognize the thoughtful and valuable contributions of the following individuals: Peg Allen; Shell Alpert; Julie Anderies; Harold H. Anderson; Francis S. Andrews; Virgil

Angerman; Hank Armstrong; Janet Bates; Mrs. Gordon Bellis; Richard Benson; Clive Bishop; Sharon Black; William McCormick Blair; Mrs. Tiffany Blake; Mary and Leigh Block; Robert Blum; Joanne Boehm; Neil Boyle; Paul Bringe; Edgar T. Britton; Ed Burnett; Albert Carriere; Ann A. Carroll; Pamela Carson; Mrs. Norman Chandler; C. Vandy Christie; Kate Coakley; George Collins; Pamela Crowley-Evans; Steven J. Dahllof; Mikell C. Darling; Jeanne Davidson; P.J. Day; Glenn Ekey; Warren Friedman; Fern M. Gardner; Richard J. Gaven; J. Jay Gerber; Milt Gershman; Thomas A. Gonser; Mary Gonyo; Jacquelyn L. Goss; Kenneth M. Greene; Norman Groh; John Groman; John W. B. Hadley; Mel Hart; Jacqueline Hayhurst; Dick Hodgson; Natalie P. Holmes; Joyce Idema; Lou Iglarsh; Wendy Katz; Anne S. Keating; Nora Kelly; Jim Kobs; Lionel Kramer; Scott Leurquin; Karen Lloyd-Amos; Jayne E. Marsh; Ed Mayer; P.J. McCarthy; David T. McCleary; Bruce McConnach; Alice Medina; Harry K. Meech; Ann E. Monnig; Dorothy Mosiman; David Narsavage; Robert E. Nelson; Nels Pierson; Fred Piet; Cletis Pride; Allin Proudfoot; Jo Rathje; Alan Reitman; Daniel Catton Rich; L. Scott Schultz; Courtney C. Schummer; Renee M. Simi; Betsy Skewes-Cox; Richard Slottow; Rod Smith; Glenn M. Solfest; Linda Starks; Elmer T. Stevens; Laura Stroup; David S. Stumph; Terry Sullivan; Peter Tagger; Larry TerMolen; Russell C. Tornabene; Charlotte Voigts; Chip Weigand; Sheila Wertz; Raymond E. Willemain; Florence R. Wolf; and Leo R. Yochim.

Also, AAA-Chicago Motor Club; The David Adler Cultural Center; American Association of Retired Persons; American Association of University Women; American Civil Liberties Union; American Society of Association Executives; The Art Institute of Chicago; The Breeden Company; Ceilings and Interior Systems Contractors Association; Chicago Symphony Orchestra; Cincinnati Zoo; The Cousteau Society; David Dawson Company; Defenders of Wildlife; Direct Marketing Association; Alan Drey Company, Inc.; Epsilon Data Management, Inc.; Evanston Historical Society; Flying Physicians Association, Inc.; Friends of the Zoo (Audubon Park, New Orleans); Friends of the Kennedy Center; Glenview (Ill.) Public Library reference staff; Group West, Inc.; Hoke Communications, Inc.; KCFR Radio; Lincoln Park Zoological Society; Monterey Bay Aquarium; The Museum Society of San Francisco; Mystic Seaport Museum; National

Association of Quality Assurance Professionals; National Carvers Museum; National Geographic Society; National Ice Cream Manufacturers Association; National Outdoor Sports Advertising Inc.; National Republican Senatorial Committee; National Restaurant Association; National Rifle Association; Newberry Library; Northwestern University; The Sierra Club; Society of Professional Journalists; Sons In Retirement; Stockton/West/Burkhart, Inc.; Transo Envelope Company; United Chapters of Phi Beta Kappa; U.S. Tennis Court and Track Builders Association; The Wilderness Society; WKAR Radio; ZIP magazine; Zoological Society of Philadelphia; and Zoological Society of San Diego.

Richard P. Trenbeth

member, n. One of the persons composing a society, community, or party.

membership, n. 1. State or status of being a member. 2. The collective body of members, as of a society.

— WEBSTER'S DICTIONARY

THE NATURE OF MEMBERSHIP

By broad definition, each of us is a member of something, just through the simple act of existing.

In fact, we may also belong to a bewildering array of voluntary organizations concerned with our personal interest and well-being, our business or profession, our families, our community, and our aspirations.

1

Just as insurance has been described as a means of spreading the risk, voluntary organizations attract members as a means of spreading *opportunities.* They provide realistic channels through which we can accomplish goals that appeal to us. Things we might not experience or achieve alone as individuals are often available to us as members of voluntary organizations.

What true membership involves. For most organizations, the definition of what membership means is fairly clear. If you're a member of the Boy Scouts, for example, you're a Boy Scout, and that's about all there is to it. But in many gift-supported institutions, membership is often mixed and even confused with annual giving; donors of various amounts are awarded appropriate levels of ''membership,'' usually without distinctive benefits and privileges. This may be a mistake.

As we'll stress throughout this book, it's the *granting* of specific *benefits* and *privileges* that distinguishes membership (as a fund-raising technique) from other forms of financial support and involvement.

In this sense, true membership is defined as a relationship between an institution and a member — a relationship in which the emphasis is on providing attractive benefits and privileges to the *member* in exchange for the payment of dues to the institution, an expression of interest in its work or an implied intent to help in that work. (Even when there is no payment of dues — as in the case of honorary memberships — the benefits and privileges are granted in recognition of interest and intent.)

WHY JOIN?

Social scientists tell us that voluntary organizations have three major functions.

- They prevent a concentration and centralization of power.
- They help individuals in understanding how political processes work.
- They are mechanisms for social change.

Beyond these broad functions are many less obvious ones that may even be more important to the individual members.

- Voluntary organizations educate. They offer members countless opportunities to learn more about the cause. And through collective strength, voluntary organizations spread knowledge far beyond the membership itself. Many of the laws that affect our lives are better because of the educational influence of voluntary organizations.

- They provide relief from loneliness. In our complex society, successful organizations offer many occasions for members to meet and mingle with other people very much like themselves. Loneliness is one of the least recognized of the problems affecting mental health, but it's especially acute among older people, many of whom have the time and money to join groups and attend functions.

- They elevate status and create a sense of self-worth. To many people, membership in certain organizations reassures them and their friends that they've achieved a level of social success. Nowhere is this more apparent than in being elected to the board of trustees of a prestigious organization, in receiving recognition as an honorary life member, or even in achieving membership in the minimum gift club of one's own university or other admirable institution.

In some cases, once we have joined an organization, we don't really have to belong any more. It's being *able* to join that's important.

The proliferation of voluntary organizations is a fairly recent phenomenon. Before the Industrial Revolution, most of our needs for human fellowship, personal security, and understanding the world in which we live were satisfied by the community, the church, and the family. As the Industrial Revolution brought sweeping changes to society, these traditional influences were weakened, creating the need for more complex organizations.

It was in America, the young nation with a government barely able to sustain itself, that the voluntary movement flourished. Early in the 19th century a young Frenchman, Alexis de Tocqueville, toured America. Everywhere he went, he marveled at the people's imagination and initiative in forming associations "to give entertainments, to found establishments for education, to send missionaries to the antipodes." Then he added: "Wherever at the head of some new undertaking you see the government of France or a man of rank in England, in the United States you will be sure to find an association."

TYPES OF VOLUNTARY ORGANIZATIONS

Probably the most comprehensive national surveys of voluntary association membership were conducted some years ago by the American Institute of Public Opinion and the National Opinion Research Center. They were later analyzed in detail by Murray Hausknecht in his book "The Joiners." These surveys provide a wealth of information about membership tendencies and potential markets. The National Opinion Research Center also breaks associations into a series of logical categories.

- Veterans, military, patriotic (and auxiliaries)
- Organizations relating to health (except sick-benefit associations)
- Civic or service (other than health)
- Political or pressure groups
- Lodges, fraternal, secret societies, mutual sick benefit associations (and auxiliaries)
- Church, religious
- Economic, occupational, professional (other than health or labor unions)
- Cultural, educational, college alumni (other than health)
- Social, sports, recreational (except specifically church connected)

Under each category, of course, could be listed thousands of different organizations. But there may be some that do not fall comfortably into any of these broad categories. Where, for example, would certain types of honor societies and fan clubs fit? Many types of welfare organizations, not related to health, perhaps deserve a more specific category than the traditional Civic or Service.

A much more detailed categorization of associations may be found in the "Encyclopedia of Associations" published by Gale Research Company, which lists detailed information on more than 15,400 associations of every type under the following categories.

- Agricultural organizations and commodity exchanges
- Athletic and sports organizations

- Chambers of commerce
- Cultural organizations
- Educational organizations
- Fraternal, foreign interest, nationality and ethnic organizations
- Greek letter and related organizations
- Health and medical organizations
- Hobby and avocational organizations
- Labor unions, associations and federations
- Legal, governmental, public administration, and military organizations
- Public affairs organizations
- Religious organizations
- Scientific, engineering and technical organizations
- Social welfare organizations
- Trade, business, and commercial organizations
- Veteran, hereditary, and patriotic organizations

Among the many pertinent observations in his two-volume "Democracy in America," Alexis de Tocqueville constantly emphasizes the role of democratic ideals in the growth of associations in America. "In aristocratic societies," he writes, "men do not need to combine to act, because they are strongly held together."

Associations, he asserts, epitomize the hopes and goals of democracy. "The principle of equality suggests to Americans the idea of the indefinite perfectibility of man. . . . Amongst the laws which rule human societies there is one which seems to be more precise and clear than all others. If men are to remain civilized, or to become so, the art of associating together must grow and improve, in the same ratio in which equality of conditions is increased."

Whether leading to "indefinite perfectibility" or not, associations are formed by people with *needs* — needs ranging from those of small boys with a club in a tree house to the most learned scientists and professionals banding together to read scholarly papers. And there are strong clues that help pinpoint the persons who will be most apt to accept an invitation to join.

2

High educational level. In the American Institute study, 39 percent of the least educated were members of associations, whereas among college graduates 78 percent were affiliated. The National Opinion Research Center survey indicated 17 percent of the least educated as members, as compared to 61 percent of the college educated. A logical corollary of these findings is that joiners also tend to have a high readership level, regularly reading newspapers, magazines, and books.

So for people who "sell" memberships, some of the most productive mailing lists tend to be those of subscribers to magazines related directly to the purpose of the association or charitable cause. Subscriber lists of magazines suggesting a high level of intellectual curiosity also work well. In the cultural field, subscribers to program guides for fine-arts FM stations and public television often produce the best results.

Income level.   As income increases, so does the rate of membership, though not quite as much as with education.

Where they live.   Although large urban communities provide the most fertile markets for memberships, the largest percentage of population involved in membership is in smaller towns and villages. Why? A large city offers many opportunities for leisure time activities that do not require membership.

Moreover, in large communities people tend to live close to others similar to themselves and can satisfy their social needs that way. But in smaller communities an association often offers the only means of satisfying these same social needs. In addition, there is reason to believe that the person living in a small town may gain a sense of personal power and effectiveness by belonging to an association — especially one that is likely to accomplish measurable good and at the same time add to his or her personal status. Income level in smaller cities and farm communities apparently has less effect on the tendency to join associations than it does in large cities.

Type of occupation.   In the past, there was a wide gap in income between blue-collar and white-collar jobs. And back then, income level seemed to explain the predominance of white collar workers as members of associations and charitable causes. Now blue-collar incomes are often higher than many white-collar incomes. But the same predominance exists, indicating that income is not as important as job and class *position* when it comes to being willing to join.

Sex.   Early studies indicated little difference between males and females in the tendency to join. But today, women may now have a slight edge — especially with some professional and civic associations. Women may feel that they gain opportunities through membership. These opportunities undoubtedly include chances for a better job through visibility within an association. More women than men now attend the national conferences of some professional and trade associations.

Age.   Membership in many associations is a symbol of "having arrived." This factor partially explains why the highest percentage of members tends to fall in the age groups between 35 and

55 years. Within this spread, under the age of 40 more men than women tend to belong; over 40 the women predominate. Women who are mothers tend to have more free time for associations after the children are in school or have left home. Men over 40, on the other hand, may prefer to concentrate on their work and narrow their association involvement to a selected few.

Marital status. With marriage and family responsibilities, comes an increase in association membership, especially in organizations dealing with community affairs and the interests of children. People who are widowed and those with broken marriages seem to continue these memberships. However, some astute organizations have been known to market programs that appeal to singles, especially programs with social events that provide opportunities for meeting others with similar interests.

Home ownership. Years ago, a far higher percentage of home owners belonged to associations than did renters. Because this difference seemed the same at all income levels, it was inferred that home ownership brings with it a sense of reponsibility — and an inclination to "join." Direct-mail fund raisers maintain that single-family units are still their most productive markets. But the situation is changing. Condominium conversion in large cities has substantially reduced the number of available apartment rental units, except among the lower income levels. So, many of today's "home owners" are actually "apartment owners." No one has attempted to compare the "joining" tendencies of people who live in single-family units with those of people who live in multiple-family units. But based on educational and income criteria, it seems likely that many apartment and condominium dwellers may be excellent candidates for your invitation to join.

Religion. Studies indicate that more Protestants belong to voluntary organizations than do Catholics — at the rate of 58 percent to 49 percent in one survey, and 37 to 31 percent in another. In one survey, 52 percent of the Jews are members of associations — higher than the Catholics but lower than the Protestants. In the other survey, 55 percent of the Jews belong — a rate higher than those of the other two groups.

It appears that the lower Catholic figures are caused by socio-economic and religious influences. Some regional and local studies, especially in Chicago and Memphis, indicate substantially higher membership participation among Jews than among either Protestants and Catholics. In the cultural field, a very high percentage of Jews tend to join — especially avant-garde museum and musical groups.

A PROFILE

Most of the key factors just recited, of course, apply best to very general types of associations that almost everyone is eligible to join. As the requirements for membership become more narrow and specific — as in the case of many professional associations, for example — these tendencies may not apply at all. Your member may have a completely different profile. And you must know what that profile is. Knowing allows you to concentrate on your most promising markets.

One national religious foundation has profiled its typical member as: "a woman 45 or over. She's married and lives in community of 50,000 or less. Her children are grown." That doesn't mean that foundation won't make it easy for many other types to belong, but it does define the market on which most of the foundation's prospecting efforts will be spent.

Of course profiling is never a precise business. If it were, we could all concentrate on our best prospects and hammer away at them until they join. It's one of the delights of the membership business that surprising pockets of "unlikelies" continue to turn up — stimulating us to find out why, what attracted them, and where more of the same can be found. Be aware that profiles tend to keep changing.

Once, as I was studying a strong membership organization, I asked a member of its board of trustees why, in his opinion, so many people had joined. "Why," he replied, "it's the thing to do."

His reply brought a smile at first, but as I thought about what he had said, his seemingly naive remark made good sense. For him, and for many like him, it *was* the thing to do, a kind of traditional obligation of his family — an obligation with strong intimations of status. And because membership did confer a kind of status, it was sought after by many primarily for that reason.

3

But his comment ignored many reasons why the organization's membership was so large and so effective. Unlike many voluntary membership organizations, this one recognized early on that once it had enrolled those who felt an obligation to join, there were still many potential less-obliged markets with other needs. And these needs could also be met effectively by this particular agency. The organization had then moved quickly and creatively to plan membership benefits and privileges that could be offered conveniently at low cost. As the membership grew and the new members continued to make known their needs and desires, new benefits and privileges were added that attracted still more members.

Probably without knowing the name for it, they were practicing marketing. They were taking advantage of the most predictable and practical reasons why most people join organizations: They want something in return that satisfies a *personal need,* or at least offers *hope* of satisfaction.

The big breakthrough comes when an organization perceives that this basic human desire — and *not* the willingness to support a cause — is the key to membership success. After that, it has only to develop and test many attractive incentives to join.

The element of hope is certainly one of the strongest motivators. A successful manufacturer of cosmetics once was asked for the secret of his success. He replied that he was not selling ground earth colors and chemical creams — he was offering hope. Dangle a vision of personal gratification in front of a prospective member, and half the selling job is done.

WHAT 'MARKETING' REALLY MEANS

After years of practicing the marketing approach to membership and writing and speaking about it, I finally found this definition in Philip Kotler's excellent book "Marketing for Nonprofit Organizations."

"The organization does not resort to force to attract resources. . . . Nor does it ask for selfless giving. It relies mainly on offering and exchanging values to the different parties of sufficient incentive to elicit their cooperation. In short, it relies on exchange mechanisms rather than threat mechanisms on the one hand or love systems on the other.

"Marketing is the analysis, planning, implementation, and control of carefully formulated programs designed to bring about voluntary exchanges of values with target markets for the purpose of achieving organizational objectives. It relies heavily on designing the organization's offering in terms of the target markets' needs and desires, and on using effective pricing, communications, and distribution to inform, motivate, and service the markets."

Why do people buy anything or contribute to or join an organization? If we are going to be successful in planning our organization's offering in terms of human needs and desires, we need to know, very realistically, what makes them reach for their check books.

A CANDID LOOK AT TRUE MOTIVATIONS

Victor O. Schwab, a legendary advertising executive in the direct-response field, stresses the importance of showing people an advantage that they want to gain and relating it to the product or service offered. In his book "How to Write a Good Advertisement," Schwab conveniently summarizes the desires most people want to achieve. He says:

People want to gain: health, time, money, popularity, improved appearance, security in old age, praise from others, comfort, leisure, pride of accomplishment, business and social advancement, increased enjoyment, self-confidence, and personal prestige.

They want to be: good parents, sociable and hospitable, up-to-date, creative, proud of their possessions, influential over others, gregarious, efficient, "first" in things, and recognized as authorities.

They want to do things that: express their personalities, resist domination by others, satisfy their curiosity, emulate the admirable, appreciate beauty, acquire or collect things, win others' affection, and improve themselves generally.

They want to save: time, money, work, discomfort, worry, doubts, risks, and personal embarrassment.

Schwab concludes his list with the comment: "And if you will check back now over the motivating forces just listed, you will realize that Napoleon was not merely being cynical when he said, 'There are two motives to action: self-interest and fear.'"

Paul Bringe, another respected direct-mail expert, continually reminds his clients and newsletter readers: "But many products are not bought for practical, common sense reasons. They are often bought for reasons that are socially unacceptable — for ego satisfaction, for emotional gratification, to satisfy anxieties with material possessions — for dozens of reasons we dare not admit to ourselves.''

If you're nodding your head in agreement, you're on the right track toward planning an effective membership program.

Of course in most nonprofit organizations this approach usually brings forth disclaimers from management and boards of trustees who will claim that people act from unselfish, constructive, and spirit-elevating motivations. In response to just that sort of protest, Shell R. Alpert, a direct-marketing consultant and columnist, writes: ''When given the opportunity to discourse on this important subject, I have exhorted agencies and advertisers to 'follow the PFEEGGLS to find the feelings' that predispose prospects to buy the product or service you're selling. This odd-looking (thus, I hope, memorable) acronym stands for what I consider the real motivations that underlie most buying decisions: Pain, Fear, Envy, Ego, Greed, Guilt, Lust and Sloth!''

To which I add another ''L,'' for ''Loneliness'' — one of the strongest motivations underlying the need to belong to groups. ''Loneliness'' is closely related to Alpert's ''Fear,'' but it's a special kind of motivation that needs emphasis and clarification.

So strong a motivation is the search for relief from loneliness that some organizations have achieved early and prolonged success simply by offering attractive opportunities for companionship as the principal benefit of membership. For example, Sons In Retirement, a California group, rocketed to a membership of more than 25,000 simply through word-of-mouth offerings of monthly meetings, golf and card groups, and travel.

Why people join organizations. After years of enticing some fairly unlikely prospects into memberships in art museum groups, I found that a knowledge of basic motivations works wonders in planning membership promotions. When we understand how human needs relate to joining an organization, many of our selling tactics easily fall into place. Here are some of the reasons why people join museums, and many of them apply to most other types of membership groups as well.

- Many people have a real psychological need of "belonging" and actually welcome the opportunity to pay dues to belong. Studies indicate that this happens most frequently in early middle age — presumably after the children have left home and, incidentally, when there is usually more disposable, discretionary income. And let me point out that these same people tend to view worthy and honorable institutions with a kind of awe. It continues to amaze me how few museums and similar institutions really comprehend the prestige and power they command when they go into the marketplace — especially when they go equipped with the right kind of membership invitation offering distinctive benefits and even such simple devices as an attractive membership card, a certificate, or a publication.

- People tend to join organizations that offer them specific benefits closely related to their personal needs, real or imagined. If these privileges include opportunities for the members to associate in a social setting with those they admire, so much the better.

- Many people are genuinely lonely and welcome the opportunity to receive regular mail, even if it's just from an institution that counts them as part of its family.

- Some people join organizations in the hope of acquiring knowledge or culture that can help them solve personal problems or bring them personal prestige. The key word here is "hope."

- Some people have strong emotional attachments to institutions in which they can get to know the directing officials. One of the reasons for this is a desire to pass along their favorable and unfavorable reactions to someone they know, rather than to an abstract, impersonal institution. Skillful handling of those reactions and complaints — even unreasonable ones — can produce generous and helpful friends for your organization.

LISTEN, ANALYZE, AND PLAN

Each organization competes with many others for the public's attention, time, and money.

Yet too few organizations regularly take a good look at themselves. Many are totally without short- and long-range objectives that inspire others to action. Few are aware of their strengths and weaknesses. Probably most damaging of all, many organizations are unaware of what their members really expect in exchange for their membership affiliation.

Sydney J. Harris observes: "Institutions of all sorts are not run for the benefit of the persons they were created for; they are run for the people who run them — not necessarily for their profit, but for their pride, their prejudice, their vanity, their hunger for the trappings of privilege and power. A large part of today's social revolution on all fronts is the mounting awareness that institutions have grown frozen, have neglected their basic human function, and operate to make their leaders look good rather than to do that good for which they were originally intended."

Adjusting programs to meet challenges.   Changing times and markets often force older membership groups to alter their programs. By monitoring the needs of special interest markets, some institutions continue to tailor their programs to meet these needs and to find national and even international sources of substantial membership support. The world of membership is full of examples of imaginative listening, planning, and promotion. Here are a few of them.

- *Local alumni club of a major urban university.* By custom, the programs of the club were limited to talks by athletic coaches and pre-game football luncheons. A new group of directors reasoned that many alumni — and especially women — were interested in much more than athletic programs. By inviting professors, distinguished alumni in many fields, university academic and administrative officials, and others to speak at the regular meetings, the club greatly increased in size and attendance and made its influence felt in many departments of the university. Tours of new campus facilities and blocks of club tickets for popular, non-athletic campus events and programs attracted still more members with the greatest increase coming from women who joined.

- *Membership of a large art museum.* Among all types of nonprofit organizations, museums have pioneered in using the membership technique to attract friends and supporters. One of the early leaders in the field had achieved a large but static membership through the years by offering such standard benefits as free admission, a quarterly publication, and a small number of lectures and gallery tours.

Recognizing that an entirely new market of educated young people existed, the museum greatly enriched its educational offerings. Guest lecturers of international renown, workshops on specialized topics, and films were added to an expanded program of lectures and tours. The museum store was greatly expanded, adding to the value of the substantial discounts already given to members.

The new benefits and privileges were widely marketed through professionally planned direct mail. The membership quickly doubled. It continued to grow as new programs and privileges were added. Every aspect of membership was constantly examined. Two types of honorary life memberships were awarded to major donors who previously had been overlooked. An annual giving program, launched just as membership began to grow, soon outstripped dues income and became a major source of income.

- *New friends for a sold-out symphony orchestra.* A major symphony orchestra whose concerts were generally sold out by subscription needed a way to attract new friends. When a development professional discovered that other attractive offerings such as chamber music concerts and training orchestra concerts were poorly attended, he recommended establishing a dues-paying membership in a new society related to the symphony.

Among the benefits offered were sharply discounted admission to the chamber music and training orchestra concerts, priority rights to subscribe to new series and to buy turned-back tickets to the major concerts, special tours to events in other cities and abroad, open houses and backstage tours (usually just after working hours), open rehearsals, and a unique record premium.

In less than two years the new society achieved a membership of almost 5,000 and had a remarkable first-year renewal rate of 67 percent. Attendance at the smaller concerts more than trebled. When the new society members were invited to contribute to the symphony's annual fund, they gave almost as much again as their dues for the year. Major donors, elected to honorary life membership in the society, greatly increased their giving the following year.

- *Meeting the needs of special interest groups.* Specialized magazines have displaced general magazines in the favor of the reading public. And imaginative, small, specialized organizations now thrive by marketing their services to special interest groups. Some of the great success stories come from small museums and libraries with facilities for research in such esoteric fields as genealogy and archaeology. In a year when many larger museums were reporting declines in attendance and membership, one such American-Indian-related small museum had its biggest year ever. Why? Because it had developed unique programs and made them known to study groups and tourist councils all over the world. At least half its visitors now come from Europe.

Some of these museums have facilities for "digs" and make use of volunteers (who pay a fee for the privilege) in excavating relics and keeping records of the findings.

Another relatively small museum with initially rapid membership growth is the National Carvers Museum in Monument, Colorado. Its guiding spirit, a retired marketing executive in the public utilities field, was quick to recognize the need for a national rallying point for all who carve wood. Its outstanding magazine, "The Mallet," provides tips and designs for carving as well as news about members.

Here, a library targets the special interests that it's best prepared to serve.

CURIOUSER
AND CURIOUSER

AN INVITATION TO JOIN THE NEWBERRY LIBRARY ASSOCIATES

Are you curious about...

Your family tree? *The Newberry Library has records and documents to help you trace your ancestors.* **Music?** *We have manuscripts by Chopin, Mozart, and other great composers, thousands of printed scores, and texts on music theory and history.* **Literature?** *We have the papers and manuscripts of Sherwood Anderson, Ben Hecht, Katherine*

Mansfield...as well as the best collection by and about Herman Melville. **Graphic arts?** *We have Tenniel's drawings for* <u>Alice in Wonderland</u>, *illuminated manuscripts, a superb collection of calligraphy, and over 60,000 maps.*

American history? *We have thousands of drawings and manuscripts chronicling the history of the American Indian, the Frontier, and the Civil War.*

If you're curious about any facet of the **humanities,** *you'll find over 1.3 million books and five million manuscripts at The Newberry Library—"An Uncommon Collection of Uncommon Collections."*

The people who join the Newberry Library Associates know that not everything intriguing about the Newberry is found on the bookshelves. As an Associate, you'll be invited to special events—in the past, Associates have enjoyed lectures by Helen Hayes, John Cheever, and Malcolm Cowley...a poetry reading by Tennessee Williams...a lecture-demonstration by Maria Tallchief and a dancer from the Chicago City Ballet...and many evenings of film, music, drama, and education.

Ａs a Newberry Associate, you also get:

☐ An insider's view of the Library's collections and research projects.

☐ A ten percent discount on our adult education classes. (This year's offerings explore everything from mythology to calligraphy, from Jane Austen to Gertrude Stein.)

☐ A ten percent discount at the Library Store. (It's a great place to buy books and unique gifts.)

☐ Free copies of special Newberry publications.

☐ A free copy of the Newberry's handsome calendar, illustrated with Karl Bodmer's 19th-century drawings of American Indians.

☐ The quarterly Newberry **Newsletter** to keep you up-to-date on all Library news and Associates activities.

Most of all, by joining the Newberry Associates you help a great institution of learning and research meet its operating expenses as well as the costs of new acquisitions, Newberry Fellowships, and scholarly publications.

SATISFY YOUR CURIOSITY. ASSOCIATE YOURSELF WITH THE NEWBERRY LIBRARY.

THE NEWBERRY LIBRARY ASSOCIATES

Most membership organizations are spawned by the desire of people to join together to accomplish common goals. But there are several other types of membership organizations — and motivations — that deserve mention.

Profit is one of the strongest motivations. Imaginative business-people have discovered how much profit can result from getting people to join an attractive group that meets their needs. In most cases, timorous nonprofit organizations will find it highly productive to follow the example of profit-oriented membership groups, especially in the ways they promote and sell affiliation.

A successful publication has aided the fortunes of several membership groups, sometimes becoming the principal reason for their existence. A pioneer in this approach in the United States is the National Geographic Society, which offers its distinguished magazine as the principal benefit of membership. Revenue from the magazine, through membership dues and advertising, has produced most of the funds for the Society's expeditions and its exhibitions.

More recently, the Smithsonian Institution in Washington transformed a small local membership known as the Associates into one of the mightiest membership groups in America. It did this primarily by publishing an exceptionally attractive magazine and vigorously promoting it — along with other desirable benefits and privileges — in a sophisticated and thorough manner, making use of the talents of skilled professionals in direct response sales.

One of the best known types of associations is the automobile club, which originally grew out of a need for information and services in the early days of the automobile. As auto insurance became more important and more expensive, the early automobile clubs recognized that they could offer their members insurance brokerage services — of advantage to the members and of profit to the clubs. There are now more than 100 competitive auto clubs in the United States. The oldest and largest, the American Automobile Association, has close to 25 million

MEMBERSHIP'S POTENTIAL FOR YOUR CAUSE

4

members, nearly double the combined membership of all other auto clubs. One reason the AAA has grown strong through the years is that it listens to the needs of its members and provides innovative solutions to these needs. Services such as insurance and travel agency business have become so profitable that the association has been able to offer an increasing number of less profitable services at low cost to the members and thus attract a constantly expanding membership.

A few groups have learned the advantages of combining membership programs and fund-raising campaigns. The Easter Seal Society, with a large national campaign conducted by local chapters just before the Easter season, began to search for additional sources of income at other times in the year. They beefed up the membership programs of their local chapters, offering minimal but attractive benefits. Many chapters discovered that by waiting until six months after the Easter Seal drive, and then inviting their donors to become members and pay annual dues, they could double their income for the year.

Properly used, the membership concept can indeed become a bottomless gold mine for many nonprofit organizations — one that regenerates itself with each new generation. Consider these advantages.

Good investment. Would you consider it a profitable investment if someone were to offer you a piece of real estate — an apartment or an office building — that, during the first year, produced as much income as your purchase price and then went on producing at the same or a greater rate as long as you owned the property and kept it in good repair? This is basically what you have when you establish a sound membership program. You can go on acquiring similar blocks of property by reinvesting your first cash outlay and watching with delight as the whole investment appreciates in value with each passing year.

All membership-marketing efforts are aimed at sifting the "joiners" out from general population. And these new members are the *real* "good investments." A loyal and interested member is far more likely to consider each new proposition from your organization than will a stranger who knows nothing about you. Various benefit events and drives to support your organization will receive most of their backing from your dues-paying members. And it's important to attract this type of support, because it will include major-gift prospects. More and more, nonprofit organizations recognize that Pareto's Law operates in direct marketing and fund raising just as in other fields: 80 percent of your profits will be generated by 20 percent of your customers. In some strong membership organizations that have life members and other higher classifications of membership, the ratio may be even more sharply drawn: as high as 90 percent of dues income and annual giving from as little as 10 percent of the membership.

Stable and predictable income.   In each year's budgeting process, many groups are unable to predict accurately what the anticipated level of annual giving will be. This is especially true if the previous year's total gift income has been skewed by a few extraordinary gifts or by a local, temporary financial disaster.

Dues income is much less susceptible to such influences. The paying of dues is an ingrained habit that can be maintained at a high level when there is an aggressive and persistent renewal effort. (After a few years of experience, at The Art Institute of Chicago we were able to predict annual dues income within 5 percent, erring usually only on the low side when membership was growing rapidly. The predicted dues income provided a strong guide for budgeting our membership-prospecting investment each year. When income ran substantially ahead of the estimate, we could immediately expand our prospecting budget and produce still more income.)

Salespersons.   Whatever an organization says about itself in public is far less credible to the stranger than what is said about it by people close to it. John Osborne has called it "the blessed alchemy of word of mouth," and indeed it is. It's highly likely that more surprise major gifts from strangers result from word-of-mouth cultivation by members than from staff-initiated efforts. There is no stronger testimonial than the word of a satisfied and excited member wanting to share his or her enthusiasm with a friend. In the early days of art museum membership, it's probable that most new members were recruited by those who had already joined. Some museums still encourage this by granting each member the right to bring one or two guests free on each visit. Many of the guests are suitably impressed when their friend simply shows a membership card for the free admission — often going in through a special entrance for members and their guests.

Two-way communication. Members are often vocal critics of their favorite organizations — quick to applaud but equally quick to let the organization know when its policies and practices are offensive (and therefore potentially dangerous to the welfare of the organization). By their attendance and involvement, members let the management know when new programs are successful. By staying away or by protesting directly, members also tell the organization about programs they find less than satisfactory. Many members like to respond to questionnaires asking for their evaluations of present programs and providing space to suggest new programs and services.

Upgraded publications. One criticism sometimes leveled at nonprofit organizations is that their publications seem to be too elaborate and expensive for groups seeking gift support. When a membership — with publications offered as a benefit of joining — is established, the members take for granted that the publication will be of high quality and applaud each time the quality improves. If the *membership* is large, the economies of printing substantial quantities that are already paid for through dues allow the organization to make these upgraded publications available to others at low cost.

Multiple appeals. A member cultivated by frequent newsletters and reports is more receptive to direct and indirect multiple appeals for gifts than any other constituent. And if your organization has a genuine emergency requiring financial support, an informed group of members will be the first to rally to help.

Volunteer involvement. In organizations that could not exist without substantial volunteer help, a membership group is a ready reservoir. Some groups offer the right to volunteer as a privilege of membership. In the early days of public television, the right to appear on camera in "marathons" and other promotions was limited to members — and many joined primarily for that privilege.

Recognition.   Canny organizations always seek opportunities to give public recognition to donors. Bestowing an honorary life membership on a non-member major donor is one of the most appreciated (and least expensive) forms of recognition imaginable. If the major gift is made by both husband or wife (or if by one, and the existence of the other is known), such honorary life membership should be given to *both.* By doing that, you have involved two prospects for additional major gifts.

Rental of membership lists.   As many mail order companies have discovered, there is often more profit from the rental of customer lists than from the sale of products. In the membership field, a total membership list of 10,000 or more may be highly rentable at rates ranging from $50 to $100 or more per thousand.

Many nonprofit membership groups, unfortunately, have board policies prohibiting list rental. But some permit list exchanges — not rentals, but exchanges — with similar organizations. In prospecting for new members, such exchanges can save money (compared to rentals).

For those who question whether it is "ethical" to put a membership list on the rental market, here is a good answer. One of the most active membership lists on the rental market is that of the American Medical Association. Its more than 300,000 members are segmented by specialty and other subgroups. Each request to rent is carefully screened and is subject to rigid policies. Income from rental fees is a source of major profit to the Association.

When a membership list is maintained by computer, there is a way to overcome board members' objections to renting. That is to print out the rental list to appear quite different from the way the list looks when used by the organization in its own mailings. For example, if your organization usually prints members' names and addresses in upper and lower case with no abbreviations, the rental format can be in all capital letters and with initials and abbreviations.

Ideal market for planned giving. Perhaps the most profitable fund-raising technique is planned (sometimes called "deferred") giving — bequests and various types of trust agreements coupled with philanthropy. As colleges and universities know from experience, the best prospects for such gifts are people who have had a continuing relationship with the institution — alumni, for example. And a strong membership group can generate "alumni" for non-academic organizations. Planned gifts are usually big gifts. It's highly probable that the value of bequests from museum members through the years far exceeds the total of all membership dues and even annual giving. Virtually all endowment funds for museums and symphony orchestras come through bequests and other planned gifts, many of which have been stimulated by articles in membership and subscriber publications.

HOW TO AVOID PITFALLS

Just as there are many advantages to having a membership group, there are pitfalls to avoid in setting one up.

- Be careful of making commitments to programs that appeal only to the vocal few. Programs cost staff time and money. If they serve the needs of many members and draw strong renewals, they'll produce a generous profit. The cost of such a program is easily justified and necessary. Occasionally, however, a vocal minority will ask for programs that may appeal only to them and will cost more than they'll ever produce in gift or dues income. Evaluate all such requests; test market them before making a full commitment.

- The same caution applies to dropping a program that's lightly attended and opposed by a vocal few. Be careful. Sometimes you'll find that a program has a value far beyond mere numbers. For example, an art museum offered its members free sketch classes. They were usually attended by a core group of the same people — a small percentage of the total membership. There were a few suggestions to drop the program, but a careful investigation revealed that the free sketch classes were a major reason why many members joined. They had the best of intentions of attending — something they had always wanted to do. But they never got around to attending. However, the program had a value as a popular incentive to join — a value far beyond the numbers it actually served.

- Avoid offering benefits and privileges that may rise drastically in cost. Here's what happened to one charitable cause. The organization started a national membership group with relatively high dues but guaranteeing a minimum of three major books a year as a continuing membership benefit. The response was so great that it enabled the organization to begin a major publications program with the assurance of a large group of prepaid customers. But as the years passed, the cost of publishing and mailing the books rose until it far exceeded the value of the dues. The dues were raised several times to the point where renewals were endangered. Eventually, the number of books was reduced, and dues were brought into a marketable-but-profitable balance.

- Be sure to make clear in the minds of your members that basic membership dues primarily pay for the benefits they receive and have little to do with general financial support of your cause. Unless this is done, membership dues may provide a convenient excuse for some potentially excellent prospects to make only minimum gifts — or no gifts at all — in addition to their dues, especially when there is no established annual giving program. Even people who are recognized as leaders of an institution will often take this easy way out, unless you make it clear that dues are not the same as straight gifts.

- Clearly establish in your bylaws that voting rights are vested in a special class of "governing" members. Many organizations start out by giving every member a vote. Then when the membership gets much larger, the leadership finds that it is vulnerable to any dissident groups that want to pack an annual meeting. It's easy to prevent this possibility through foresight and the establishment of a class of governing members who must be elected by the board, usually in recognition of a substantial annual gift or life dues.

When a business sets out to sell a product, it pays close attention to the specifications of what it is offering. Once they are determined, the business then test-markets its product at various price levels. If repeat business is important, it plans methodically to go back to the markets with repeat offers.

But for some reason, many membership programs pay scant attention to such vital details, and this often seriously limits their sales potential. As we'll see in following chapters, the appeal of a membership offer is based primarily on the benefits and privileges offered. But there are some important product-specifications that can seriously affect the first sale of a membership and the all-important renewal. Let's consider these questions.

- How many classes of membership should there be?

- What should be the price of the dues for each class?

- What are the best permanent starting and renewal dates for a membership — dates consistent with the customer's convenience and ease of handling in the membership office?

- How do membership dues relate to annual giving, cumulative giving, and classes of major contributors?

If there is an almost trackless wilderness, it's the wide variety of membership classifications and levels of dues offered by different types of organizations. Sometimes these reflect some original thinking. But more often, they're just copied from others, usually with little regard for the appropriateness of such imitation. For you, as an explorer in this wilderness, here are some guideposts to help you chart your own path to success.

You can range from a single, basic membership category with fixed benefits and privileges, to a wide choice of levels and benefits. Most memberships are renewable annually, though as we shall see, many organizations should also consider the value of life and governing memberships.

Many large national membership organizations in the United States, such as the National Geographic Society and the Smithsonian Associates, concentrate on a single class of annual membership with relatively low level of dues. However, after building a very strong base of one classification, the Smithsonian began an upgrading process — suggesting a Contributing Membership category with dues that were more than four times the basic rate.

On the other hand, most art museums start life as membership organizations, usually without any other kind of annual fund raising. Probably because of this, some offer up to 13 different membership classifications. This practice results in unnecessary confusion and probably reduces profits. If you've inherited one of these unwieldy structures, you'll want to take a good look at other, more profitable options.

Basic considerations. The number of membership classifications and the appropriate levels of dues can best be determined by answering several questions.

- Is there, or will there be, a separate annual giving program?

- Are there, or will there be, classifications of major contributors, based on cumulative giving?

- Is there a broad — even national — market for membership in the organization?

If the answers to at least two of these questions are "yes," you may want to limit the number of annual classifications to not more than three or four — especially if you have one or more life or major-gift classifications. And be careful what you call the lower classifications. You're likely to run out of suitably impressive names for the highest classes of donors if you're not careful. When a broad market for your membership exists, your first sales approach should be at the basic membership level. Your goal is to sell, not confuse. After the sale, you can start talking about your higher classifications and their benefits.

The nature of your organization may help determine your membership classifications and dues. Pick out some of the leading organizations in your field, and ask to see their membership structures. You're apt to find that the most successful ones lean toward a simplicity and logic that you can apply to your own situation. Meanwhile, here are a few guidelines.

General membership organizations.   Museums, public television stations, zoos, and similar organizations in which there are substantial membership benefits, tend to have two types of basic annual membership classes: "Individual" and "Family" (with Family dues from 50 to 100 percent higher than Individual dues). Most of these groups, including those with annual giving programs, also have at least one higher annual classification — usually at around five times the cost of the Individual dues, and with special privileges.

Governing and Life members.   As described earlier, most membership organizations begin as small groups of friends. Their original bylaws often bestow voting rights on all members. But as the association grows, the right to vote can threaten the continuity of the leadership and even the basic purposes of the organization. Dissidents can take over. Foresighted groups have forestalled such threats by establishing a "Governing" membership, usually requiring election by the cause's board of trustees and almost always requiring either a substantial one-time dues payment or somewhat smaller (but still large) minimum annual dues. Voting rights for the organization are vested in these Governing members. Because they are elected, Governing members usually consider their status an honor and take their voting and contributing responsibilities seriously. Some organizations wisely bestow "Honorary Governing Life membership" on those who have contributed fairly large amounts.

The Chicago Symphony Orchestra defines its Governing memberships as shown on the next page.

Not all organizations should have Life memberships. Yet, for the right group under the right circumstances, Life memberships can attract substantial current financial support and bequests. How do you decide? For Life memberships to be effective, your organization must have:

- Strong and attractive membership benefits and privileges;

- Vigorous annual fund raising (in addition to membership dues), with published recognition of gifts at the higher levels and especially for donors to minimum gift clubs;

- A fairly sophisticated planned giving program and a policy of publicizing such gifts; and

- A core of past and present leaders whose interest is to be retained for life.

Governing Members are the voting members of The Orchestral Association and elect Trustees and Governing Members at the annual meeting of the Association. A full term for a Governing Member is five years, though to fill vacancies caused by resignation or death, some may be elected to shorter terms. A person may be elected a Governing Member for a succeessive term or terms without limit as to the number of such terms.

On the recommendation of the Nominating Committee, Governing Members are elected each year from among those friends of the Chicago Symphony Orchestra who have shown a high degree of interest in the welfare of the Symphony and support it generously. Each Governing Member is expected to contribute a minimum of $500 a year to the annual Sustaining Fund.

In addition to their legal duties as voting members of the Association, Governing Members serve a number of other important functions as active volunteers working to maintain the excellence of the Chicago Symphony and its many unique services to the community. Acting as goodwill ambassadors for the Symphony, the Governing Members

1. *encourage the public to become acquainted with the work of The Orchestral Association, to attend Symphony concerts, to inquire into the opportunities for strengthening the services of the Symphony, and to give encouragement and counsel;*

2. *engender a spirit of friendly cooperation between the Symphony and the community, including business firms and governmental agencies;*

3. *increase the influence of the Symphony in national and international music and education; and*

4. *build, through gift and bequest, an endowment and annual operating income commensurate with the present and potential role of the Symphony in a city noted for outstanding cultural achievement.*

Life memberships work well for such organizations, because they offer a bargain to those who are already interested and intend to stay interested. Once a person has become a Life member, he or she generally takes a more active part in the affairs of the organization and feels a responsibility for giving each year, usually at a substantial level. This fact is often overlooked by some observers who see the "expense" of servicing a Life member as a drain on operating funds. (After such a protest, one development officer was able to point out that year after year, annual giving from members in the Life categories accounted for at least 70 percent of total annual giving.) Most bequests and other planned gifts to institutions with strong Life memberships come from Life members, even when there is no major program to encourage planned giving.

A Governing membership may require annual dues of at least 50 times the cost of an Individual membership. When the Governing membership is for life, the one-time fee can be considerably higher, often two or three times more. Ordinary Life memberships generally are pegged at 10 to 50 times the cost of Individual dues.

How will you deal with major contributors who have neglected to enroll as members (or perhaps have never been invited to join)? Once, when The Art Institute of Chicago wound up a capital campaign, it was discovered that many who had made the largest gifts were not members and consequently were not receiving membership benefits. It took only a little persuasion to convince the board to elect every person (or couple) who had made cumulative gifts of at least 10 times the Life membership dues to a new classification of Honorary Life Member. It's likely that this thoughtful and inexpensive form of recognition led to more additional gifts and bequests than any other single way of expressing gratitude.

On the next page you'll see how the bylaws of The Art Institute of Chicago define the classes of membership, the dues of the Life categories, and various responsibilities and privileges. (Note that Section 8 also defines the cumulative-giving qualifications for the classes of major contributors. Inflation can make it necessary to revise your bylaws from time to time, upgrading the required gifts as needed.)

SECTION 1 Members of the Art Institute of Chicago shall be of five (5) classes: Governing Life, Honorary Governing Life, Honorary Life, Life, and Annual.

SECTION 2   All Governing Life, Honorary Governing Life and Honorary Life Members shall be elected by the Trustees from among those persons who meet the qualifications as set forth in this ARTICLE I, except that all living Benefactors shall become Honorary Governing Life Members without payment of dues and shall have all the privileges of Governing Life Members.

Two negative votes at the duly constituted meeting of the Board of Trustees at which such election is proposed shall reject a nominee. Only Governing Life Members and Honorary Governing Life Members shall have the right to vote for or be elected Trustees. The total number of Governing Life Members shall not exceed 650, exclusive of Honorary Governing Life Members, and such members shall be exempt from the payment of dues.

SECTION 3   Governing Life Members shall be elected from among such Life Members as shall have made a donation to The Art Institute of Chicago in the sum of $1,000.00 or more, which sum shall be credited to an unrestricted endowment fund.

SECTION 4   Honorary Governing Life Members and Honorary Life Members shall be chosen from among persons who have rendered eminent services to The Art Institute of Chicago or have attained distinction as artists, patrons of art, or educators.

SECTION 5   Any person may become a Life Member upon the payment of $1,000.00 to The Art Institute of Chicago, which sum shall be credited to an unrestricted endowment fund.

SECTION 6   Any person may become an Annual Member upon such terms as may be fixed from time to time by the Board of Trustees.

SECTION 7   All Members with their immediate families shall be entitled to free admission to all public exhibitions of The Art Institute of Chicago, except as otherwise provided by the Board of Trustees.

SECTION 8   Donors and Benefactors of The Art Institute of Chicago shall be classed as set forth in this Section. Evaluations are on the basis of gifts of money, securities, and objects of art, or a combination thereof:

        Distinguished Benefactor......................$1,000,000 and over
        Major Benefactor.............................   300,000-$999,999
        Benefactor...................................   50,000-$299,999
        Patron.......................................   25,000-$ 49,999
        Sponsor......................................   10,000-$ 24,999
        Friend.......................................   5,000-$ 9,999

With the exception of those qualifying as "Friends", any donor within any of the foregoing classifications may be elected to such classification by the Board of Trustees and the name of the donor, including the donor's spouse, listed on the plaques in the entrance hall or other such area of The Art Institute of Chicago.

Be specific and clear when you're describing your membership classifications, and be sure they are spelled out in your membership materials and also in *bylaws* and similar statements of policy. Don't relegate such descriptions to memoranda or resolutions, which are often overlooked or disregarded as staff members change.

Some institutions prefer to avoid clear statements of policy and membership definitions. Some have an unstated practice of making every donor above a certain minimum level an automatic member in an appropriate annual or life classification. But then they often fail to notify the donor that he or she is indeed a member. This practice complicates the renewal process and may very well decrease the amount of the donor's next gift.

Some causes offer low-cost Student (or Junior) memberships and special rates for senior citizens. The principle of offering reduced membership dues to both young and old is commendable. But the institution that gives them then has a responsibility for creating programs related to the needs of these groups. Special classes and programs seem to appeal to children and seniors alike. In theory, at least, the Student or Junior members will get into the membership habit and continue for many years. So they're a good investment. (But make sure you ask for each Junior member's age so he or she can be moved up to the more profitable regular status at the proper time.) And older members often are your best planned-gift prospects.

If your institution is in a large city visited frequently by people from all over the country, don't overlook the possibilities of starting a special classification of non-resident membership. The Museum of Modern Art in New York City has had one for many years with great success. The Metropolitan Museum of Art in the same city created the National Associates of the Metropolitan for people who live 150 miles or more from New York; it gives most of the basic membership privileges but for dues that are less than half those charged for the normal membership.

When to renew?   The timing of your invitation to a member to renew his or her membership is not a decision to make casually. The timing can affect the response to your invitation. And it can also affect the ease with which your office accomplishes the renewal job.

Despite the importance of the decision about the renewal date, some causes clearly have a policy to do the renewal work only when it's most convenient for the staff. Others can't even tell you why their renewal policy is what it is! One of the strongest museum membership programs went to the absurd extreme of dating every membership from the day the application was received; another museum has a single enrollment date for a whole year: January 1. If you're designing or changing such policies for your organization, here are some realistic options for you to consider.

- Make the effective date the first of the month *following* the month in which the member joined. This makes sense to the member and lets him or her in on a small bargain of extra days. It also enables you to carry on membership promotion and renewal all year long.

- If monthly enrollment seems too much for you to handle, try quarterly enrollment dates — January 1, April 1, July 1, October 1 — moving each new applicant up to the nearest *future* date. Again, there is a bargain involved for the member, and your renewal processing can be spread out in advance during slack times. After the first year, not many members will recall exactly when they first joined, either month or year.

Professional and trade associations.   Trade associations and professional societies are different from museums, schools, and zoos. They have a stronger claim on their members. Most have a single class of membership with relatively high fixed dues, sometimes running into many hundred dollars a year. Some trade groups break membership classes into "user" and "supplier" groups, usually with higher dues for suppliers. Sometimes the level of dues may be pegged to the member firm's annual volume of business or number of employees. This provides an incentive for new and smaller potential members to join. It also places the major responsibility on the larger companies. Many professional and trade associations with local and state affiliates require people to belong to the local affiliate before they can be eligible for membership in the national group. In such cases, the terms of the national and local memberships and renewal dates coincide to minimize confusion about eligibility.

How to increase dues.   You'll be surprised how readily loyal members will accept logical changes when the reasons behind them are carefully explained — just once — and comments are invited. Small increases in annual dues usually don't have to be explained at all. People are used to paying a little more for things every year or so.

But sometimes it's necessary to make dramatic increases in membership dues, especially in life membership dues that haven't been changed for many years. And when that happens, you have an opportunity to earn the respect of your membership and possibly reap the biggest harvest in dues in your history.

Announce the increase six months in advance of the effective date. If you have a large and loyal annual membership, many members will rush to become life members before the fee goes up. And many who are already life members will buy life memberships for their children and grandchildren at the old, bargain rate.

Try to tie a "bargain" aspect into every change in dues and invite people to take advantage of it before the deadline. When *annual* dues are being increased substantially, offer your present annual members a special rate for two or more years at the old level. This will complicate your records a bit and require changes in your renewal cycle, but the increased revenues may be worth it.

Here now is how several organizations spell out the benefits of their various levels of membership.

MYSTIC SEAPORT MUSEUM®
MEMBERSHIP BENEFITS

Annual
Dues

INDIVIDUAL

$20
—Free admission for the member
—Guest card which upon presentation at the gate will allow members' guests admission at a discount
—10% discount at Seaport Stores on purchases of $5 or more (excluding sale items)
—Discount on dockage
—Use of the Membership Building
—The *Log* and the *Wind Rose*
—Notice of special Museum programs: seminars, workshops, courses, lectures, tours and special events, some for members only
—Eligibility to purchase Mystic Seaport burgee, members' scarf, tie and patch
—Purchase of guest ticket books (limit 3 annually) which allows members' guests free admission

FAMILY

$30
—All of the above, and in addition,
—Free admission for member's spouse, their children or grandchildren 18 and under

PARTICIPATING

$50
—All of the above, and in addition,
—Upon joining, a profile and sail plan of the Friendship sloop, *Estella A.,* will be given

SUSTAINING

$100
—All of the above, and in addition,
—Free dockage for two nights each visit
—Choice of complimentary Mystic Seaport burgee, members' tie, scarf or patch, upon joining
—Card issued for one free dinner (with purchase of one dinner) at Seamen's Inne

ASSOCIATE

$250
—All of the above, and in addition,
—Private tour of the Museum (or any part) upon request, with 2 weeks notice
—One free guest ticket book upon joining

BENEFACTOR

$500
—All of the above, and in addition,
—Curatorial consultation on maritime collecting, upon request with 2 weeks notice
—Upon joining, a reproduction of maritime art will be given

Single
Payment

LIFE

$1000
—All of the above, and in addition,
—Annual free guest ticket book
—Private tour of the Museum given by the Director with 2 weeks notice
—Upon joining, one photograph by Oliver Denison III will be presented

One adult admission may be credited toward a new membership if applied for within a year of the last visit. (Gate admission receipt is required.)

LEVELS OF SUPPORT

SPONSORING $500
- An invitation to an Associate event
- A Museum publication

SUSTAINING $300
- Free subscription to
- Special tour

SUPPORTING $125
- Reciprocal privileges at fourteen other museums in the U.S.A.

CONTRIBUTING $60
- Free admission for a guest ten times a year

HOUSEHOLD $40
- Two adult cards and cards for all children under 18

INDIVIDUAL $25
- Free admission to the Museum, Museum,
- New Members' Morning
- Invitation to previews of special exhibitions
- Free subscription to *Calendar, Magazine & Bulletin*
- Special lecture series, programs, trips and films
- Behind-the-Scenes tours
- Free   lectures
- Reduced magazine rates
- Discounts in the Museum Shop
- Special sale days in the Museum Shop
- Art Sales and Rental Gallery privileges
- Free use of Library

This art museum shows six membership levels and the cumulative benefits for each.

Make no mistake about it, people join organizations because they want to get something in return. We call that something a "benefit."

In some rare cases, what they want to get may be only a good feeling about helping a worthy cause. But people who join for that reason represent less than 5 percent of your market. It's the other 95 percent you really have to work for. How? By offering the most attractive membership benefits and privileges your organization can reasonably afford. Surprisingly, some of the best benefits may cost very little — and may even produce profits on their own.

Some organizations — especially those that confuse membership with annual giving — tend to offer unattractive and unimaginative membership benefits. Often they make no distinction between the benefits given to basic members in the lower classifications and those in the higher levels.

It's essential that attractive basic benefits be given to *all* classifications, but after that there is almost no limit to the benefits that can be given to top levels of membership. The highest classifications may be given voting rights and an attractive annual meeting party at which to exercise that right. Some trade associations and major museums go a step further and require belonging to a high classification of membership to be able to hold office.

More common special privileges at the higher levels include invitations to exclusive parties and special events, premiums and awards, listings in directories, and listings on honor rolls or plaques. The variety of benefits is limited only by the nature of the organization, its imagination, and the funds available to carry out the membership project. Once again: The relatively few people in the highest membership classifications provide most of the money. And they feel *entitled* to being treated well and recognized for their generosity and interest. But you've got to deliver what you promise, and that usually costs money. It's surprising how many organizations overlook the necessity for

BENEFITS THAT MAKE PEOPLE JOIN

6

budgeting for such things as prompt handling of membership transactions. Sometimes they even forget the costs of membership benefits. It's a good idea to examine each proposed benefit and avoid those that can escalate greatly and quickly in cost but not in profit. But remember: Even the simple ones require expenditures.

POPULAR BASIC BENEFITS

Free admission and services.   The most attractive word in all advertising is "free," followed closely by "new" and "improved." Prospective members all want to know what they're going to get. That's probably the most important reason why they'll want to join. Some organizations, such as museums, offer "free" admission as the principal membership privilege. It's easy to show prospects how much they will save in admissions for themselves and their families when they become members. Unquestionably the most attractive membership privilege in a motor club is "free" emergency road service, in which a single use may easily justify a year's dues.

Membership Benefits

JOIN THE LINCOLN PARK ZOO NOW FOR THESE BIG BENEFITS!

- **Free Subscription to Animal Kingdom**
  Full color magazine with photographs and articles about wildlife and Lincoln Park Zoo.
- **Caroling to the Animals**
  Chicago's newest holiday happening.
- **Super Zoo Picnic**
  Members' Night in June. Behind-the-scenes tours, bands, popcorn— and the Zoo all to yourselves.
- **Country Picnic at the Farm-in-the-Zoo**
  Down-home fun every August for the whole family.
- **Free Zoo Guide Book**
  50 pages of photos and information on Lincoln Park Zoo animals.

- **10% Discount at the Zoo Shops**
  Filled with wonderful gifts and books for all animal lovers!
- **Calendar of Zoo Events**
  All the activities for adults and children. Mailed to members five times each year.
- **Free Wildlife Programs**
  Films, lectures and seminars.
- **Members-Only Previews**
  Special invitations to preview new exhibits at the Zoo.
- **Adult Classes, Seminars, and Behind-the-Scenes Tours**
  Special parties and classes for children too.

Closely related to free admission are *priority tickets* and "express" admission for very popular events. Many museums discovered how attractive this privilege can be years ago when the King Tut exhibition toured the United States. In some places, members not only got free tickets but were able to request the exact time when they would be admitted. At that reserved time they simply marched past the long lines and met King Tut on their own terms. At less popular exhibitions, a separate (short, fast-moving) "express" admission line for members can stimulate on-the-spot sale of memberships. Priority tickets and admission are highly visible membership privileges that make members glad they joined — and others wish they had. Regularly repeated surveys of Friends of the Zoo at Audubon Park in New Orleans, for example, show that free admission and a members-only gate on weekends and holidays consistently rank at the top of the reasons for joining.

Discounts.   Savings again! Some of the most popular discounts are those given on: convention and seminar fees; tickets to theatrical, musical, and athletic events; magazine subscriptions; and merchandise sold in the institution's store or through its catalogs.

One professional association with a very popular (and expensive) annual conference sells a lot of memberships by offering a combination of membership and the conference at a discount. And the discount continues through numerous special seminars offered throughout the year.

If your organization attracts members interested in a special field that's well represented by magazines, check with the publishers about offering your members discounts on magazine subscriptions. The Art Institute of Chicago offers its members discounts on subscriptions to 2l different magazines in art and related fields. It's good business for all concerned, and it costs you nothing except for handling and for printing the announcements and coupons. Less common but worth exploring is the practice of a few magazines that rebate part of the subscription charge as a contribution to the institution.

Discounted tickets to performances and events offer a wide variety of additional opportunities. Some causes arrange discounts at restaurants before the event, for example, and sometimes free bus service from the restaurant to the event.

Discounted merchandise can be an attractive privilege. Motor clubs often offer their members substantial discounts on luggage and other travel-related items. Most museums now have stores in which members are given discounts (usually about l0 percent) on merchandise. Large museums offer similar discounts on merchandise in their catalogs. Trade associations that publish or distribute professional publications often offer their members special discounts. Tours and other travel projects (we'll talk more about these in a moment) can also be discounted to members if they are offered to both members and non-members.

Publications. Even the smallest organization can and should have at least a newsletter as a membership benefit. Content and copy can be of high quality — and of optimum interest to the membership — even in a simple mimeographed newsletter. When a cause has the potential of a wide national membership, a quality magazine can often be the most important single membership benefit. For example, few members of the National Geographic Society ever get to go on an expedition, but they all receive their magazines. Certainly Smithsonian Magazine is the major reason the Smithsonian Associates suddenly grew from a small local group to a national membership approaching two million. For years, Opera News has

been the principal benefit of membership in the Metropolitan Opera Guild. And Modern Maturity is a major attraction of the American Association of Retired Persons.

Beyond the basic membership publications, some organizations have found that their membership base has enabled them to publish important books, usually at substantial discounts to their members.

Reduced Subscription Rates for Members on Selected Art Magazines

Mail application coupons and checks directly to the magazines at the addresses indicated.

Members of The Art Institute of Chicago should use these coupons to enter their subscriptions to any of the magazines listed at the special Members' price. These special rates are applicable only on Members' own subscriptions, not gifts. This offer is effective through June 1, 19

AFRICAN ARTS
African Studies Center, University of California,
Los Angeles, CA 90024

I am a Member of The Art Institute of Chicago and wish to subscribe to *African Arts* (4 issues) at the special members' rate.

Regular annual subscription rate	$18.00
Special members' rate	$16.00

My check for $16.00 for one year is enclosed.

_____
Name   Membership exp. date

_____
Street

_____
City   State   Zipcode
☐ new   ☐ renewal

AMERICAN INDIAN ART MAGAZINE
7314 East Osborn Drive, Scottsdale, AZ 85251

I am a Member of The Art Institute of Chicago and wish to subscribe to *American Indian Art Magazine* (4 issues) at a special members' rate.

Regular annual subscription rate	$16.00
Special members' rate	$14.00

My check for $14.00 for 4 issues is enclosed.

_____
Name   Membership exp. date

_____
Street

_____
City   State   Zipcode
☐ new   ☐ renewal

APOLLO
P.O. Box 47 N. Hollywood, CA 91603

Members rooms.   Organizations that attract large public attendance, such as performing arts groups and museums, find that many people enjoy the privilege of spending free time in a special members room. Usually free coffee and tea are served there. The rooms — attractive and comfortably furnished — are generally convenient to the main areas and conspicuous enough to suggest that non-members, too, might enjoy this special privilege. Admission to the room for members and their guests requires only the showing of the membership card, a privilege that impresses guests.

Invitations to special parties for new members — held in the members room — not only introduce them to the room's use but also reaffirm the members' feelings that joining was a sound decision. If the room is large enough, special meetings for members can be popular. When it first opened its members room, The Art Institute of Chicago held a series of "Curator's Choice" lectures. At each lecture, a curator displayed a specific work and talked about it, answering questions from the members. Eventually the Institute had to discontinue the series, because the crowds became too large for the room — a problem many museums would welcome.

Volunteer opportunities.   Quite a few institutions have found that some volunteer activities are so popular that they have to be limited to members. Special courses for gallery guides and docents at art museums are great attractions for some potential members, and of course they produce valuable volunteer help to serve the public and save staff salaries.

Reciprocal arrangements.   A number of similar groups have banded together to give the members of each the right to some of the free benefits offered by all. Whether or not members actually use the benefits, it's an attractive offering to contemplate and thus it stimulates sales. Many museum members, for example, are offered free admission to certain other museums throughout the nation. Or, another example: Every member of the American Automobile Association is advised that his or her membership privileges are honored by other AAA chapters throughout the world. Such reciprocal arrangements are low-cost benefits, worth considering and adapting for your group.

Special membership services.   Especially in the professional and trade association field, exclusive membership benefits can be real inducements to join. The American Hotel Association accepts listings and advertising in its "Hotel Red Book" only from member hotels. The Direct Marketing Association and the American Association of Advertising Agencies are among several trade groups that conduct studies resulting in valuable reports available only to members, or to members at a substantial discount.

Special merchandise offers.   Many large membership organizations offer attractive merchandise and services to their members several times a year. Especially popular for years has been the offer of distinctive holiday cards and gifts. A few organizations offer a discount-buying service to their members. More often, organizations make arrangements with manufacturers and distributors to sell members attractive merchandise at break-even prices. Known in the trade as "self-liquidating premiums," these items sometimes bear the organization's logo. Golf organizations, for example, may sell impressive bag tags, golf towels, reproductions of old golf paintings, photos of historic golf courses, etc. Motor clubs sell driving safety equipment, luggage, driving caps and gloves, and vacation equipment. The Metropolitan Opera Guild sends its 64,000 members (and 30,000 subscribers to Ballet News) an attractive mail order catalog offering everything from rare recordings, to opera memorabilia, to tote bags, jewelry, and accessories — all tied in to an operatic theme. Members of most groups welcome an opportunity to buy such items from a reputable source at a bargain price and consider it a valuable membership benefit.

Special programs and seminars.   Many museums and performing arts groups offer lectures and seminars to their members. Usually, these are free or at a sharply discounted price. When a wide variety of such educational offerings is test-marketed, the institution can quickly identify the most popular ones and add more of the same type. Art museums and cultural centers often offer film and music programs unavailable elsewhere in the community and attract many new members who are initially interested only in those special programs.

When the Chicago Council on Foreign Relations wanted to expand its membership, it reached a whole new market of young singles by scheduling a series of after-work cocktail parties and special lectures — a cultural alternative to the popular Thank-God-It's-Friday parties in the singles bars. Many members joined primarily to meet other young people with similar interests. The success of this program moved the Council into expanding its adult education programs, just in time to tap a rich market.

Most large museums offer a special "members night," at which tours are conducted behind the scenes in such normally private areas as conservation laboratories, storage areas, study rooms, even shipping rooms.

Symphony orchestra groups are invited to an annual backstage tour of the hall and to open rehearsals, sometimes several times a year. Theater and dance groups also offer their members attendance at workshops and rehearsals. Lyric Opera of Chicago has an annual dinner for major contributors — on the stage of the opera house and attended by outstanding opera stars.

Lincoln Park Zoo in Chicago has done such imaginative things as holding a ball in the lion house.

Take a good look at your own organization and its resources and then let your imagination zoom.

Reading lists, libraries, and study rooms.   Remember the study that found that people who join organizations are apt to like to read? It's true.

Their curiosity constantly seeks ways to find out more about the subjects in which they're interested. And many organizations have expert knowledge about source materials — current books and periodicals, films, etc. — on those very subjects. Some causes maintain circulating libraries and study collections to be borrowed — by mail — and returned after a fixed period. Some have created videocassettes on fascinating aspects of their work, and those cassettes can be rented or purchased. What a rich and attractive membership benefit it can be to have access to all of this material! And that's just what many causes offer.

Phi Beta Kappa provides recommended reading lists to its members — publishing them in its newsletters and other publications. The Association for Research and Enlightenment, with a membership of 38,000 followers of the teachings of Edgar Cayce, maintains a large library and circulating files available to all members. And the Association offers access to even more advanced reference files, books, and newsletters to its upper levels of membership. The Direct Marketing Association has an extensive circulating collection of prize-winning mailings and other direct-marketing items.

When the space in a specialized library is too small to accommodate the general public, an effective way to control the use of the library is to make it a membership privilege. Museums with study rooms for prints and drawings, photography, and other specialized fields make them available to members only — sometimes even requiring membership in a special interest group within the general membership.

reading recommended by the book committee

humanities ROBERT B. HEILMAN, LAWRENCE WILLSON, FREDERICK J. CROSSON
social sciences EARL W. COUNT, LEONARD W. DOOB, ANDREW GYORGY, MADELINE R. ROBINTON, VICTORIA SCHUCK, ELLIOT ZUPNICK
natural sciences RUSSELL B. STEVENS, RONALD GEBALLE

RUSSELL B. STEVENS

The Cropland Crisis—Myth or Reality? Ed., Pierre R. Crosson. Johns Hopkins. 1982. $27.50; paper, $10.50.
Although the number of U.S. citizens who are directly engaged in farming is shrinking dramatically, most Americans have come to accept uncritically the assertion that available cropland is in short supply and its fu-

Krimsky's work affords a detailed, convenient account of the remarkable events of roughly the 1970s. He takes pains to set this cluster of events in the political and social context of the times and to examine the specific roles of the principal players in the drama. In the main, the author holds to a neutral stance and contents himself with a documented, dispassionate account. The result is

can sense an impending e doing so, he convinces hi nomenon is valid and ama anecdotal evidence of its r portant, he postulates an e nism—electrically charged which animals can detect happen. Thus he provides opportunity to put the ma though the author dwells tribulations of those who tional scientific questions, appreciably marred by thi cupation.

Chimpanzee Politics: Pow Apes. Frans de Waal. Har $16.50.
In this volume the author what impresses me as a ve fashion, his detailed obser breeding colony of chimp Zoo in Arnhem, Holland.

Phi Beta Kappa's reading list, published as part of its newsletter, The Key Reporter.

Special classes.   In addition to general-interest lectures, classes, and seminars, some organizations have been successful in offering extremely esoteric classes in related fields. These membership benefits are sometimes free, but more often there's a tuition fee. The Adler Planetarium in Chicago, for example, has courses in grinding telescope lenses and making telescopes. The Evanston (Illinois) Historial Society finds great interest in courses on refinishing antique furniture. Even small art museums that offer no other type of art instruction have attracted members through sketch classes for beginners — providing creative outlets for many who have long nursed a secret desire to learn how to draw.

Take a good look at what your organization is doing or could be doing. Then draft a list of special classes you could offer, and circulate the list in a questionnaire to your members, inviting their own suggestions. That way you also end up with prime mailing lists, ready to use when the courses are ready. Despite all of the competition for leisure activities, the continuing education movement grows with each year. It can bring you many new members.

Tours and travel.   Back when a travel boom was just beginning, the Council on Foreign Relations in Chicago sought advice on how to build its membership, then just a few thousand people. It was advised to offer unique tours taking advantage of the Council's international connections. One of the first was a world tour that included interviews with Nehru and other world figures; it sold out immediately and is still mentioned fondly by those who made the tour. As more Council tours and eventually charter flights were offered, the membership swelled to some 25,000 — with a high renewal rate.

Museums of all types have found tours for members one of their most popular membership privileges. One natural history museum divides some of its tours into two sections: one led by a curator of anthropology, the other by a curator of botany. The Chicago Symphony Society takes its members on the Symphony's tours to Europe, Asia, and American cities as well as to special musical events throughout the world. Zoos and botanic garden societies offer tours to Africa and to attractive areas in this country and abroad. The Smithsonian Associates, with its large national membership, publishes in each issue of Smithsonian magazine a wide selection of domestic and foreign study tours, inviting inquiries.

But even small organizations can offer a wide variety of interesting tours to its members without getting involved in complex travel commitments. Here are a few suggestions.

- House and garden tours. These can be planned within a limited area, permitting walking between the houses and gardens.
- Architectural tours, locally and in nearby concentrations of outstanding architecture.
- Tours of ethnic neighborhoods, often followed by dinner in an ethnic restaurant.
- Tours of private art collections and studios of artists, usually not available to the public.
- Tours to outstanding nearby trade or professional facilities.

Preview receptions and social events.   Most art museums have discovered the value of exhibition previews for their members. These are often attended by the artists and important local collectors. Although the exhibition itself is a major drawing card, the reception following it may be even more attractive to many lonely members whose principal reason for joining is to associate with people they admire.

One of the most effective ways to increase the renewal rate of new members is to offer them a "new members reception" a few months before their membership is to expire. The principal reason new members don't renew may be that they haven't taken advantage of their membership benefits. The reception for new members brings them in under happy and usually flattering circumstances. This is especially true when local social leaders on the board are in the receiving line and act as hosts and hostesses for the event.

Group insurance opportunities. Especially in trade and professional associations, many individuals and sole proprietors of businesses welcome an opportunity to get economical group insurance coverage. Many motor clubs offer their members "free" accident insurance policies with their membership, provide complete insurance-brokerage services, and from time to time tell their members about other group insurance of possible interest to them. In many cases the clubs make a substantial profit from the insurance in addition to offering their members an attractive membership privilege.

Free parking and checking. When being a member involves attending large public gatherings (such as exhibitions, athletic events, or arts performances), convenient and free parking or valet parking can be a very attractive benefit. A windshield parking sticker can bring a surprising amount of free advertising for the cause wherever a member's car is parked. (And there may be unexpected benefits, too. Many years ago at Northwestern University, a prominent and genial man came to the development office with a special request. It seemed that a few years back he had been a guest in the president's box at a Northwestern-Notre Dame football game and had received a parking sticker for his windshield. For obvious reasons, these stickers issued by Northwestern were good for just one game, were usually printed in the opponent's colors, and carried the opponent's name in large block letters. His sticker, in bright green ink, had read: "OFFICIAL - NOTRE DAME." When he sold the car, he couldn't remove the sticker, so he was there to ask if they had a duplicate he could put on his new car. When the development officer asked him why, he replied, "I never got a parking ticket in Chicago with that sticker on my car.")

Free checking of bulky parcels as well as coats and hats is another welcome membership benefit, especially in large cities where the cause is headquartered close to shopping. Often the little things that make a person's life easier and more gracious are best remembered and valued by your members.

SPECIAL BENEFITS FOR HIGH-LEVEL MEMBERS

If you've provided strong benefits for your members in the lower classifications, you can safely do much better for the highest level members without danger of resentment or criticism.

In fact, knowing of these higher benefits may lead smaller donors to higher aspirations. When the Chicago Symphony Orchestra made its first European tour, governing members and trustees were invited to go along. Included in the arrangements made for these two special groups were tickets to concerts and parties in each city, plus side trips to places of interest. The price of the tour was not low. However, friends and neighbors of governing members started discreetly inquiring if they could become governing members and go along, too. The high price was clearly no problem, considering the excellent benefits.

The Lyric Opera of Chicago has a special "green room" in which high level members and contributors enjoy an intimate cocktail service at the intermission of each performance. The Art Institute of Chicago, with the largest art museum membership in the world, generally precedes each members' preview of a major exhibition with a dinner for its Governing Life members and Honorary Governing Life members.

Even when the general membership is eligible to attend prestigious and expensive balls and similar events, the fact that the first invitations go to people in the higher membership classifications often inspires others to move up. (Always remember, people do and buy things for reasons they won't even admit to themselves.)

Have you noticed how quickly most people leaf through published directories of distinguished groups to see who is listed? As expensive as they may be to prepare, such directories are well worth almost any expense, because of the recognition they give to those who provide the bulk of the organization's financial support. This is so even when the directories have a very limited circulation. The Chicago Symphony publishes a directory (complete with photographs) of its officers, trustees and governing members. Each listing provides titles, home and business addresses, name of spouse, and name of secretary. The directory is a valuable aid to many for both social and business reasons. To be listed in it is an attainable goal for many others.

Consider awarding special membership cards and certificates to high level members. A surprising number of people welcome them and display them with pride. When the Chicago Symphony Society recognized major donors by electing them to be honorary life members, they created a distinctive gold engraved membership card with a blind-embossed cover flap. The member's name was filled in by calligraphy. They came in a special clear vinyl sheath. (One member asked for a duplicate because he had had his original framed for display in his office!)

Chicago Symphony Society

Mrs. William R. Od

HONORARY LIFE MEMBER

WITH ALL OF THE RIGHTS AND PRIVILEGES

THERETO APPERTAINING

Tax deduction.   Most dues for nonprofit organizations are charitable gifts, deductible from the member's income taxes. And dues for professional and trade associations are almost always totally deductible as business expenses. Members have come to expect this tax-deductibility as a membership privilege (though deductibility usually ranks far down the list of reasons why people join or give to an organization).

But if a part of the dues is used by the organization to provide substantial, continuing benefits to the member, that part cannot be deducted as a charitable gift.

The Internal Revenue Service tends to be lenient about the deductibility of basic membership benefits and privileges, and it's likely that the membership dues of more than 90 percent of the charitable membership organizations in the United States are fully deductible. But if the continuing membership benefits also include tangible items of considerable monetary value — such as elaborate magazines, books, or tools and equipment — the organization has an obligation to make its members clearly aware of what portion of their annual membership dues is deductible and what part is not. The National Geographic Society, for example, specifies on the bottom of its membership acceptance form that 80 percent of the basic annual dues is "designated" to pay for the member's subscription to the National Geographic magazine.

This is a grey area in the nonprofit world, and that's possibly why so many membership groups more or less ignore it. ("Dues are tax-deductible to the extent allowed by law," is one way many groups handle this greyness, very often on the advice of their legal counsel.) But the real solution is found in discussing the question with your attorney and very possibly with your accountant as well. They should be able to define, for example, how much of your elaborate magazine is counted toward your organization's public information mission, and how much is counted as a non-deductible, "substantial, continuing" benefit to the member.

Why this emphasis on tax deductibility? Well, there are two reasons. First, in the long run it's best for you to make it clear that you operate an ethical membership organization. And it's equally important for you to help your members avoid violating the tax laws.

When you and your professional advisers have arrived at an honest and clear statement about the tax-deductibility of your dues, make sure that all of your membership staff people and the officers and directors understand the specific details (which may have to be updated from time to time). Then describe those details in print at the bottom of the membership acceptance form, to be read after the prospect has already made a positive decision to join and is taking action on that decision. It's also a good idea to print the same information on the receipt for membership dues. Some members with a long record of renewal may resent being told that a part of their dues is not deductible. But some others will respect your frankness and your ethics.

WHICH BENEFITS?

The cause that offers all of the benefits we've discussed so far would probably be so overwhelmed by carrying them out that it wouldn't have time for the main business of the organization.

So, how do you pick the ones that you'll offer? First of all, you should probably start small. Initially offer the inexpensive, attractive, easy-to-produce benefits. Later, increase the desirability of your membership program with more sophisticated offerings. And think carefully about each proposed benefit. Ask yourself whether it's really right for your type of organization. A Food and Wine Society might offer discounts on wine, but maybe your type of organization should offer something else. Test your ideas on a few people who are close to your organization and typical of its majority thinking. They'll like a few of the ideas, but they'll politely scratch some of the others as not being "appropriate."

And remember at all times that you are marketing your memberships — selling them on the open market. So do as marketing people do. Don't just dream up all the arrangements for your program and its benefits, print them in an attractive brochure, and mail them to 400,000 names. Rather, pick a small test group of those 400,000 names and send them a questionnaire asking which of the ideas seem most attractive to them. The results may surprise you, but it's better to be surprised then than to have the surprise come after you've put postage on 400,000 non-productive membership solicitations.

Market surveying like this, of course, is not something you just do. You've got to know something about doing it. If you're not an experienced market researcher, then get help. Hire an experienced firm or consultant, or try to find a volunteer — perhaps through a board member. At the least, read an authoritative book on the subject.

Market research takes time and budget. But properly done, it can give you fairly solid facts on which to base your decisions about which benefits to offer and even what prices to charge for membership. These decisions are crucial to the future of your membership program. And working from facts is far safer than taking a guess.

Few nonprofit groups ask themselves questions like these. Who are we? Where are we? What future do we want for ourselves? What are the best ways to achieve that future?

The questions are simple, but the answers may be very complex. And they will affect your membership program. How many members, for example, do you really want? You may have physical limitations for meetings and events.

A few organizations, of course, have very finite limitations on the ultimate size of their memberships. Some professional associations have only so many eligible prospects. But consider, on the other hand, the market opportunities for such national organizations as the Smithsonian Associates, which in less than 20 years grew to an international membership of almost 2 million persons. Still broader is the market for the American Association of Retired Persons with countless millions of eligible prospects and more than 19 million members — an outstanding example of growth built on substantial membership benefits and the willingness to invest in top quality membership promotion.

Acquiring new members, year after year, is the lifeblood of any organization. People tend to move. For local organizations, this alone can deplete even a strong membership in less than five years. So can deaths and cancellations, even when the renewal rate is very high. New members mean more money, and with each additional dollar, the organization can strengthen its programs and services to attract still more new members.

There's a marketing term called *positioning.* It means how you make the public — especially your present and potential members — know what your organization stands for. When they hear the name of your group, what do they think of? That's your market "position." You can't be all things to all people. It's your marketing "position" that determines what you are and to whom — whom you target to recruit as members and how you present your offer to them. It's also how you develop your prospect lists.

7

MARKETS AND LISTS

Every organization knows how important lists are. In most cases, though, they tend to think of their own membership list and not of the wide variety of *prospect* lists that are out there, waiting to be found and tested.

It's an old adage that even a poor offer sent to a good list will do better than a strong offer sent to a poor list. Why is this so? Every buying decision (and that includes "joining" decisions) is made by someone who is *predisposed* to consider the offer favorably. Such a person needs only to be invited to "buy" your group's offer of an attractive way to act on that predisposition. That's what good lists are all about — names and addresses of people whose interests, lifestyles, incomes, homes, buying habits, and countless other factors suggest they might be willing to consider favorably your offer of attractive benefits.

When you get involved with testing lists, you're apt to hear many references to demographics and psychographics. Demographics are the measurable indicators of a life pattern: age, income, occupation, value of home, location and duration of residence, value of car, size of family, level of education, etc. Psychographics are also measurable. The term simply refers to the psychological profile of a person. In our case, the profile contains such important information as the way a person spends his or her disposable income and how he or she sees himself or herself in relation to others.

In the list business, there are countless examples of strong lists that clearly exhibit certain psychographics. The best list ever used to promote membership for The Art Institute of Chicago was a relatively small list of people who regularly attended high fashion shows. They probably didn't buy much high fashion, but they saw themselves as part of a group they admired — and enjoyed the company. The same psychographic was demonstrated when the Playboy Club membership list first came on the rental market. In those days, the Playboy members were upwardly mobile young men who, among other needs, wanted to acquire polish and sophistication and to impress their friends by taking them to the Art Institute. The list tested well for the Art Institute.

Another psychographic of great importance is called "mail-responsiveness," which means a propensity to order through the mail. If two lists match all of your other indicators and only one is made up of mail order buyers, the chances are strong that you'll get far more responses from the mail-responsive list. If you can, try to determine how recently they've bought, how frequently they've bought by mail, and the dollar volume of their orders. These are the recency/frequency/monetary value indicators you're likely to hear about when you deal with list people.

How to start looking for lists. Before you dig into the many types of rented lists available to you through list brokers, list managers, and compilers, you should know more about who and where your best prospects are and some effective ways of generating your own prospect lists.

- Analyze your membership list. If you already have a strong membership list, you'll find there are many clues in it that will direct you to new prospects. As a starter, break down your list by city, state, and ZIP. Many large business mailers have been able to cut their prospecting mailings (and, hence, costs) in half without losing response simply by knowing the most responsive ZIP codes. Whether your organization is local or national or even international, you simply must know where most of your present members live. From that base, you can also analyze your list for such vital information as approximate income level (by matching the ZIPS with census data) and even educational level.

  In the list business, this matching of your own list with outside lists is known as using "overlays." Another list containing information not found on yours is "laid over" (matched against) your list to pinpoint those prospects who are most like your current clients. Those, then, are the only ones you solicit on the new list. A good example: A motor club that knows where its members live and the kind of cars they drive can "overlay" lists of all owners of similar makes of cars and living in the same or similar ZIP codes to develop a highly targeted list. The more overlay information you can build into your own file the more valuable it becomes in analyzing the available rental lists.

By knowing where your present members live, you can also practice the simplest form of effective list building: "clustering," which is mailing to their neighbors. This can be especially effective for building membership in cultural organizations, because people who live near each other tend to have the same kind of interests. You can do this manually in small quantities or by hiring a list compiler when you're looking for large quantities.

If you seek new members for a trade association, match the businesses of your present members with lists of people in similar businesses. (You do this with the help of directories that list Standard Industrial Classifications.) You pick names in the best classifications and then address the most productive ZIP codes among them.

- Ask your members for referral names. Referral names are recommendations about people who are likely to become new members when they learn of the benefits and privileges available to them. Members who are pleased with your services really like to help, and the names they send will be among the best prospects you can possibly find.

On several occasions The Art Institute of Chicago invited all members to send in names. It offered them an attractive but inexpensive booklet as a reward. The response was overwhelming; about 20 percent of the membership returned names — thousands of them. After duplicates and current members were eliminated, a prospect list of almost 10,000 names remained. Over a period of about three years the Institute sent them several invitations and finally followed up by telephone, netting almost 6,000 new members — a 60 percent response!

The offer of a gift for sending in names almost always helps the response, sometimes significantly if the gift is especially attractive.

One motor club asked its members to recommend just one prospect to become eligible to win a sweepstake prize. The first prize offered was a mini-car, made popular on a television program. This brought in more than 10,000 referral names, of which 54 percent were converted to memberships within six months. A later offer of a portable television set as a sweepstake prize pulled 20 percent fewer referral names.

```
๚ธ เ  เ    
 10 S Hick
    isda    Il 6C
```

```
                                              May 1, 19
```

Dear Mr. i. r   :

```
    May I ask a favor of you?  It's an easy way of putting the Golden
Rule into action, and at the same time you'll be earning yourself a very
useful free gift.

    Your Club has grown strong through the years and has been able to
offer all of our Members an ever-increasing variety of benefits and
privileges because of one vital fact:  Members help.  Satisfied and
loyal Members such as you tell their friends about the Club and often
send us their names and addresses so we can send their friends an
invitation to join.

    Almost every day Members tell us they would like to do more to
help their Club grow stronger still.  Some, I suspect, correctly
reason that as Members grow in number, your Club will be able to
offer still more attractive services to each Member and also increase
the number of handy branch offices.

    Among your friends there probably are quite a few who share your
interest in safe, convenient driving.  Many would welcome an opportunity
to save time and money and enjoy your freedom from on-the-road worries
through belonging to the world's largest association that provides all-
around assistance to car owners.  Probably a fair number have had their
children's lives protected by Club-sponsored School Safety Patrols
and also want a powerful influence watching over their best interests
on legislation affecting motorists.

        The favor I ask is that you send me today the
    names and addresses of five friends of yours who
    would appreciate receiving an invitation to join
    your AAA-Chicago Motor Club.  As soon as their names
    are received here, we'll be happy to send you as a
    token of our thanks the handiest little map-magnifier
    you've ever seen.  It's small and flat and tucks

                                              (over, please)
```

easily into your road map case--even into a wallet
or a purse--and doubles as a bookmark when you're
not using it to read fine print.

You will be especially helpful to your Club by giving us permission
to mention your name in extending the invitation to your friends. They
will then know that you value their safety and convenience just as much
as your own. And because they value your judgment, they will welcome
the invitation and give it careful consideration.

So please take a few minutes now and send us the names and addresses
of five of your friends who will most appreciate having the protection
enjoyed by all Members of your Club. We'll rush your handy magnifier
to you along with our thanks for your valued help.

                                    Sincerely,

                                    Nels L. Pierson
                                    President

P.S.   For each of your recommended friends who joins the Club, you'll
        also receive your choice of the Club's coveted Honor Awards.
        We are enclosing a descriptive brochure of our awards to assist
        you in making your selections on the reverse side of the
        Recommendation List. We'll let you know when they join and
        send your awards in your order of preference. But remember,
        in any case, you'll have your handy magnifier to help you read
        the fine print on maps, telephone books, and your daily
        newspaper--plus the good feeling that you've helped your
        friends learn about the protection and convenience of belonging
        to the AAA-Chicago Motor Club.

NLP
Enclosures

RECOMMENDATION LIST

To: Nels L. Pierson, President
AAA-Chicago Motor Club
66 East South Water Street
Chicago, Illinois 60601

Date_____

Yes, I want to help my friends listed below learn more about the convenience, savings, and protection of membership in the AAA-Chicago Motor Club. You may mention my name when you invite them to join (except those I have marked with a check).

MY NAME (Please print):

Mr./Mrs./Miss/Ms._____

Address _____

City_____State_____Zip Code_____

Membership No._____

Please invite the following to join the AAA-Chicago Motor Club:

(Please print)

Mr./Mrs./Miss/Ms._____

Address_____

City_____State_____Zip Code_____

Mr./Mrs./Miss/Ms._____

Address_____

City_____State_____Zip Code_____

Mr./Mrs./Miss/Ms._____

Address_____

City_____State_____Zip Code_____

Mr./Mrs./Miss/Ms._____

Address_____

City_____State_____Zip Code_____

Mr./Mrs./Miss/Ms._____

Address_____

City_____State_____Zip Code_____

_____
Member's Signature

(Over, please, for your HONOR AWARD selection)

I understand I will receive the honor award(s) I have marked below in the order of my preference as soon as each of my recommended friends enrolls as a new Master Member.

(Please indicate your selections in the order you prefer to receive them by printing numbers 1 through 5 in the appropriate boxes and checking your color choice, where applicable.)

☐ A. THERMAL CUP SET (12)

☐ B. LADIES COWHIDE BILLFOLD
_____ BLUE (04) _____ RED (05)

☐ C. POLISHED METAL ASH TRAY (03)

☐ D. FRENCH PURSE
_____ BLUE (11) _____ RED (10)

☐ E. MEN'S BROWN LEATHER BILLFOLD

☐ F. DOUBLE DECK PLAYING CARDS
_____ BRIDGE (07) _____ CANASTA (08) _____ PINOCHLE (09)

☐ G. NYLON TOTE BAG
_____ _____ LADIES (13) _____ MEN (14)

☐ H. TWO-PIECE VALET SET (15)

The following new awards are also available but **not illustrated** in the folder:

☐ TENNIS BALLS—Three to Can (16)

☐ GOLF BALLS—Package of Three (17)

☐ FLASHLIGHT (18)

☐ COMPASS (19)

☐ FIRST-AID KIT (20)

☐ COIN KEY HOLDER (21)

☐ AAA EMBLEM (22)

☐ PHONE DIRECTORY (23)

☐ ROAD ATLAS (24)

How to WIN CHICAGO MOTOR CLUB HONOR AWARDS

Recommend a friend for membership in the CHICAGO MOTOR CLUB-AAA

Yes, you can win Chicago Motor Club Honor Awards simply by recommending friends for master membership in the Club. You will receive the handsome Honor Award of your choice just as soon as your prospect has been enrolled as a new master member.

You'll enjoy using these distinctive Honor Awards and you'll be doing your friends a favor by introducing them to the many advantages of membership in the Chicago Motor Club-AAA.

Recommend your friends for membership today!

SELECT YOUR HONOR AWARD
you have your choice of one of these beautiful Honor Awards

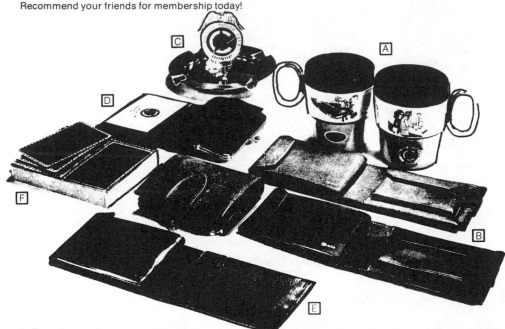

A. **Thermal cup set** — attractively designed—ideal for home or outdoor use.

B. **Ladies' blue or red cowhide billfold** — smart styling — by leading manufacturer.

C. **Polished metal ash tray** — eye-catching gold-red-white-black Club emblem — perfect for home or office.

D. **French purse** — red or blue — distinctive, compact "clutch" purse — perfect for everyday use — holds coins, credit and identification cards.

E. **Men's brown leather billfold** — secret compartment — by leading manufacturer.

F. **Double deck playing cards** — attractive, distinctive, red-blue with gold Club emblem — Pinochle, Canasta, Bridge.

How many names should you ask for? In one of the few documented tests in the field, it was determined that it's best to ask for no more than five names. The fourth name was only 49 percent as responsive as the first. Usually it's a good idea to ask for three names and provide space for four. Test various combinations and keep careful track of the results.

The documented test also showed the advantage of mentioning the name of the person who made the referral. In this test, the mailings using the name of the person who made the referral outpulled the mailings using no name by three to one. It's easy to obtain permission to use the name of the person doing the referring. You provide a box to be checked, or better still, simply say something like, "We will assume it is all right to mention your name when we write."

If your membership invitation mailing to referral leads is fairly small, you may want to send personal letters with the lead sentence reading, "You have been recommended by your friend John Jones." Test it by using an automatically typed letter or a word processing machine, and if that works well, consider going into computer letters.

If you plan to make several follow-up approaches, there's a definite advantage to creating a computer record that includes the name of the person making the referral. This allows you to produce a personalized membership form that also mentions the name of the person who made the referral.

If you prefer to use a mass-produced printed letter as the first in the series to the prospective new member, you can still get the important personalization by using a "hanger" — a slip folded over the top of the prospect letter, with text along the lines shown here. By leaving the space for the referrer's name, the "hanger" can be used whether or not you have a name to add.

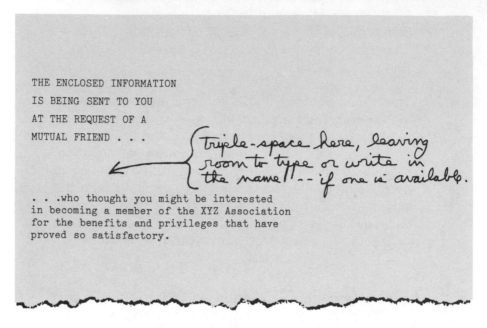

Whether or not you offer a gift to referrers for sending in names, by all means rush them a letter of warm thanks; and tell them that the friends they referred will thank them too. You might enclose another form and reply envelope for future use as new names occur to them. Some motor club members receive as many as four referral forms a year, especially as new premiums become available.

Here's a computer letter follow-up to a referral lead. It's designed to be printed along with a personalized membership enrollment form, which also mentions the name of the referrer. When the referrer doesn't want his or her name used, the one-line second paragraph is deleted and the paragraph spacing is closed up by the computer.

- List brokers/managers/compilers. Eventually, you'll exhaust all the prospect lists you can generate for yourself through directories and referrals. At that point, you'll want to test some of the thousands of lists available on the rental market — and you'll want to *rent* them for a one-time use, not buy them. This mysterious world of lists is made easier if you use directories of available lists to get ideas and then work directly with three unique suppliers.

List broker. A professional counselor to renters of direct mail lists. The broker acts as your agent in dealing with the list owner, expediting delivery, arranging merge/purge with other lists, etc. You pay no more by dealing with a broker, who makes his or her income from a commission paid by the list owner. If you're in or near a large city, look in the phone directory yellow pages under "Mailing Lists" for the names of list brokers (who may also be list managers and compilers as well). Ask another organization similar to yours for recommendations; some brokers specialize in lists for nonprofit organizations. Your

CHICAGO MOTOR CLUB

```
Mr. Robert P. Sample
1606 Embassy Avenue
Evanston, Illinois  60201

Dear Mr. Sample:

You have a true friend who cares about your safety and
convenience.  As a loyal and satisfied Member of the
AAA-Chicago Motor Club, your friend has asked us to
send you this special invitation to join the Club for
year-round peace of mind and protection.

Your thoughtful friend is Albert J. Killingsworth.

Membership in the AAA-Chicago Motor Club can save you
time, money, and a lot of trouble--as your friend knows
```

broker need not be located near you; contact is mainly by phone and mail.

List manager. A person or firm who, as an agent paid by the list owner, promotes a list for its owner and solicits rentals. Requests to rent (perhaps from a broker) go directly to the manager, who may have the power to accept or refuse the rental or may need the owner's permission.

In the cultural field, there are some consortiums of cooperating institutions that maintain unduplicated databanks containing the mailing lists of all consortium members. In a way, they act as a list manager. Working through such a databank, you can rent all the lists (or parts of several lists) in one transaction. For a fee, some consortiums will check your own list against the databank and make recommendations about the databank lists and ZIP codes you should test.

When you get ready to put your own membership list on the rental market, talk to a few list managers and ask for their proposals.

List compiler. A person or firm that compiles lists from directories, public records, registrations, and other sources. These lists do not guarantee any sort of past buying activity. They show only that the people share something in common, such as automobile ownership by make and year, or place of residence (often by median income in ZIP code or census tract). Many compilers can offer "overlays" — education level, income, etc. — on a basic geographic list that's usually compiled from telephone directories. Such lists can be very helpful in "clustering" — mailing to close neighbors of your present members. Your list broker can advise you on compiled lists and rent them for you, or you can go directly to the compiler.

When you get involved in renting lists, you'll hear talk about primary markets and peripheral markets. Both types can be "target" markets for you. Primary markets for a museum membership program, for example, would include lists of contributors to cultural organizations, buyers of books, records, and cultural magazines, and subscribers to concerts or the theater. But you shouldn't overlook such peripheral markets as buyers of expensive merchandise and credit card holders. The fashion show list mentioned earlier is a good example of a successful peripheral market.

How to rent a list.   Once you've decided to test a few lists of prospects and you've talked with your list broker, you'll have to submit a sample of your proposed mailing piece with your order to get the list owner's approval. Then you have to decide whether you want the list printed on pressure-sensitive labels, or prepared for "Cheshire" mailing labels (computer print-out sheets that can be automatically cut up and glued to your mailing piece by a machine in your mailing house), or on computer tape for computer-letter printing. If your own list is on computer tape, you may then ask to have the rented lists "merge/purged" against your list to eliminate duplications. (They merge the lists, and then purge the duplicates.)

You are renting at a fixed cost-per-thousand for a one-time use. (Every rented list is loaded with "decoys," dummy names, to alert the list owner if the list is copied and used more than once. So follow the rules.) You'll want to code every mailing piece to show from which list it resulted so you can measure response. If you use pressure sensitive or Cheshire labels affixed to a membership response form, you can have the computer print the code directly on the label. That's called "key coding," and it costs just a little extra.

YOUR SALES TECHNIQUES

Once you've determined the markets you want to test, you'll have to decide which methods of selling will get the best results for the smallest investment. And there are many techniques for you to consider.

Any selling method you use must be considered cost-effective if it returns as much as *80 percent* of the *selling cost* through first-year dues. This is a concept you'll have to be sure your board understands and becomes comfortable with. Just about every business, and especially the magazine publishing field, knows how significant it is to acquire a new customer and is usually even willing to lose a little to make the first sale.

In membership, as in business, you should plan to start making a profit on the first renewals, and the profits continue to grow the longer you persuade each member to renew. This is especially true if you have other services and products to sell along the way — books, conferences, seminars, and other opportunities that may be available to you. (Later in another chapter we'll show you how to compute the long-term "value of a member" through the Allowable Order Cost Formula.)

But as you examine the many selling methods available to you, just keep in mind that you're likely to have a first-year gap between selling cost and dues income. It's okay. It happens to almost every organization.

Direct mail. Even if you're just a small local organization, direct mail is the best way, and probably the only way, to contact a large audience — identifying those who are predisposed to consider your offer favorably.

You may even want to arrange advance mass-media publicity and advertising to alert prospects that a mailing is coming and to arouse their curiosity enough to get them to open your envelope.

If direct mail is such an effective way to acquire new members, why don't more organizations use it? Well, most of them do. But some don't. Why? Part of the reason is *unreasonable expectations,* both about dollar return and percentage of response. Many board members and staff professionals cling to "the myth of 2 percent" as the average response they should receive. Very few membership programs do that well, and many have built strong memberships at .8 of one percent or less. Remember, the only true measurement of response rate is to determine what is profitable after you know your renewal rate. Then you keep mailing until the response drops below that profitable level.

Direct mail is a very demanding and complex way to sell. Yet interest and activity in it grow each year. Fortunately, there are dozens of good books on direct mail basics and still more on special aspects of the field. There are also several excellent trade magazines and newsletters in the field, most of them covering the broader aspects of direct marketing.

It's an excellent idea to join a local direct mail or direct marketing club, so you'll get notices for seminars on subjects like lists, direct mail mathematics, production, copy, etc. Write to the Direct Marketing Association (6 East 43rd Street, New York, NY 10017) for information about local clubs and about membership in the DMA itself. DMA publishes and distributes excellent books, manuals, and booklets on direct marketing and also sponsors many seminars and several national conferences. You may find DMA dues to be high (though they're scaled according to whether you're a "user" or a "supplier" and also by the volume of your business). But the manual that comes with membership and the continuing information you'll receive as a member can improve your efficiency and save you from many costly mistakes. The manual includes one of the best bibliographies available on direct marketing publications.

Space, radio, and television. Large national organizations promote membership with paid advertising in regional or national magazines and newspapers or on radio and television. They usually tie the advertising to direct-mail saturation of the targeted markets.

Some small cultural organizations with attractive membership programs have also found it profitable to use paid or public service ads in the media. They advertise special events, mentioning membership discounts and other membership benefits. Sometimes they include a coupon "for more information" in newspaper or magazine ads or an address or telephone number on radio and television.

Celebrity endorsements can be helpful in mass media advertising. The Cincinnati Zoo enlisted the help of the star of a popular television show associated with Cincinnati. She appeared in television and radio commercials. She was also featured in a follow-up mailer. And a bonus of a full-color wall poster of her was offered to those who became members before a deadline. The first three months of the campaign increased basic memberships by 27 percent.

Direct sales of memberships through any type of mass media advertising are relatively rare. But advertising exposure tends to make prospects aware of your organization, predisposed to accepting your mailed offer or interested in requesting more information.

It's usually a good idea to include a code indicating the source of the response in all the addresses given in your ads. For example, an ad in a newspaper could include in the address: Dept. LP520 (for a May 20th ad in the Logan Post).

Some of your best media opportunities have nothing to do with formal paid advertising. Every press release or interview should include some strong reference to your membership program — especially if the benefits and privileges are newsworthy. During the King Tut exhibition in many United States cities, for example, the media gave museums' membership programs many thousands of dollars worth of free advertising by mentioning that there were special viewing times and priority tickets for members. Information like that, in news and feature articles, can be more effective than paid advertising.

When an organization is new and unique, the willingness of national media to cooperate by giving massive, valuable publicity can often astound even seasoned public relations people. Here's an example. As plans for the Monterey Bay (Calif.) Aquarium began to unfold a year or two before it opened, the staff received calls from news media from all over the nation. A regional magazine featured a long cover story. National news magazines and network television and radio news programs gave extensive coverage to the opening. And newspapers throughout California reported on attendance, which ran nearly double the estimates in the first year. This publicity helped to build an initial membership of more than 13,000, representing nearly 30,000 individuals.

But that was just the beginning. One of the major privileges of membership was free admission and a separate members' entrance, with priority admission for members and their guests

at all times. As huge crowds forced the Aquarium to limit week-end attendance by non-members to specific reserved times, this priority admission greatly increased in value as a membership privilege. At the end of less than a full year, the aquarium's membership had swelled to 38,000 — representing more than 100,000 individuals and attesting to the continuing value of excellent publicity and promotion.

Telephone.   Use of the telephone, known as "telemarketing," to sell memberships is far from new. In the 1930's, The Art Institute of Chicago already depended on telephone sales for most of its basic annual memberships and for upgrading people to life membership. Some of the most successful telephone selling was done to new arrivals in high-income neighborhoods and also to business people whose promotions were reported in the media. The technique can be effective all by itself in small markets and as a selective follow-up to mailings in large markets.

When the telephone is used by volunteer callers, the costs can be substantially reduced. But be sure that volunteers are carefully coached and provided with a script written by an experienced professional. Sometimes a local company will contribute the use of its telephones for selling memberships after business hours. Many colleges and universities have found phonothons, using alumni volunteer callers, to be one of the most effective ways of persuading other alumni to make annual gifts and to join minimum gift clubs. As we'll explore in a later chapter, the telephone can be especially effective in getting renewals of memberships after less expensive mailings have failed.

Counter sales and 'take-ones.'   When a person is interested enough in your organization to visit it, you have to assume that he or she has a predisposition to become a member — if invited. So, remember to extend the invitation.

Some organizations — such as museums, cultural centers and theaters — have a membership-sales counter staffed whenever the crowds are passing through. These counters are most effective if they're positioned so that the prospect approaches them before he or she reaches the ticket booth. They're even more effective if they advertise discounts or priority lines for mem-

MONTEREY BAY AQUARIUM

886 Cannery Row
Monterey, California 93940
408-649-6466

For Information Contact:
Hank Armstrong
Public Relations Manager
John C. Racanelli
Director of Marketing

News Release

FOR IMMEDIATE RELEASE
October 12, 198

<u>Monterey</u> <u>Bay</u> <u>Aquarium</u> <u>Memberships</u>
<u>Proving</u> <u>Tremendously</u> <u>Popular</u>

Response to the Monterey Bay Aquarium's initial
Charter Membership campaign has been overwhelming,
with nearly 9,000 memberships likely to be sold by
its opening on October 20.

Caught somewhat by surprise, aquarium staff have
been working around the clock at times to meet the
demand.

All those who join prior to opening will have
their memberships honored on opening day, even if
membership cards have not been mailed to them by
October 20. A list for those will be kept at the
aquarium's Group and Member's Entrance and identification will be requested.

At $35 for individuals, $40 for couples, $45 for
families and $25 for students and seniors, memberships
are an attractive alternative that offer people a year's
free admission, a quarterly newsletter and other benefits.

Membership forms are available at many businesses on
Cannery Row and Fisherman's Wharf as well as the aquarium.

bers. Most membership-sales counters would be too expensive to operate if they didn't use volunteer staffing on a steady basis, as most organizations do. But some membership-sales counters are combined with merchandise-sales facilities, which are operated by paid staff.

Even when there is a membership sales counter, you should also explore other ways for visitors to become members or at least to express interest. At The Art Institute of Chicago, members receive a 10 percent discount on purchases at the museum store. A small sign in the store mentions this discount. And the Institute receives hundreds of membership inquiries each week as a result. Would-be members simply fill out a small form available at the store (using a pencil on a chain) and drop the completed form into the slot of a box provided just for that purpose.

Many organizations find it profitable to develop a "take-one" folder describing membership benefits and including a membership form with reply envelope. These can be placed on lunch room tables, in hospital lobbies and in other convenient places throughout an institution. In short, when they're visiting you, make it easy for people to discover the additional benefits you offer.

Package inserts and statement stuffers. Sometimes there are opportunities to get the help of cooperative businesses that send a lot of merchandise to their own customers. The Prorodeo Hall of Champions and Museum of the American Cowboy made such an arrangement with the manufacturer of a brand of men's jeans. They put an application for membership into the hip pocket of each new pair of jeans. Sometimes you can make such an arrangement at no cost; usually you have to pay, but often not much.

Banks, utilities and some other firms often mail huge numbers of statements to customers each month. Sometimes they will consider enclosing your membership folder in their mailings. The Art Institute of Chicago once persuaded a merchandiser to enclose a "send me membership information" card with one of its credit-card-statement mailings. As expected, the response was fairly light because of the nature of the market. Slightly less than 2 percent of the recipients returned the cards. But more than 10 percent of those people became members. The only cost to the Art Institute was for printing the card and for return postage.

Salespeople.   A few large professional and trade associations and motor clubs use salespeople to approach prospects in person. This can work when membership dues are relatively high and there is an opportunity to sell the new member additional, profitable services — such as automobile and casualty insurance, attractive professional publications, or seminars. Salespeople can be effective in following-up referral leads. Members who have failed to renew after a full series of renewal mailings may respond to a direct sales call.

'Member-Get-A-Member' campaigns.   Some organizations run campaigns in which all current members are invited to sign up one or more new members. Many offer a premium to a member who recruits a new member. But others do equally well by just publicizing the member's performance as a new-member recruiter — usually in a membership newsletter. The Petroleum Equipment Institute asks members to write to friends, enclosing a folder that explains membership benefits. The folder includes a membership form on which the recommending member can enter his or her name as "Presented by." It's small enough to fit a standard size, #10 envelope. The Institute of Internal Auditors provides a brochure for current members to use in recruiting new members and awards a prize to the member who brings in the most new members. Also, for each new member obtained, the recommending member's name goes into the bowl for a grand prize; the drawing is held at the Institute's annual conference.

Recruitment events.   Many small organizations regularly schedule events designed solely to recruit potential members — a sort of "Tupperware" approach to membership promotion. These events can take the form of: pool parties, cocktail parties, teas and coffees, pot-luck suppers or luncheons, exhibitions, local tours, slide shows, lectures, etc. Active members invite friends to come and meet the other members and guests, often in an attractive private home or an exclusive club. Prospective members are introduced to the organization's leaders and given flattering personal attention. Some groups make no attempt to enroll the prospect at the recruitment event itself. They prefer to send a formal membership invitation after the event. Others prefer to have a membership-sales table right there at the event, manned by a member who is skilled at describing the benefits of membership and in making the sale a warm and friendly experience. The volume of membership resulting from a recruitment event is likely to be light, but for some organizations, this technique may be the best.

HOW TO PICK THE BEST SALES METHODS

If nothing else, this chapter demonstrates that there are lots of ways to sell a membership program. But which of these represent the best, most efficient, most acceptable, methods for your organization?

This question is answered two ways: part by intuition, part by experience. It probably makes a great deal of sense, for example, that a zoo should avoid recruiting new members by personal visits from paid salespeople. Intuition tells you that. So you pick the sales methods that seem best for your group, and you gain experience with them — you test them. If your pool party, say, is a flop, you cross that technique off the list.

But remember: For almost all types and sizes of organizations, direct mail is almost certain to produce the most new members at the lowest cost.

However, don't hesitate to test such things as magazine ads, television public service announcements, membership-sales counters, etc., if they seem promising. You may do better with mail, but you may not do badly with many other techniques. You can mix techniques. Pay special attention, for example, to combinations of telephone and mail.

In your testing, keep accurate records of the results for each technique. Without records, testing becomes worthless and expensive. And watch timing carefully: pool parties work best in the summer; museum memberships sell best when a super-exhibit is coming to town.

Before you can start selling memberships, you have two more crucial steps to take. You must decide what you're going to sell: the specific sales points you're going to emphasize. And then you must decide how you're going to sell them: your sales package — the actual letters, phone scripts, brochures, party invitations, events, schedules, etc.

The what determines the how, so let's begin by looking at the various things you have available to sell.

WHAT DO YOU HAVE TO SELL?

Your proposition is called the "offer." It explains what you will give the prospect if the prospect takes the action you have asked him or her to take. In membership, the offer includes an accurate description of the benefits given to members and the payment terms under which the prospect may become a member. It also includes any conditions attached to membership and possibly special incentives (such as a free gift or a discount for prompt response).

How important is the offer? Extensive testing shows that different offers can produce profoundly different results. Even when the same basic offer is presented in several different ways, one will often produce much better response. If your market is relatively small, you may not have the ability to test many variations of your offer. So you'll just have to build what you think to be the most attractive features into your offer. Then later you can test other variations. Your most basic offer is simply that of your benefits and your price. But the advertising trade provides many ways to gild a basic offer to make it more attractive. You are, in fact, about to advertise something for sale. So here are some of those gilding techniques.

Free gift and free trial.   Even with sophisticated markets, the word "free" has a magic appeal. With merchandise, the free trial works especially well. And so it is with memberships, too.

Many large associations have found that issuing a temporary membership card, entitling the prospect to all the membership benefits during a fixed trial period, is one of the best inducements to membership. The temporary membership card becomes valid for a full term as soon as the prospect sends in the dues. But he or she has the option of cancelling for a full refund of dues any time within the trial period. This offer usually is combined with a time bonus — enjoy the temporary membership for a month and then get a full year's membership (or a total of 13 months) for the price of 12. The AAA-Chicago Motor Club gets great results from the temporary membership card/free trial offer, especially if the mailing is made in seasons when emergency road service is most needed.

Even more attractive to many prospects is the free gift offer or premium for "joining now." The key lies in making prospects feel they are getting more than a simple gift. It must be a gift that arouses their hopes and dreams of still better things to come. When it began, the Chicago Symphony Society offered a free gift for becoming a charter member. It was a unique collector's record that would never be offered for sale at any price, complete with a 14-inch baton imprinted "Chicago Symphony Society" to inspire the Walter Mitty fantasies in the new member. The record bonus was announced in "teaser" copy on the outer envelope of the mailing package. It was developed fully on the second page of the letter, after all the other benefits had been spelled out on the first page. The record was created by combining the Chicago Symphony Orchestra's recording of Beethoven's Symphony No. 9 with fascinating commentaries by Maestro Sir Georg Solti and by Margaret Hillis, conductor of the Chicago Symphony Chorus, which is also featured in the recording. A free gift should have an unmistakable relationship to the basic offer, as was the case with the record.

Chicago Symphony Society

220 SOUTH MICHIGAN AVENUE   CHICAGO, ILLINOIS 60604

Your invitation
to Membership and
collector's record bonus

Mailing envelope

Chicago Symphony Society

(312) 427-7711   220 SOUTH MICHIGAN AVENUE   CHICAGO, ILLINOIS 60604

Dear Friend of Great Music:

You and your immediate family have a great treat in store for you.
When you join more than 4,000 others as a Charter Member of the year-old
Chicago Symphony Society, you will have many opportunities to share in the
varied programs of our great Symphony and several special privileges which
alone are worth far more than the modest fee for membership.

This is _your_ invitation to _Membership_ in the Society.

You will find many strong reasons why you should consider joining
the Society immediately for family pleasure and unique advantages. High
on the list of reasons is to establish your eligibility for the special
Members' Tours now being planned for 19 ; and on into 19 ;.

Established in October 19 ., just as the Chicago Symphony was
returning from its triumphal tour of Europe, the Society extends to its
Members and their immediate families many special benefits and privileges,
including:

* Free admission with two seats to Civic Orchestra Chamber Music
     concerts up to the capacity of Orchestra Hall

* Substantial discounts for unlimited seats at Chicago Symphony
     Chamber Music concerts and Civic Orchestra concerts; also
     on up to eight seats for the three-concert series of Chicago
     Symphony University Nights. You save up to $2 per seat, a
     discount that can more than pay the modest cost of your
     Membership the first time you order tickets.

* Open rehearsals of the Chicago Symphony and the Civic Orchestra.
     Watch and hear distinguished conductors as they prepare the
     orchestras for major concerts.

* Top priority for new season subscriptions

* Announcements of all Symphony events

* The Annual Report and occasional newsletters

* Eligibility for Chicago Symphony Society Members' Tours. Last
     year's first tour to the Aspen Music Festival was an unqual-
     ified success. See the enclosed preference sheet for proposed
     19 ; and 19 . tours to Europe and major American events.

The first page of the letter outlines the basic membership offer.

* A "hot-line" for Members to call for unsold and turned-back seats for regular and special concerts

* Parties and special events (last year's Governor's Reception, for example)

As a special bonus for new Members, we are planning the biggest surprise of all. Maestro Solti and London/Decca Records are working on an absolutely unique "collector's record," one that will never be offered for sale at any price--but will be given to you FREE when you become a Member of the Society. Last spring the Orchestra and the Chorus and a cast of distinguished soloists recorded Beethoven's magnificent Symphony No. 9. Your special bonus record, which we hope to have ready for delivery within a short time, will feature the maestro's own comments on various parts of the recording. Your Member's bonus record will have an heirloom value far beyond anything yet published by the Chicago Symphony.

In addition, if you are a member of that great fraternity of armchair-Soltis who feel moved to conduct when listening to great records, you'll especially enjoy the extra gift of a perfectly-balanced 14-inch baton, imprinted "Chicago Symphony Society," which you'll receive with your bonus record. The baton could bring out the Walter Mitty in all of us. At any rate, it will add an element of fun to those solitary nights when we're alone with our stereos and the records we enjoy most.

All of these unique benefits and privileges, plus the bonus record and baton, are yours for a little more than a nickel a day. For just $20 you and your immediate family can take part in a most unusual program for an entire year.

Please accept this warm invitation and send us your check for Membership dues today.

Sincerely,

John W. B. Hadley

John W. B. Hadley
Chairman
Membership Committee

P.S. If you are already a Member of the Chicago Symphony Society, please pass this invitation along to a friend who shares your interest in great music. Better still, why not use the application to give a Membership to a friend or relative for some special occasion or just to show your high regard. It's a gift that will remind the recipient of your thoughtfulness all year long.

The second page "gilds" the basic offer with the promise of a free gift.

more

pleasure

(and savings)

for you

and your family

through membership

in the new

Chicago Symphony Society

The gateway to your enjoyment of great music

You and your immediate family can now share in an exciting new program designed to heighten your enjoyment of music and the many events involving the Chicago Symphony Orchestra and its unique training organization, the Civic Orchestra. As a Member of the Chicago Symphony Society, you will be entitled to a number of specific benefits and privileges that can be worth many times the modest membership fee.

There is only one class of renewable Membership, appropriately called Annual Membership, with dues of $20 a year. Contributors of gifts to the Symphony having a cumulative value of $1,000 or more will be elected to Honorary Life Membership with no dues to pay during their lifetime.

Initially, all Members of the Society and their immediate families are entitled to the following specific privileges:

Ⓖ **Free admission** with two seats to Civic Orchestra Chamber Music concerts up to the capacity of Orchestra Hall. The Civic Orchestra, founded in 1919 by **Dr. Frederick Stock** to train young musicians for careers as symphony artists, is selected by annual auditions and is rated as one of the finest organizations of its kind anywhere. Members will be sent coupons for ordering tickets to each concert, either by mail (enclosing a self-addressed, stamped envelope) or by showing their Membership card at the box office.

Ⓖ **Reduced prices** on an unlimited number of seats for all Chicago Symphony Chamber Music Series events and Civic Orchestra concerts. You save up to $2 each for as many tickets as you wish to order.

Ⓖ **Top Priority** for new Symphony season subscriptions. Each year the increasing demand for new season subscriptions to Symphony concerts makes it more desirable to be "at the head of the line." Your Symphony Society membership card number on your application will assure you that your order will receive the earliest possible consideration.

Ⓖ **"Hot-line"** number to call for unsold and turned-back tickets. As a Member, you get first consideration on a special priority list.

Ⓖ **Announcements** of all Symphony events will be sent to you as soon as they are published, giving you an early opportunity to make your plans.

Ⓖ **The Annual Report** and two newsletters, Chicago Symphony News and Development Report, will keep you informed on all activities of the Symphony throughout the year.

Ⓖ **Eligibility** for Chicago Symphony Society travel program and group flights. Members of the Society will be invited to participate in a variety of tours within the United States and abroad. Plans include tours to music festivals and Chicago Symphony tours to other cities. You travel with congenial fellow Members, attend special parties, and save as you go.

Ⓖ **Discount** of 10 percent on all Chicago Symphony records and tapes at several leading record shops. Your Society is exploring other attractive discount possibilities for you as a Member.

Ⓖ **Parties** for Members only will be offered at lowest possible prices. You will also receive invitations to special events at Orchestra Hall.

The Chicago Symphony Society will become, through the years, the kind of organization you want it to be. Your suggestions for program development and special events will be welcome at all times.

AN IDEAL YEAR-ROUND GIFT

Annual Membership in the Chicago Symphony Society is the perfect gift for every occasion, reminding the recipient of your thoughtfulness all year long. Allow at least three weeks before the birthday, anniversary, or other event to permit processing and timely announcement of your gift on a special card sent by the Society. Each gift Membership will also include the bonus record and baton.

Chicago Symphony Society

Orchestra Hall
220 S. Michigan Avenue, Chicago, Illinois 60604

(312) 427-7711

Date_____

Yes, I accept the invitation to become a Member of the Chicago Symphony Society with full benefits and privileges for one year. I enclose my check for $20 made payable to the Chicago Symphony Society.

Mr.
Mrs.
Miss_____
(Please print)

Street_____ Telephone_____

City_____ State_____ Zip Code_____

☐ Please send additional Membership card for my wife (husband):

Name_____

The membership form is on the rear of the wallet-flap envelope.

SPECIAL
BONUS
RECORD

Yours . . . FREE
when you become a Member of the
Chicago Symphony Society

"The Making of a Masterwork," a *unique record* produced exclusively as a *membership bonus for Members* of the Chicago Symphony *Society, will be sent to you* with your own 14-inch baton *when you enroll.*

Featuring the comments of Sir Georg Solti and Margaret Hillis on the *making of the widely* acclaimed London *recording of the Beethoven* Symphony No. 9, the *special bonus record provides a rewarding experience in the understanding* and enjoyment of great *music*. This is truly a "collector's record" and *will not be sold in* record shops at any price.

The record and baton are yours—**FREE**—*when you become* a Member of the Chicago Symphony *Society for just $20 a year.* Get yours while the limited supply lasts.

An attractive, three-color enclosure underscores the free offer.

Another version of the free offer is to tie the value of the gift to the level of the membership. The National Carvers Museum offers eight different classifications of membership, each with gifts of a different value.

MEMBERSHIPS

Members join under 10 different instructional membership categories, most with different types of tools and instructions. The most recent membership categories are the Charter Junior Membership program for Boys & Girls Ages 5-15, and the charter Senior Membership for senior citizens. The Foundation has recently received approval for funding by a local support organization to develop an instructional membership for handicapped children.

$98.45 Dremel PowR-Carve Membership #2 — the same as the above membership with the exception that the Dremel #232 Moto-Flex Tool with the 34" long reach flexible shaft is substituted for the Dremel 380 Moto Tool.

- ☐ **($10) Charter Junior Membership.**
- ☐ **($10) Charter Senior Membership.**
- ☐ **($15) Contributing Membership**
- ☐ **($29.95) Free-Form Sculpture Membership**
- ☐ **($34.95) Warren Instructional Membership**
- ☐ **($49.95) Warren Instructional Membership with Cutouts**
- ☐ **($88.45) Dremel PowR-Carv Membership #1**
- ☐ **($98.45) Dremel PowR-Carv Membership #2**
- ☐ **I am including an extra $2 donation to the National Carvers Museum Foundation to help support its programs.**
- ☐ **I am including an extra tax-deductible donation in the amount of $_____**

Enclosed is a check or money order in the amount of $_____ made out to the National Carvers Museum Foundation.

Please charge $_____ to ☐ Master Charge ☐ VISA No. _____

Expiration Date _____ 4 numbers over your name — Master charge only _____

Legal Name _____ Signature _____

Tel. No. _____ Address _____

City _____ State _____ Zip _____

Mail to: National Carvers Museum Foundation, Woodcarver Rd., Monument, Colorado 80132.

There are many other kinds of tangible premiums you can think about. Some groups have offered free rides in hot air balloons. Golf and tennis clinics — featuring a chance to play with, and receive instruction from, a celebrity star — can be attractive to the right markets. Use your imagination, and you're sure to come up with something appropriate and profitable for your organization.

Discounts.   Sometimes the offer of discounts can be even more effective in moving people to action than the free gift or free trial offer. When someone is predisposed to consider joining an organization, the promise of savings, like an initial discount on dues, is a bargain that's hard to pass up. When an organization has a fixed membership year, it should consider an introductory offer to prospects of a bargain discount on dues for the remaining months in the current year. For example, when the membership year begins on January 1, a prospect may be offered an introductory 50 percent dues discount in August.

Another effective discount for some organizations is a combination offer of reduced dues and a lower registration fee for an annual conference. Or you might offer a time-bonus discount: Join now but get more than a full year's benefits in return for only one year's dues. It's an inexpensive discount for the organization to offer. It can be offered at any time, but it's especially effective when the time bonus is connected with charter membership in a brand new organization. When The David Adler Cultural Center announced its membership program less than a year after its founding, it offered charter members two additional months of membership and found many takers.

Another discount possibility is to offer discounted dues in the principal organization when the prospect is already a member of an affiliated or satellite organization. There's extra work in determining eligibility (whether the dues have been paid in the satellite organization) and also some possible problems in terminating the discount eventually, but the results may be well worth the trouble.

Still another form is the refund certificate — actually a delayed discount. With each new membership, you offer a refund certificate worth, say, $10 or more on the registration fee for one of your future seminars. In your promotional material, list some of the most attractive past seminars and also those planned for the future. The certificate costs the organization nothing more than the printing until the refund is used (and it may never be used), but it may nonetheless provide that extra nudge to join now.

Time-limit offers. Apathy and procrastination are hard to overcome; prospects want to join but never get around to it. One of the best ways to make a membership offer move is to give the prospect a time limit for accepting. If you're offering a free gift or a discount, the time limit is especially believable and makes the offer even more imperative. The prospects know they must make up their minds now if they want to get in on the discount or free gift you're offering.

Time limits must always be stated in terms of specific dates. To be believable, for example, you must say, "This free gift offer expires on October 15," rather than "expires in 10 days." If you use direct mail to make your offer, make certain that the expiration date occurs at least a month after your mailing is likely to be received.

The
DAVID ADLER
Cultural Center
Established 1980

William McCormick Blair, *Honorary Chairman*
Gilbert W. Stiles, *Chairman*
Mrs. George W. Boehm, *President*
Douglas Miller, *Vice-President*
Mrs. Robert Lunde, *Secretary*
Robert O. Dunn, *Treasurer*

1700 NORTH MILWAUKEE AVENUE / LIBERTYVILLE, ILLINOIS 60048   TELEPHONE: 312/362-0707 ■ 312/362-0384

Dear Friend of the Arts:

    Have you ever dreamed of learning to draw or paint? Or play a guitar or banjo? Or simply to view art or listen to music among congenial people? Today you have an exciting opportunity to do all of these things and more in a charming landmark setting, just minutes from your home. It's ideal for children and families or singles of all ages.

    We cordially invite you to become a Charter Member of The David Adler Cultural Center in Libertyville, now offering outstanding classes and programs for children and adults in the visual arts, music, film,and folk dancing. As a special _bonus_ for joining now as a Charter Member, your annual dues will include two _additional_ months of membership (14 months in all) at no additional cost.

    And as your tastes and interests lead you into the wide variety of programs offered, you'll save even more through your Member's

Another time limit offer is for "charter membership" in a new organization. There is great appeal to some people to be in on the ground floor and to be known as a "charter member." The appeal heightens if the "charter" designation is shown on the membership card and certificate. Charter membership is usually awarded within the first year of the new organization. Sometimes it includes the assurance that charter members will receive special consideration for certain membership benefits.

Guarantee offer. Although money-back guarantee offers can be a little risky in the membership field, they certainly do reassure the hesitant prospect that he or she is risking nothing by enrolling now. (The danger, of course, is that if the new member — through apathy or procrastination — does nothing to take advantage of the major benefits, he may ask for a return of the dues.) Usually the guarantee is for an extended period, most often for six months or up to a year. There is some reason to believe that the longer your guarantee period, the higher your response to the offer will be. One attractive way for a membership organization to make a guarantee is to offer to refund the *unexpired* portion of the membership dues any time within the term of the membership. Few, if any, are likely to ask for such a refund, but the fact that the offer is made is a reassurance that the new member is joining a quality organization that has pride in its programs.

Philanthropic offer. Membership in organizations that raise funds to carry out philanthropic objectives carries an inherent feeling with it — the feeling that at least part of your membership dues is helping to support those philanthropic objectives. In some organizations, this "philanthropic benefit" may be a substantial part of the benefits received. In fact, if few other benefits can be offered, this feeling can be stressed in your offer. Such emphasis can set the stage for future appeals to upgrade the membership level or to offer support through annual giving as well.

Gift membership offer. The membership benefits of cultural organizations make attractive gifts. And many organizations make a point of offering gift memberships, frequently in special mailings at holiday time. The organization announces the gift to the recipient in an attractive card or letter, giving the name and address of the donor. A few groups even give discounts for multiple gift memberships, just as many magazines do for gift subscriptions. If a free gift is offered to a prospect for joining, the same gift may be included in the gift membership offer — tangible evidence to the recipient that he or she is receiving something of immediate as well as continuing value.

Sweepstakes offer.   If you have a large potential constituency, you might consider a sweepstakes offer: "You may already have won a valuable prize...." These offers have been used successfully in many magazine and merchandise promotions and also in some national direct-mail fund-raising programs. But be sure you understand the fairly rigid rules and laws governing sweepstakes. For example, all prizes must actually be awarded, and the prospect must be eligible to receive a prize whether or not he or she joins the organization. Most people think they have a better chance of winning if they do join, so if the prize is really attractive to them, they may join just to be sure. In some cases, a sweepstakes may improve results by 50 percent or more. But there is a strong probability that the subsequent renewal rate may be lower than for other types of offers.

One of the most attractive membership sweepstakes offers was the inspiration of the American Association of University Women. It's shown on the next pages. Join the AAUW, and become eligible for a sweepstakes prize of $2,000 a year, paid into your Individual Retirement Account until you are 70½ years old. This prize ties in nicely with the AAUW's other benefits of low-cost hospital and life insurance and annuity plans. Any female graduate of an accredited four-year college or university could enter the AAUW IRA Retirement Nest Egg Contest without joining the AAUW. (This stipulation is necessary to avoid turning the sweepstakes into an illegal lottery.) But it's likely that most respondents joined. Check your plans with your cause's legal counsel, if you are thinking of a sweepstakes.

American Association of University Women

2401 Virginia Avenue, NW
Washington, DC 20037

Non-Profit Org.
U.S. Postage
PAID
Washington, D.C.
Permit No. 9347

*Open immediately:
You could win a carefree
retirement!*

AAUW LIFETIME IRA NEST EGG SWEEPSTAKES

American Association of University Women

2401 Virginia Avenue, NW, Washington, DC 20037
(202) 785-7700

IRA RETIREMENT NEST EGG SWEEPSTAKES

Dear graduate woman,

Your signed entry blank will make you eligible to win a fully paid IRA retirement account.

This means you could win $2,000 per year until you are 70 1/2 years of age, toward a secure retirement. Just think. You'd never have to worry again about making deposits from your present income.

Now I know you're busy.

And you're probably not in the habit of entering sweepstakes.

But to win a $2,000 per year payment to your IRA you don't have to buy anything.

And you don't have to spend a lot of time figuring out how to enter.

All you have to do is sign your name to the enclosed entry form.

Just imagine how secure you'd feel knowing that $2,000 a year would be deposited automatically to an IRA account in your name.

Most of us put off planning for retirement and many women don't do it at all.

And frankly that's why the American Association of University Women spent hours in strategy meetings to come up with the very best way of showing that we care about you--now and in the future. The IRA sweepstakes is our way of introducing you to the wealth of information and benefits AAUW members enjoy.

As an AAUW member you will have access to information most women overlook or don't even know is available. AAUW wants to share its knowledge with you.

over

AAUW membership, a MUST for you as a graduate woman, provides:

- Low cost group rates in hospital and life insurance,

- Annuity plans designed especially for you as a graduate woman,

- Group travel plans,

- Strong vocal representation on Capitol Hill by experienced women lobbyists,

- Invitations to participate in special women's leadership seminars,

- Strategies for best employment opportunities, and

- A subscription to Graduate Woman, AAUW's every member publication packed with up-to-date information on major issues confronting women.

You'd think membership would cost at least $25.00, but full membership entitling you to all the benefits listed above, PLUS a one-year subscription to the Graduate Woman, is only $12.75.

If you're proud of your ability to get a lot for a little, AAUW membership is the right choice for you. So before you start juggling your third project for the day, do two quick simple things for yourself right now.

1. Sign your IRA retirement income entry form. You could win $2,000 per year until age 70 1/2.

2. Invest $12.75 in your own success and become an AAUW member.

Even if you don't win the IRA retirement, you'll still have the satisfaction as an AAUW member of knowing you've made a great investment in your best asset-- yourself!

Sincerely,

Mary H. Purcell
President

P.S. Don't forget to fill out your IRA Retirement Entry form. You must enter to win! You'll have the satisfaction of knowing you're one step closer to a worry-free secure retirement. Be sure to see official rules enclosed.

To qualify for the sweepstakes and/or for AAUW membership, entrants must be female graduates of an accredited four-year college or university.

☐ Yes, I want my chance to win an IRA RETIREMENT NEST EGG.

☐ Count me in as a new member of AAUW for only $12.75.
☐ Check Enclosed   ☐ VISA   ☐ MasterCard   ☐ American Express

Card Number _____ Expiration Date _____

Name _____

Address _____

City _____ State _____ ZIP _____

Phone (_____)_____
       area code

College or University _____

Year of Graduation _____ Degree earned _____

☐ Check here if you want information about the AAUW branch in your area.

☐ No, don't count on me as a new AAUW member, but please include me in the IRA RETIREMENT NEST EGG Sweepstakes.

Name _____

Address _____

City _____ State _____ ZIP _____

Phone (_____)_____
       area code

College or University _____

Year of Graduation _____ Degree earned _____

AAUW American Association of University Women
2401 Virginia Avenue, N.W.,
Washington, D.C. 20037

If you are already a member of AAUW, please pass this on to a friend.

The prospect is given several options on this "Membership/Entry" form.

IRA RETIREMENT NEST EGG
S W E E P S T A K E S

Imagine winning a $2,000 payment per year towards your IRA (Individual Retirement Account).

WIN A CAREFREE RETIREMENT!

AAUW MEMBERSHIP HELPS YOU GET WHAT YOU'RE WORTH

The American Association of University Women is looking for women on their way to the top. We are equipped to help you reach your goals through outstanding member benefits.

Over the decades we've developed an impressive network system through 1900 local branches to help you solve even the most complex issues confronting active women today.

AAUW provides fellowships for doctoral and post-doctoral work and grants to return to school.

Confused about annuity and insurance plans? AAUW offers good low cost group rates on hospital and life insurance designed especially for women.

Looking for discounts? AAUW offers price cuts on group travel plans. We also have good discounts on books in our current collection.

Frustrated looking for work? AAUW has a great job hunters kit.

Feel your views are never heard or heeded? AAUW runs the nation's largest corps of experienced women lobbyists on Capitol Hill.

Don't miss out on these great benefits and services. Join AAUW now.
Just fill out the enclosed membership form and mail it today!

A   A   U   W
IRA RETIREMENT NEST EGG
S W E E P S T A K E S

OFFICIAL RULES
NO PURCHASE NECESSARY

Fill out the enclosed Official Sweepstakes Entry Blank with your name, address, city, state and zip and mail to:

> **AAUW IRA RETIREMENT NEST EGG SWEEPSTAKES**
> American Association of University Women
> 2401 Virginia Avenue, NW
> Washington, DC 20037

> Entries must be received by October 1, 19 .

This sweepstakes is open only to residents of the United States except employees of American Association of University Women, their agencies, Marden-Kane, Inc., and their immediate families.

To qualify for the sweepstakes, entrants must be female and graduates of an accredited four year college or university.

The prize, $2,000 per year for life up to age 70½, will be paid directly into the existing IRA (Individual Retirement Account) or Keogh Plan of the winner. If the winner has no IRA or Keough Plan the $2,000 will be paid directly to the winner. Payments will be made by the American Association of University Women the first calendar week in December each year beginning 19 .

Winner will be selected from the entries in random drawings conducted by Marden-Kane, Inc., an independent judging organization whose decisions are final. No substitutions permitted. Taxes, if any, are the sole responsibility of the winner. The prize will be awarded. Not responsible for lost or misdirected mail. Void where prohibited by law. Winner may be required to provide eligibility affidavits. Odds of winning are determined by the number of entries received.

For a list of major prize winners send a self-addressed stamped envelope to:

> **AAUW IRA RETIREMENT NEST EGG SWEEPSTAKES**
> Winner List
> PO Box 294
> New York, New York 10046

Negative option. This type of offer is popular with book and record "clubs." You are notified of new offerings and are required to send in a rejection card by a certain date if you don't want the offering. Otherwise the club has the right to ship the book or record and bill you. One of the most clever uses of this "negative option" in membership has been the renewal procedures of some motor clubs. It's based on cooperating oil companies and their credit cards. Each year the club's renewal fee shows up as a charge on your oil company credit card, unless you notify the motor club that you do not want to renew your membership.

Price and payment offers. Although not as significant in membership as in merchandise offers, this method is still worth considering in membership promotion. It simply involves offering several ways for the member to pay the dues.

- Cash with order. Just as it says, you enclose your check. Usually coupled with this method, though, is an incentive, such as a free booklet or an extra month of membership.

- Bill me later. There's nothing to do but fill out the reply card and drop it into the mail. The bill is sent with the new membership card and other credentials. Because no valuable merchandise is shipped before payment, there is little credit risk. But the convenience encourages *impulse* enrollment. There is, of course, an extra cost to following up on the billing.

- Installment terms. Some organizations that offer life memberships and other high levels of affiliation also offer prospects such options as quarterly payments. It's an upgrading technique that frequently allows members to elevate their sights.

- Charge card privileges. This payment option gives the buyer both convenience and delayed payment. With the rise of bank cards, such as Visa and MasterCard, and credit cards, such as American Express and Diners Club, this option has come into common use for membership offers. However, results have been mixed. The most productive form, as mentioned earlier, has been the use of oil company credit cards by motor clubs for automatic membership renewals.

HOW TO CREATE YOUR SALES PACKAGE

The term "package" is appropriate. It implies taking all the decisions and elements we've discussed so far, and wrapping them up as a working recruitment tool. That tool is usually a direct-mail package, so we'll use that variety of sales package as our model. It employs virtually all the elements that any other type of sales package (phone, personal solicitation, etc.) will use.

Timing. The schedule on which you put your sales campaign into action can be crucial to its success. Most organizations figure out a good time and more or less stick to it, year after year. But this doesn't mean that you should feel locked into a specific schedule. It does mean that you should research what have been the best times for other similar organizations, and then consider how the activities of your organization may alter those times. In the mail order field, the heaviest mailings are usually made in January, next heaviest in the months immediately before Christmas, which also is the traditional best time for most fund-raising organizations. But if you have an attractive annual conference or a special seminar or a trip or a major exhibition or some other event in which membership privileges are significant and attractive, by all means plan to sell early enough before these events to capitalize on their appeal.

Sometimes you need a little experience before you can make sound judgments about timing. The Art Institute of Chicago tested several time periods. Then they analyzed the results and settled on four basic times that seemed most productive. But when a very popular Andrew Wyeth exhibition was scheduled at another time, they shifted gears and put on one of their most successful membership promotions. It made sense, and the new members agreed. Many professional associations are locked into a fixed membership year that limits their timing to a few specific months, but most other types of organizations with much broader markets and ranges of activities should test membership promotions in at least 10 months during their first several years. Then concentrate the heaviest promotions in the months and even the weeks that have worked best.

Elements of the package.   The classic direct-mail membership package is composed of these elements.

- The letter. This is the single most important part of any membership offer. It's one person talking to another person (*never* use a plural salutation such as "Dear Alumni" or "Dear Friends"). It should come from a top official (the higher the better) of your organization and be signed by that official. We'll get into letter copy a bit later. But decide right now that you'll develop the best letter or letters you can. Don't let an advertising "expert" drafted by a board member try to persuade you to skip the letter and concentrate on an elaborate brochure. More than anything else, the letter is what sells.

- The enclosure. It's usually a brochure or folder, but it also could be something like the formal invitation used so effectively by the National Geographic Society for many years. For some organizations, the most effective enclosure may be a reprint of an article from a newspaper or magazine that tells the organization's story effectively from a third party's point of view. The brochure is the place to go into detail about membership benefits and privileges and to show good photographs and other illustrations of people enjoying themselves at membership activities. If a fine magazine is one of the major membership benefits, the brochure may show samples of the kinds of articles that are in store for the new member. If you offer trips, give the itineraries in your brochure.

- The mailing envelope. It should be at least a #10 (standard business size) in size, and some organizations find a 6x9" envelope still more effective, especially when the stock has interesting color and texture. Some widely known organizations need no more copy on the mailing envelope than their names and addresses in distinctive typography. Others find that the right kind of teaser copy and attractive drawings help to get the envelope opened. (As widely known as the Chicago Symphony was, you'll remember that it felt its new Society needed to be introduced by teaser copy on the mailing envelope — copy pointing out that this was an invitation to join and that there was a collector's record bonus. Another well-known group, the Lincoln Park Zoological Society, makes effective use of attractive drawings of animals on its outer envelopes.) No matter how attractive your membership offer is, if the envelope isn't opened, your prospect will never know about it.

Here's a tip to help get your envelope opened. If possible, don't print indicia for nonprofit bulk-rate postage on the mailing envelopes. It's much better to *meter* nonprofit bulk-rate postage on your envelope, or better still, you might try using stick-on, "live," nonprofit-rate U.S. Postal Service stamps. Your lettershop can do the metering for you, and it usually can affix the stick-on stamps by machine quickly and inexpensively.

- Membership response envelope. This is vitally important, and I share the late FRI founder Bill Sheppard's firm convictions about it. He said:

    1) It should be large — a #9 size or at least a #7¾ size.

    2) It should have a wallet flap, providing space for a restatement of the offer and also covering the membership form when it is sealed.

    3) Postage for it should be paid by the organization.

    4) It should be colorful and possibly made from textured stock.

The response envelope should contain enough of your message to stand on its own after the letter and enclosures are tossed away and the response envelope is tucked into the prospect's bills-to-be-paid file. At the crucial time, when the check is about to be written, the response envelope may be your sole surviving spokesperson. Color and texture will make your envelope stand out from the rest in that file. And why make the prospect look around for a stamp? So use a business-reply envelope. Make it as easy as possible for the prospect to drop a check in the envelope and send it today.

- The membership form. And call it a "membership form" or "acceptance," *not* an "application." It should briefly restate the offer and benefits in clear, simple terms, provide plenty of room for the new member's name and address, and state the classes of membership and appropriate dues.

HOW TO WRITE YOUR SALES MESSAGE

Unless you are a professional writer, you should seriously consider investing in the services of an expert letter writer or even several. It could be a profitable investment. The Smithsonian Associates, with one of the best track records in the business, uses the services of four or five of the best writers in the direct-marketing field.

But whether you do your own writing or hire a professional, here are some pointers that will help. And you'll find some excellent examples of these pointers at the end of this chapter.

The letter. A letter is a one-to-one communication. It is addressed to one predisposed person, and the salutation should be as individualized as you can make it: "Dear Friend of the Arts" or "Dear Motorist" or "Dear Friend of Great Music" or "Dear Conservationist" or "Dear Mr. Trenbeth" or "Dear Dick."

It should look like a letter, in *typewriter* type with a ragged right margin, preferably with indented paragraphs. It should have short opening paragraphs and plenty of white space. Some people believe that the second most read part of a letter is the postscript; it's a great place to suggest *gift* memberships, for example. A signature printed in blue ink is usually more effective than one in black ink.

About length. You'll hear a lot about how long a letter should be — and most of the advice from nonprofessionals will be wrong.

The letter should be as long as it takes to present the offer and a strong description of the benefits. It's almost impossible to write a good membership letter in less than two pages, and you may need as many as four. Those who consistently use long letters really know what they're doing. They've learned from constant tests of long copy against short copy. You can be assured that their long letter works better. The higher the price of the product or service, the more words are needed to sell it. The copy may not be read completely by many buyers, but they want to see lots of words, which they equate with the importance of the expenditure to them.

Is there a formula for copy? Two of the most-quoted formulas for letter copy are AIDA (sometimes with an extra "C" between the "D" and the second "A") and KISS (Keep It Simple, Stupid). This last formula is added in a half-joking way, but there's truth in it. In any case, AIDA or AIDCA means:

> Get .... **A**ttention
>
> Arouse ...... **I**nterest
>
> Build .... **D**esire
>
> Develop .... **C**onviction
>
> Ask for ...... **A**ction

The best attention-getting word of all is "you." Immediately relate your offer to what "you" is going to get out of it. Readers are interested primarily in themselves and in their own problems and ambitions. They want to know what you are going to do for them to help them solve their problems and realize their ambitions. Remember Victor Schwab's list of human desires in Chapter 3? Go back and review them each time you set out to write or review copy about membership. They'll tell you what the prospect is predisposed to buy. Make clear in your letter that you're selling it.

Once you have attracted the reader's attention, paint happy word pictures of the way the benefits and privileges you are offering are going to improve his or her life. Build the reader's desire to be a part of what you're offering. Then convince the reader how easy and thrifty it is for him or her to take the action you're asking for, how much he or she will enjoy being a part of the membership. Then, unmistakably, ask the reader to take action: Complete the form, write out the check, and send it today. It's this last step of asking for the order that's so often overlooked in writing letter copy.

Use short, simple, personal words, and action verbs. Rudolf Flesch recommends using four times as many words of one syllable as polysyllabic words. Put the words into short, simple sentences. If you want to emphasize a point, try to make the sentence eight words long, or less.

To emphasize a point further, make that short sentence stand as an independent paragraph.

And keep most of your other sentences within the range of 11 to 17 words. If the word picture you paint is easy to read and inviting, you'll hold the reader's attention right to the end, when you ask him or her to join and tell how to do it. Use a simple, easy, conversational style; don't try to impress the reader by writing "literature."

Even when your letter copy is written by a top pro, give a draft to four or five people who know nothing at all about your organization, and ask them to read it. Then ask them if they understand what is being offered and, if they were interested, how they would go about enrolling as a member. Don't ask them if they would want to join; simply ask if they *understand* what the letter is saying. What you're looking for is an unbiased judgment on the clarity of your message. Too often we write copy for ourselves, not for the prospect we're trying to reach.

The enclosure.   Pictures of people enjoying their membership privileges are usually more effective than even the best words. The enclosure is the place for pictures, and it's also the place in which to elaborate on the membership benefits you've perhaps just touched on in the letter. You may lose the reader's interest by going into too much detail in the letter; but anyone searching for more detailed information should be able to find it, and the place to put it is the enclosure.

By all means print the full name, address (including ZIP or postal code), and telephone number of your organization prominently on the back cover of the enclosure. Those basic pieces of information should appear on *every* piece of the package. The prospect may lose the membership form and response envelope and later want to get more information or to join. Make it easy for the prospect to find you.

In the enclosure, good graphic design is almost as important as the copy and illustrations. The design alone should tell the reader that he or she is being invited to join a distinguished group, or a fun group, or a simple group, or whatever you're selling. Get your design done right by an expert who understands your organization and has a record for knowing what's appropriate and for attracting the reader's attention. The designer should understand that you are usually approaching mature, "bifocal" markets where the prospect's vision may not be quite as good as it once was. (Advise the designer to use dark inks on contrasting stock, reverse printing only for large letters in headlines, and 10- or 12-point type for body copy.)

Can a brochure stand alone as an effective selling tool? Not likely. But there are some exceptions. The National Geographic Society, for example, often has used a somewhat formal invitation format on the front cover of a brochure that, itself, is written in warm, letter style. But most of us should play it safe with a letter and an enclosure.

The membership form.   Copy for the membership form is crucial. But too often it's lightly considered or poorly planned. Whether the membership form is printed on the back of a wallet flap envelope or as a separate card, it should: be easy to fill out; contain your basic selling message; and have all the facts the prospect needs to "sign up," even if all other parts of the package are lost. Certain elements should be on virtually every membership enrollment form.

- A line for the date. This establishes the term of the membership in the mind of the new member and also serves as a reference in your records.

- An affirmative statement: "I want to participate in the many benefits and privileges of membership in the

Blank Association." It's often a good idea to preface the statement with a boldface "Yes" and a box to check.

- Classes of membership and dues listed in simple table form, with boxes to be checked. Make this easy to understand and to fill out.

- If gift memberships are offered, consider providing space for at least one gift membership and a place to indicate how the gift card should be signed.

- At least a short summary of the most important benefits and privileges.

- Information on how the check should be made payable. If the name of the organization is very long, you may want to give a shortened, legal version for writing the check.

If the membership form is a card and not a wallet flap envelope, the full name and address of the organization should be printed on the form, so there's no question about where to send it. If yours is a qualified, tax-exempt organization, you might want to add a line explaining that dues are tax-deductible to the extent authorized by law — perhaps also spelling out details of that extent.

You may want to design your membership form so that the mailing label can be attached to it, showing through the window of the mailing envelope. Doing this assures you of getting your label back again with the gift (along with any possible coding you have included on the label). It also eliminates addressing the envelope. And it has the added advantage of making it extremely easy for the prospect to reply; his or her name and address are already on the form — with plenty of space to make corrections, if necessary.

You and your graphic designer must always keep in mind that the ease and convenience of the customer are paramount — not subject to the whim of a data processor or a mailing house. By all means avoid making the prospective member write each letter of his or her name and address in a separate box for the convenience of the data processors on the receiving end. One reason the use of credit cards as a membership payment option has been sometimes disappointing probably is the requirement for writing the account number and expiration date on the application.

Work hard to keep the membership enrollment form as simple as possible. In some professional and trade associations, especially those that require the prospect to provide credentials, this may not be easy to do. But remember, much of the required information can be obtained at a later date, when the member is enrolled and enthusiastic about all of the benefits. So don't discourage the applicant's early impulse to join by making the membership form an unpleasant chore.

Save examples of membership forms that come your way and put them in your sample file. And to start that file, several good examples follow.

IDEAS IN ACTION

Reading about direct-mail membership appeals is one way to learn the needed skills and techniques. But perhaps a better way is to see those techniques in action, and that's what comes next. On the next pages is a gallery of direct-mail membership material — some recent, some historic — chosen because each illustrates one of the ideas, tips, or theories you've just read about. The full mailing packages are not always reproduced here — only the parts that illustrate the helpful points. As you study these examples, you may well find that your own direct-mail package is taking form in your mind's eye.

If you sell ice cream for a living, the NICRA offers 19 membership fees, based on the number of stores you own and operate.

APPLICATION FOR MEMBERSHIP

☐OK, we want to join NICRA RIGHT AWAY!!

NICRA
NATIONAL ICE CREAM RETAILERS ASSOCIATION
1800 Pickwick Ave. • Glenview, IL 60025
312/724-7700

Please Check
☐ Active   ☐ Associate (supplier/mfr.)

Name_____
Title_____
Co. Name_____
Address_____
City_____
State/Zip_____
Phone_____/_____
No. of Stores_____ No. of Plants_____

ACTIVE MEMBERS:
ELIGIBILITY—Active Membership is open to any retail store organization where the sale of frozen dairy prod[...] item of business. One or more retail stores must be owned or operated by the applicant. A manufacturing p[...] is considered as one store. Part-year operated stores are considered as full time store in computing dues pay[...]

DUES SCHEDULE—(Please check and list stores on back of this form).

1 Store	$ 75	5 Stores	$150	9 Stores	$200	13 Stores	$245	☐ 50-74 Stores
2 Stores	100	6 Stores	165	10 Stores	210	14 Stores	255	☐ 75-99 Stores
3 Stores	120	7 Stores	175	11 Stores	220	15-24 Stores	300	☐ 100 or more
4 Stores	135	8 Stores	190	12 Stores	235	25-49 Stores	310	

Membership begins when application and payment for one year are received.

Active Member Calssification—List number of each type operation:
MP___Manufacturing Plant   **FR** -___Ice Cream Restaurant Waitress Service   **FD** ___Ice Cream Dippin[...]
WD___Wholesale Distributors   **P** ___Ice Cream Parlor (no food) Waitress Service   (with food) Count[...]
DC___Dairy & Convenience   **D** ___Ice Cream Dipping (no food) Counter Service   **O** ___Other_____
                                                                                         (please specify)

ASSOCIATE MEMBERS:
ELIGIBILITY—Associate Membership is open to any person, firm or corporation engaged in the business of ma[...] turing, selling or distributing supplies, equipment, materials or ingredients used in the manufacture of and ret[...] distribution of ice cream and related products.
DUES RATE—The annual membership dues are $100 payable in advance.
PRIMARY PRODUCTS OR SERVICE_____

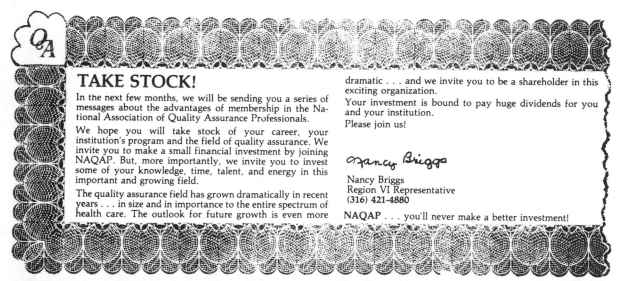

TAKE STOCK!

In the next few months, we will be sending you a series of messages about the advantages of membership in the National Association of Quality Assurance Professionals.

We hope you will take stock of your career, your institution's program and the field of quality assurance. We invite you to make a small financial investment by joining NAQAP. But, more importantly, we invite you to invest some of your knowledge, time, talent, and energy in this important and growing field.

The quality assurance field has grown dramatically in recent years . . . in size and in importance to the entire spectrum of health care. The outlook for future growth is even more dramatic . . . and we invite you to be a shareholder in this exciting organization.

Your investment is bound to pay huge dividends for you and your institution.

Please join us!

Nancy Briggs

Nancy Briggs
Region VI Representative
(316) 421-4880

NAQAP . . . you'll never make a better investment!

This is the first shot in a membership-recruitment-mailing series.
The benefits of NAQAP membership are itemized on the back.

The Lincoln Park Zoological Society

The Lincoln Park Zoological Society is a not-for-profit organization providing supportive services and funds to Lincoln Park Zoo.

Enjoy the benefits of zoo membership and at the same time help the zoo fulfill its 111 year old commitment to protect and care for the world's wildlife.

All contributions are fully tax-deductible.

Many employers sponsor a "matching gift" program. Your gift may qualify; please check with your employer.

☐ New Member   ☐ Renewal

Name _____

Street _____

City _____ State _____

Zip Code _____ Tel. No. _____

Charge to ☐ Visa/BankAmericard ☐ Master Charge

Account No. _____

Expiration Date _____

Signature _____

Annual Memberships:
☐ Individual $20 ☐ Sustaining $ 50
☐ Family $30 ☐ Contributing $100*

Permanent Memberships:
☐ Life $ 500*
  (may be paid in $100 installments over 5 years)
☐ Patron $1000*   *Voting Members

I cannot join, but would like to make a contribution in the amount of $ _____

Checks payable to:
The Lincoln Park Zoological Society
2200 North Cannon Drive
Chicago, IL 60614

Share our commitment to wildlife

The top panel of this gift envelope repeats the offer, while the bottom carries the membership form.

115

THE ART INSTITUTE OF CHICAGO

MICHIGAN AVENUE AT ADAMS STREET   CHICAGO ILLINOIS 60603   TELEPHONE CENTRAL 6-7080

Office of the President

Dear Friend of the Art Institute:

      To my surprise the other day I found that one of my friends was not a member of the Art Institute. Knowing his tastes, I asked him why he hadn't ever joined. His answer was equally surprising: "No one ever asked me to."

      In case we have made the same oversight with you, let me hasten to correct it. I am writing to ask, indeed to urge you to join the Art Institute.

      Here are just a few of the reasons why you and your family will enjoy Art Institute membership:

- Free admission to all special exhibitions, of which some notable ones are scheduled for the early future. (Admission fees for non-members range up to $1.00 for adults and 50¢ for children under 18.)

- The comprehensive Annual Report and a free subscription to The Calendar, listing exhibitions and events

- The new Members' Room, where you may relax and enjoy a cup of coffee in comfort

- Free admission to the Thorne Miniature Rooms

- Lectures and sketch class for adult members

- Reduced rate for Subscription Lecture Series

- New season subscriptions to Goodman Memorial Theatre at special rates now available only to members of the Art Institute. Reduced rates for Children's Theatre performances on Saturdays and Sundays

- Discount of ten percent on purchases amounting to one dollar or more in the Museum Store

      In addition, through the cooperation of a leading art publisher, we are able to offer you a FREE art volume if you enroll now as a member of the Art Institute. The book itself is one of the handsomest volumes on the luminous paintings of Claude Monet that I have ever seen.

The Art Institute's many benefits come early in the letter, but the offer is strengthened by a free-gift bonus.

It contains 78 illustrations, including 51 plates in full color, and a clear and fascinating text by the French art historian Yvon Taillandier. The reproductions include five oils in the Art Institute's own collection (one of the most extensive on Monet in any museum in the world) and two of our early caricature drawings. You'll enjoy a wide range of subjects, including Monet's incomparable water lilies, distinctive portraits, and glowing landscapes. The book's hard covers, bound in cloth and jacketed with two color reproductions, measure an impressive 8½ x 11¼", providing ample size for the reproductions inside.

The chances are that you have known about the Art Institute for years, but only needed some special reminder to move you to become a member. Once you have joined, you will find this vast museum is an inspiration and a tonic. Every wall has something challenging or rewarding. There are exhibitions to illuminate every taste. Here are riches for the spirit, so necessary in these days of tension and concern.

Send us your membership check now, and come soon to see for yourself. You'll think that you have never, never invested $15.00 more wisely. And the superb book on Monet will be sent to you at once.

Very sincerely,

Frank H. Woods
President

If you are already a member and wish a copy of the Monet book, enroll two new members and send us the names and dues. Each of you will then receive a copy. By the way, nothing could be more fitting for young people than a gift membership in the Art Institute and a copy of the Monet book.

And notice how the P.S. handles the problems of current members who might want a free book, too.

REPUBLICAN PRESIDENTIAL

TASK FORCE

RONALD REAGAN
Founder

July 6, 19C

Mr. John D. Sample
N.R.S.C.
404 C Street, N.E.
Washington, D.C. 20002

Dear Mr. Sample:

As your President, I am calling upon you to make a most unusual sacrifice.

Not the kind of sacrifice that a national emergency might require of you or your children or your grandchildren to protect our shores from invasion.

I pray that will never happen -- but today I still must ask you to volunteer.

And I must ask you to sacrifice for your country -- in order to keep our Republican majority status in the Senate.

For this reason, I am personally inviting you to become a member of the "Republican Presidential Task Force."

And you are urgently needed. Here's why:

And the "Republican Presidential Task Force" is a must for every Republican who is serious about keeping a Republican majority in the Senate.

I am calling upon you to become a charter member of the Task Force.

In honor of this occasion, I have ordered a special Medal of Merit to be struck.

And Senator Bob Packwood, Chairman of the Task Force, will present you with your Medal of Merit.

I think it's beautiful and impressive...though a bit large for informal wear, so there's a lapel pin (an exact reproduction of the Medal of Merit) to be worn proudly everyday.

Also, your name will be entered in my "Honor Roll" book and remain with my permanent papers.

I am placing a copy of this Honor Roll on file so that everyone can see your name on this vital document, along with the other true Republicans who are making this country strong again.

Equally exciting, I've commissioned Senator Packwood to dedicate a full size American flag at a special ceremony in the Rotunda of our Nation's Capitol Building.

And I've asked Bob to send this personal memento to you so that you can proudly fly it as I will on every day that's important to America.

And as a member of the Task Force, Senator Packwood will also be sending you a Task Force Membership Card with a toll-free, unlisted, members only Washington hot-line number on the back.

It's not for constituent services...there are regular channels for that.

But Task Force members can call or write any day to get an accurate up-to-date report on issues that are being discussed in the Senate.

3

You will also be receiving a special insider's report called "The Force" so you can know exactly what is happening on Capitol Hill and across the country.

And Bob is planning on writing you special personal letters to keep you informed of any issues that he feels the Task Force should be taking immediate action on.

I believe that the "Republican Presidential Task Force" will be one of the strongest action groups in America.

That's why Bob Packwood and I decided to launch the "Republican Presidential Task Force." We must maintain our Republican majority status in the Senate!

And that's why I'm asking you to become a Task Force member and send $120 a year (i.e., $10 a month) and more when possible. I realize this is a sacrifice -- but sacrifice is what made this country great.

I cannot carry this burden alone. I am only one man. It will be your regular monthly contribution that will carry us to victory.

So I urge you to check the "YES" box on the enclosed Acceptance Form and mail it with your check today.

Remember, this is an exclusive club -- and every member is dedicated to keeping a Republican majority in the Senate. And the Democrats are coming after us in 19C . They want to defeat our 12 Republican incumbents up for re-election.

So tough days are ahead...days that call for sacrifice!

That's why I'm hoping you'll accept my personal invitation now to join this Task Force by sending your contribution of $120 (or $10 for the first month) without delay.

Sincerely,

Ronald Reagan

Ronald Reagan

P.S. If you truly share my vision of America then I urge you to join the "Republican Presidential Task Force."

Thanks so much for reading my letter, and, please, I need your answer within 10 days.

Ronald Reagan

Always try to have the letter come from your top person.

REPUBLICAN PRESIDENTIAL TASK FORCE
Acceptance Certificate

Dear President Reagan: Q00197

☐ YES, I accept your personal invitation to join the Republican
Presidential Task Force.

I'm excited that together we're seizing this once in a lifetime
opportunity to maintain Republican control of the U.S. Senate.

☐ I pledge $120.00 for Charter Membership.

☐ Enclosed is my $120.00 payment in full.

☐ Enclosed is my first payment of $10.00. And I promise to pay
the balance over the next eleven months.

I understand my name will be added to your special "Honor Roll."
And that this historic document will be kept forever with your
permanent papers.

_____
Signature

Mr. John D. Sample
N.R.S.C.
404 C Street, N.E.
Washington, D.C. 20002

367G

Please make your check payable to **Republican Presidential Task Force.**   (over please)

BUSINESS REPLY MAIL
FIRST CLASS   PERMIT NO. 10782   WASHINGTON, D.C.

POSTAGE WILL BE PAID BY ADDRESSEE

Ronald Reagan
PRESIDENTIAL TASK FORCE
408 C Street, N.E.
Washington, D.C. 20002

NO POSTAGE
NECESSARY
IF MAILED
IN THE
UNITED STATES

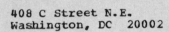

408 C Street N.E.
Washington, DC   20002

Mr. John D. Sample
N.R.S.C.
404 C Street, N.E.
Washington, D.C.   20002

To help assure that the mailing envelope is opened, it bears a first-class postal stamp, glued on. To pique the prospective members curiosity, there's a return address but no name.

Friends *of the Kennedy Center*

WASHINGTON, D.C. 20566   202-254-8700

————— Membership Application Form —————

YES, I've reviewed the membership categories. Please sign me up as a (an) _____ member of the Friends of the Kennedy Center. This entitles me to a complimentary copy of John F. Kennedy Center for the Performing Arts, a subscription to *Kennedy Center News*, and many other benefits.

☐ Payment Enclosed $_____Amount
Please bill my: ☐ American Express   ☐ MasterCard   ☐ VISA
Account # _____ Expiration Date _____
Signature _____
Phone (Home) _____ (Office) _____

```
Wm Balthaser
~   , ჟo ¹ Rcʜd
Ambler, PA 19002
```

PPP130

————— Please make check payable to and mail to: Friends of the Kennedy Center, Washington, D.C. 20566 —————

Kennedy Center members can charge their membership dues to the same convenient credit cards to which they probably charge their theater tickets.

Friends
of the Kennedy Center

WASHINGTON, D.C. 20566
202-254-8700

February 24, 19

Wm Balthaser
̄ ̄ ̄ ̄woo ̄ Road
Ambler, PA 19002

Dear Friend:

I'm writing you today to invite you to become a member of a unique organization called the Friends of the Kennedy Center.

Your first reaction to this invitation might well be, "Why are they inviting a resident of Ambler to join a cultural group in Washington?"

Probably the best answer to this question relates to your current involvement in the arts. Think for a moment of the cultural activities you enjoy in Philadelphia. Whether it's the Philadelphia Orchestra, the Philadelphia Museum of Art, or the Pennsylvania Ballet, you enjoy them because of their high artistic standards and because you can make convenient arrangements to attend.

By joining the Friends of the Kennedy Center, you can <u>avail yourself of the very same benefits</u>.

As a Friend, you will enjoy <u>advance notice</u> of upcoming events at the Kennedy Center through a special Friends edition of the "Two on the Aisle" calendar, enabling you to <u>plan weeks ahead</u>. This way you assure yourself of seats for popular shows.

Then when you've decided what you want to see, simply attach a special Friends <u>priority handling</u> sticker on your mail order ticket request. This helps to move your order to the top of the stack, so you stand a far greater chance of getting the seats you want on the date you want!

This season's performances include the United States premiere of the world-famous operetta theater, the Vienna Volksoper, and the great Pulitzer Prize winner, American classic, "Death of a Salesman," starring Academy

---

Sophisticated computer personalization not only fills in the name of the prospect's community (paragraph 2), but also, based on the ZIP code, chooses the appropriate regional paragraph (paragraph 3) for the Philadelphia area.

The Kennedy Center has been able to showcase the very finest of American talent, as well as bring renowned performers from all over the world to American audiences. The Friends have helped take the dream from blueprints to opening nights with ovations and beyond.

Which brings us to the most rewarding benefit of all -- knowing that your valuable support is enriching the lives of so many through the Center's national outreach and public service programs.

This is quite impressive when you consider that the Kennedy Center receives virtually no federal assistance for its wide range of artistic and public service programming.

It's up to concerned individuals like yourself to guard and promote the high artistic standards that have earned the Kennedy Center its international reputation. And you can do this by becoming a Friend of the Kennedy Center at any membership level you choose. In return, we offer you a handsome edition of the 159-page John F. Kennedy Center For The Performing Arts and a wealth of valuable benefits.

Whether you enclose your contribution or charge it -- remember your gift is tax-deductible. I look forward to greeting you as a Friend very soon.

Sincerely,

Thomas J. Mader
Executive Director

PS: I hope you'll return the acceptance card right now while you're thinking about it. But by all means R.S.V.P. within two weeks to receive the Brendan Gill book being held for you -- with our compliments.

Benefits and privileges of membership

Friends
of the Kennedy Center

Associate $25.00
- A complimentary copy of John F. Kennedy Center for the Performing Arts
- Advance notice of upcoming performances
- Priority handling of mail order ticket requests
- A subscription to Kennedy Center News
- Gift shops discount
- National membership card

Sustainer $50.00
- All of the above, in addition to:
- Admittance to the Friends Lounges during specified theater hours
- Invitation for two to a working rehearsal

Contributor $100.00
- All of the above, in addition to:
- Backstage tour of the Kennedy Center
- Additional invitation for two to a working rehearsal (total of two)

Donor $250.00
- All of the above, in addition to:
- Friends Telephone Desk for performance and ticket information
- Additional invitation for two to a working rehearsal (total of three)

Sponsor $500.00
- All of the above, in addition to:
- Name listed periodically in Stagebill
- National Benefactor's Certificate

Patron $1,000.00 and over
- All of the above, in addition to:
- Name in Stagebill on a continuous basis
- Invitations to special Friends events

Membership Benefits

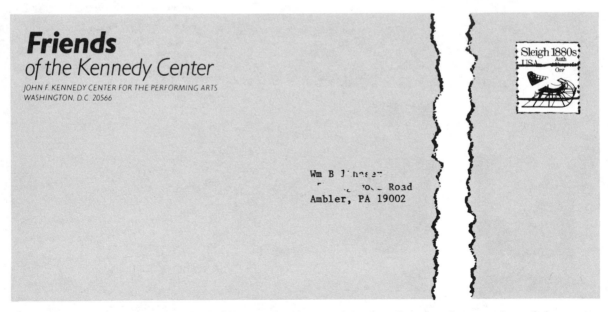

Friends
of the Kennedy Center
JOHN F. KENNEDY CENTER FOR THE PERFORMING ARTS
WASHINGTON, D.C. 20566

Sleigh 1880s
USA Auth
Onv

Wm B J^hnse^
^ ^o^_ Road
Ambler, PA 19002

No headlines or teasers for this mailing envelope; rather, it relies on: the prestige of the Kennedy Center name, computer-generated addressing that looks like individual typing, and a U.S. Postal Service stamp pasted in the corner by a high-speed machine. Nonetheless, postage is at the nonprofit, bulk rate.

Dear Friend,

    We need your support.
Your contribution means we can
reach influential leaders and
continue our critical research.

    Please, join me now as a
member of The Cousteau Society
at a special introductory rate.

Yes, Captain Cousteau,

I care, too. And I want to do my share to help you carry on your much-needed work to protect this planet, its waters, its environment, and its people. Please enroll me as the newest member of The Cousteau Society.

☐ My **$15 annual membership fee** is enclosed.
☐ My **$25 family membership fee** is enclosed.
☐ Because The Cousteau Society is so important I want to make an additional contribution of:
   ☐ $10 ☐ $15 ☐ $25 ☐ $50 ☐ $100
   ☐ Other $_____.
☐ I am already a Member. This is an additional contribution.
My contribution totals $_____.

862

Christopl... ... ...
... ...y ...o... Dr...ve
Ambler, PA 19002

Your membership benefits include:

- Quarterly issues of the *Calypso Log*, the colorful, enlightening magazine that keeps you in touch with The Cousteau Society's ventures.
- Seven issues of the *Calypso Log Dispatch* to keep you up to date on the most recent developments in environmental matters.
- Family members receive the *Dolphin Log* quarterly, packed with stories, facts, games, and experiments to interest young readers.

- Books, calendars, Society art prints, posters, T-shirts—at a discount from The Cousteau Society Book Service.
- Your Cousteau Society membership card and a decal for your car window.

Join The Cousteau Society today!
Box 11313 Norfolk, Virginia 23517

A copy of the last financial report filed with the New York Department of State may be obtained by writing to: New York State Department of State, Office of Charities Registration, Albany, New York 12231, or to The Cousteau Society

The six-page cover letter from ocean explorer Jacques-Yves Cousteau spends all but the last few paragraphs describing the problem: man's abuse of his watery environment. But this membership form carries a triple impact: an additional letter from Capt. Cousteau complete with signature, a recital of the membership benefits, and a powerful photo of the Captain himself.

NOMINEE: 2R06

        MR. WILLI__ _._H_.
             _O__ DR
        AMBLER, PA 19002

REGISTRATION
NUMBER: **41208**

GUARANTEE: If at any time, for any reason, you are less than completely satisfied we will refund your
        entire dues payment—regardless of how many months you have been a member

Please RSVP within 10 days.

*On this "Membership Acceptance Form," the registration number,
printed in red (the rest is in brown), gives an aura of individuality and
officialism. And note the guarantee.*

> *On behalf of the Board of Trustees,*
> *I would like to invite you to join*
> *a select group of Americans in*
> *a significant cultural endeavor.*

Dear Member-Elect:

    _'_ has always been a part of my daily life.
Like you, I can't imagine what real life would be like

"Dear Member-Elect. . . ."

OFFICIAL
Membership Nomination Certificate

The Board of Trustees hereby certify
that you have been nominated
to participate as a
National Member
of

*One is not simply asked to join; one is "nominated." This theme runs
through the entire membership sales package.*

The ACLU offers a variety of membership prices, but it indicates the one it wants most.

Membership Acceptance Form

☐ I accept your invitation to become a member of the American Civil Liberties Union. I care about my civil liberties and those of my fellow Americans. I want to help the ACLU fight the Reagan Administration's information control campaign and stand guard against all other threats to our civil liberties.

☐ To help keep the ACLU strong and vigilant I am enclosing my voluntary membership dues.

American Civil Liberties Union

Membership	Individual	Joint
Basic	☐ $20	☐ $30
Contributing	☐ $35*	☐ $50
Sustaining	☐ $75	☐ $75
Supporting	☐ $125	☐ $125
Life	☐ $1,000	☐ $1,000

* Every membership in this amount makes our fight that much easier!

```
1366
CHRISTOP     .   .L .
             DRIV.
AMBLER, PA                  19002
```

As a member of the ACLU, you will receive . . .

■ A subscription to *Civil Liberties,* to keep you up-to-date on major challenges to your rights and freedoms.

■ Membership in the local ACLU chapter in your area and all periodicals and bulletins published by your local chapter.

■ Voting rights to elect the members of the Board of Directors of your ACLU chapter.

American Civil Liberties Union   132 West 43rd Street   New York, New York 10036

Attention: Ira Glasser
             Executive Director

NO POSTAGE
NECESSARY
IF MAILED
IN THE
UNITED STATES

BUSINESS REPLY MAIL

FIRST CLASS   PERMIT NO. 7031   NEW YORK, NEW YORK

POSTAGE WILL BE PAID BY ADDRESSEE

American Civil Liberties Union
132 West 43rd Street
New York, New York 10036

The gift envelope is marked to go back directly to the ACLU's top person.

With vast computer personalization, this mailing uses an upcoming special event, the "Family ZooNite Festival," as the peg on which to base the membership offer. The prospect is urged not to miss the event, which is a creation of the Zoo itself. The "family" theme runs cohesively through all of the mailing's many pieces. The package initially seems a bit complex; it has many pieces and many ideas. But as you read, you see how convincing it is.

The Zoological Society of Philadelphia

Cordially Invites

C ⁀ꓭL Tꓯ⁀ꓭL

and Family

to attend our special annual

Family ZooNite Festival

on May 4, 19

4:00 PM to 8:00 PM

at the

Philadelphia Zoo

R.S.V.P.
Using card below
Entertainment provided
free of charge

Please present Invitation
at the Gate with your
valid Member's I.D.

088588

the Zoological Society of Philadelphia

On May 4th, the entire
Ba_____r Family is
invited to a special
sneak preview . . .

March 21, 19

463 CAR-RT SORT** CRO1
Mr. Christopher W Ba_____ger
~   c_ Drive
Ambler, Pa. 19002

Dear Mr. Bal h__er:

Among all the families at the Philadelphia Zoo, can you
guess which one will be most important to me this year?

Sure the <u>Kangaroo and Emu families</u> are causing a lot of
excitement due to the grand opening of our newest modern exhibit
designed especially for them . . .

And, of course, the <u>primate family</u> of chimpanzees and
orangutans, the <u>feline family</u> of cheetahs and tigers and the
<u>reptile family</u> of snakes and lizards will still draw the big-
gest crowds to their natural wilderness exhibits .

Yet, there's one family I consider even more important to
America's First Zoo this year!

Yes, the <u>Balth____r Family</u>!

And that's why I am so eager for you to accept my personal
invitation (for you <u>and</u> your family) to become a Family Member
of the Zoological Society of Philadelphia today -- right now
-- in time for <u>May 4th</u>.

What's May 4th, you ask?

Why, it's the biggest Springtime celebration in the whole
Delaware Valley -- <u>Family ZooNite Festival</u>!

For one very special evening, our gates will open <u>solely</u>
and <u>exclusively</u> for one special group of Philadelphians -- the
friends and supporters who help our Zoo keep its rank as one
of "America's Finest" -- our Zoological Society Members.

I'll be on hand to personally welcome you and your family
for an evening of entertainment and fun which I know everyone
in the Bal_____r Family will treasure.

(Over, please)

America's
First Zoo   34th Street and Girard Avenue ● Philadelphia, Pennsylvania 19104 ● 215/243-1100

Amidst the springtime splendor of flowering dogwoods and blooming azaleas, our jugglers, clowns, magicians and musicians will create an evening of magic and clean family fun that's become the most eagerly-awaited outdoor celebration in all of Philadelphia!

Children, parents and grandparents alike are sure to enjoy the non-stop, strolling entertainment and behind-the-scenes tours set in one of Philadelphia's most beautiful botantical gardens as twilight creates a spirit of magic and joy.

Yet, there's even <u>more</u> to Family ZooNite Festival than just fun, food and festivity!

You see, May 4th is your chance to see all of the Zoo's newest animal additions <u>before</u> they are seen by the general public.

From the new diving ducks on Bird Lake and the beautiful Blesboks on the African Plains to the new curious Brown Bears in Bear Country and our majestic reticulated giraffe, Family ZooNite Festival gives you a <u>private premiere</u> to the debut of our latest additions.

And, you can take part in the grand opening on May 4th of our newest exhibit -- our Australian Kangaroo/Emu Outback.

We've taken down the old cages and have given our 'roos a natural outdoor enclosure where they can hop, skip and jump while surrounded by Australian Emus -- the funniest looking bird you've ever seen.

I even have a special <u>commemorative poster</u> so you'll remember this big day!

It's special privileges like these -- plus the fun and enjoyment of the Family ZooNite Festival -- that you receive absolutely free when you become a <u>Family Member</u> of the Zoo!

For less than 10¢ a day ($35 per year) you and your whole family can enjoy 365 days of clean, family fun and education, plus these special benefits:

-- Your family gets to pass through our Zoo's private "Members Only" gate as many times as you'd like, all year long -- <u>absolutely free</u>!

-- We'll give you five extra free passes to take care of out-of-town guests and relatives who want to visit America's First (and most historic) Zoo.

-- Parking won't be a problem -- we'll provide you with <u>free parking passes</u> (and a special windshield decal).

(There's more)

-- You'll receive our full-color quarterly magazine ZooOne <u>plus</u> our regular "members only" newsletter, ZooToo all year long to keep you abreast of Zoo events and educational programs and activities.

-- And, you'll be able to take advantage of a 20% discount in our Zoo Shop plus attend lectures, movies and travelogues presented by world-renowned authorities.

All of this -- plus more -- is yours for one whole year once you become a <u>Family Member</u> of the Philadelphia Zoo!

But let me tell you what I consider to be the most important "benefit" of all that stems from your $35 annual Membership dues:

<u>The preservation of rare and endangered wildlife</u>.

Right at this moment, there are over 265 endangered animals such as lowland gorillas, Indian rhinos and Siberian tigers for which the Zoo is a haven in the on-going struggle to save endangered species around the globe.

Last year alone, the Zoo's conservation fund spent over $300,000 protecting these rare animals from extinction.

Without the help of Family Members who've joined us in the past <u>that simply wouldn't have been possible</u>.

As you can imagine, it takes many, many Member donations of $35 and more to raise the urgently needed $300,000. And our only hope of doing more rests with your willingness to help, too. That's why I am so <u>eager</u> to enlist you now as a Family Member.

When I think how much fun your Family Membership contribution of $35 can bring -- and when I consider how so many of those dollars go directly toward helping us protect threatened wildlife -- I know that your Family Membership is one of the best "bargains" in town.

But don't just take my word for it! <u>See for yourself</u>!

Because I am so keen on adding your name to our list of Family Members in time to join us for Family ZooNite Festival, I'm extending you a <u>special limited-time offer</u>.

Here's the deal:

1. I have enclosed with this letter a Free Pass in your name to the Philadelphia Zoo. You can use this Free Pass <u>any</u> <u>time</u> between now and May 1st to see for yourself the pleasure and enjoyment that America's First Zoo can bring you and your family.

(Over, please)

OR

    2. Use your Free Pass as a "discount coupon" and take 10% off the regular $35 cost of Family Membership by mailing it to me today before May 4th celebration.

Your Free Pass coupon is worth the full $3.50 price of an adult admission. So, you can use it when you come to the Zoo before May 1st, and avoid paying the usual admission fee.

Or, sign it and mail it to me with your Membership Application (and your check for $31.50) and take 10% off the regular price of annual Family Membership for the entire Baltimer Family.

Remember, in order to use your Free Pass coupon (for admission or to receive a 10% discount on Zoo Membership), you must act now before May 4th.

So, I hope you'll sign and mail your Family Membership Application right away!

Then, I'll send your personal 19 Family Membership card, your 5 free guest passes, your free parking passes and windshield decal in time for you to join us at Family ZooNite Festival.

Even if you feel you may not be able to attend Family ZooNite Festival, I do hope you'll consider joining or helping the Zoological Society of Philadelphia.

That's why I am so eager to make sure the entire Baltimer Family becomes the "latest addition" to the Philadelphia Zoo!

The time between now and Family ZooNite Festival is running out . . . and I'm running out of paper!

So, use your free pass (or take advantage of our limited time discount of 10%) and join us today!

We want you as a Member. And we need your help.

See you on May 4th!

               Sincerely,

               Wm V. Donaldson

               William V. Donaldson
               President

P.S. As I said, $35 guarantees you all the rights and privileges of regular Family Membership. But you can help the Zoo even more (and receive greater benefits) by joining us as a Contributing Member ($45) or as a Sustaining Member ($100). Every extra dollar is so important! So, please let me list the Baltimer Family as Members for 19 !

Membership Acceptance Form

```
        Mr. Christopher W Bal......
        ˉ ˉ ˉ ˉ oˋ Drive
        Ambler, Pa. 19002
```

Dear Mr. Donaldson:

    I am pleased to accept your invitation to become a Family Member of the Philadelphia Zoological Society. To validate my Membership, I have enclosed the following:

☐ $35.00, which is the full Family Membership fee for the year.

☐ $31.50 + my Free Pass to serve as a 10% discount off the regular Family Membership fee.

☐ I want to help more! Enclosed is my check for the following amount:

    ☐ $45 Contributing   ☐ $250 Patron

    ☐ $100 Sustaining   ☐ $500 Benefactor

                ☐ I do not wish to become a member at this time. However, I would like to make a contribution in support of the Zoo: $_____ .

the Zoological Society of Philadelphia

_____
Signature of Authorization

34th St. & Girard Ave., Philadelphia, PA 19104 (215) 243-1100 **RD54**

---

yes! My Family and I would like to be a part of the Family ZooNite Festival at the Philadelphia Zoo on May 4th and enjoy all the privileges of membership for the entire year!

There are _____ people in our family, and those of us attending will include:

_____ _____

_____ _____

_____ _____

Don't Forget...

Members also receive these exciting benefits as well...

THANKS FOR YOUR SUPPORT!

	INDIVIDUAL $30	FAMILY $35	CONTRIBUTING $45	SUSTAINING $100	PATRON $250	BENEFACTOR $500
Preview of Exhibit Openings						
Art and Architecture Book						
Invitation to Zoobilee						
Free Parking						
Invitation to Zoo Trips						
Discount in Zoo Shop						
Invitation to Members' Events						
Members' Newsletter Zoo Too						
Full-Color Magazine Zoo One						
Guest Passes						
Free Admission						

From the Desk of William V. Donaldson

TO: The Bal̲ᵢ̲ ᶜᵒʳ Family

As I said, I'm especially eager to enlist you as a Family Member this year.

That's why I have attached the special free pass below, printed in your name.

You can use your Free Pass any time between now and May 1st and skip the regular $3.50 individual cost of admission. . .

. . . or, sign your Free Pass and mail it back to me (along with your check for $31.50) and get a 10% discount off the regular cost of $35 for an annual Family Membership.

Since Family ZooNite Festival is coming up soon (May 4th, 4-8 p.m.), you'll want to join now, then load up the car with your picnic dinner and get ready for an evening of fun, magic and music that's reserved exclusively for Family Members of the Zoological Society of Philadelphia.

Please, let me hear from you soon!

Sincerely,

Wm V. Donaldson

FREE PASS

This FREE PASS entitles

Mr. Christopher W Balchᵤₑr
̲ ̲ ̲ ̲ ᵖc. Drive
Ambler, Pa. 19002

to one free visit to the

Philadelphia Zoo

(or 10% off the Family Membership Fee)

This offer expires May 1, 19

Number of people in party: _____.

Date of visit: _____

RD54

ADMIT ONE

Remember...
the Zoo is for People, too!

Present this Pass to the Gate attendant
for your FREE visit to
America's First Zoo!

(Or sign below and return it with
your check for the 10% discount
off the family membership fee!)

_____
Signature of Authorization

The Philadelphia Zoo is open daily
from 9:30 AM to 5:30 PM

☐ **Family Membership
Contribution Enclosed!**

BUSINESS REPLY M

FIRST CLASS   PERMIT NO. 5103   PHILADEL

POSTAGE WILL BE PAID BY ADDRESSEE

The Zoological Society of Philadelphia
Membership Office
34th St. and Girard Ave.
Philadelphia, Pennsylvania 19104

*A final, subtle prod to action in the upper corner
of the gift envelope.*

The patriotic color combination of this piece is red and blue ink on white paper. The text is in black. The individual-looking "number" is in red, as is the rubber-stamp-looking "urgent" text. Benefits described in the four-page letter include the NRA's lobbying efforts on behalf of gun owners. These are aimed against the "anti-gun and anti-hunting forces."

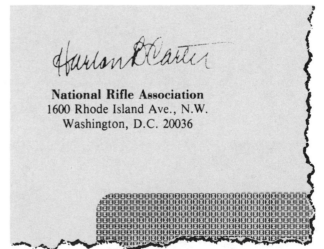

The signature in blue, above the black return address on this window mailing envelope, is that of the NRA executive vice president.

Which of our FREE Sportsman's
Gifts will you choose for your own?

Please let me know your decision today.

Dear Member-Elect:

The Board of Directors and I cordially invite you to choose
one of 2 Free Sportsman's Gifts we have selected for your enjoyment.

But first, the Board and I--along with the more than 2 and
one half million NRA members--invite you to accept active membership in the National Rifle Association of America.

Because NRA has already been working for you, and because
you have missed out on many new and valuable NRA membership
benefits, I'm enclosing a Temporary Membership Card for you.

Your "YES" and signature on the enclosed Temporary Membership Card today will make you an NRA member entitled to receive
your Free Gift and to share the remarkable benefits and services
of The New NRA.

I call it The New NRA for one simple reason: today's NRA
gives you so many valuable new shooter and hunter benefits that
old-timers like myself can hardly recognize it!

You know, I'm sure, that NRA is still the foremost guardian
of your Constitutional right to keep and bear arms. And I'm
sure you're aware that NRA has more programs for shooters and
hunters (and more members) than any other gun owners' group in
America.

But you probably don't know just how many benefits you now
receive when you sign that NRA membership card and slip it in
your wallet.

(over please)

The Officers
and Board of Trustees
Cordially Invite You
to Enjoy the Benefits of

MEMBERSHIP

in the
National Geographic Society

Membership Year 19

There are more wonders in this world than any of us could ever hope to see

. . . but the enclosed booklet will tell you how you can see your full share . . . and then some!

Each year at this time, selected candidates are invited to join the National Geographic Society, the world's largest non-profit scientific and educational organization.

Since all memberships are on a calendar-year basis, we invite you to join now. Then—beginning in January 19____—you'll enjoy a whole year of membership—*including* your 12 monthly issues of NATIONAL GEOGRAPHIC.

NATIONAL GEOGRAPHIC will introduce you to fascinating people in the United States and in the far corners of the earth. You'll experience the thrill of daring adventures and amazing discoveries . . . extend your knowledge of nature's enchanting ways . . . and gaze with awe upon the sheer beauty of our world, beauty too often missed in the frantic pace of life today.

NATIONAL GEOGRAPHIC has been a family reading habit for more than four generations. In millions of homes it enlivens conversations around the dinner table, helps students with their homework and special assignments, suggests great vacation ideas, and gives every member of the family a better understanding of our ever changing world.

Other Society benefits include multicolor wall maps in selected issues. Planned for your 19____ Geographics: *Europe, The Universe, The Arctic Ocean/Arctic Peoples.* Plus three in a new series of U. S. historical maps: *The Deep South, The Central Rockies,* and *The Atlantic Gateways.*

You'll be able to examine—without obligation—lavishly illustrated, full-color books and other Society products and purchase them, if you'd like, at modest prices . . . nominate friends for membership . . . and take pride in knowing you are helping to sponsor the Society's worldwide research and exploration projects.

. . . *all for dues of $15.00.* Surely that's a remarkable value these days! And when you join, you'll receive a distinctive membership certificate, a brief history of the Society, and a catalog of National Geographic member-priced gift suggestions for any occasion.

This may be the only invitation you'll receive to join the National Geographic Society in 19____. So please fill out and mail the enclosed acceptance form today with your membership dues.

Membership Acceptance

Please detach this portion of card.
Then mail this acceptance form in the envelope provided.

NATIONAL GEOGRAPHIC SOCIETY ☆ ☆ INCORPORATED A D 1888

ANNUAL
MEMBERSHIP
DUES
$15.00

CAR-RT SORT **CR 02 33L7L

J H TRENBETH
DR 6002
GLE.WI.W IL

I accept with pleasure the invitation to become a member of the National Geographic Society. I enclose my payment for dues for the calendar year 19___

The membership dues (80% of which is designated for the subscription to NATIONAL GEOGRAPHIC magazine starting with the January issue) are for the calendar year 19___. Please forward this acceptance with check or money order payable to the National Geographic Society, P.O. Box 1224, Washington, D. C. 20013.

D

The fine print at the bottom explains that your subscription to National Geographic magazine is valued at 80 percent of the cost of the membership. This gives the new member helpful guidance concerning the amount of his or her dues payment that may be considered a tax deductible charitable gift.

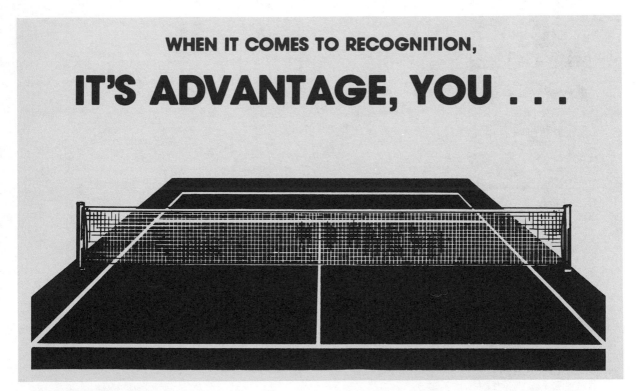

A "take-one" membership promotion. A business-reply-mail panel is printed on the rear of the perforated reply card.

. . . when you join BUILDERS ASSOCIATION

The association has developed a voluntary Builder Certification Program in an attempt to help raise the professional standards and practices of tennis court construction. To become a certified builder, a member must pass a written examination that demonstrates a high level of knowledge of tennis court construction. Over twenty builders have already earned the CTCB (Certified Tennis Court Builder) designation.

Industry-wide cooperation and recognition is achieved by USTC&TBA's active participation in liaison committees with the U.S. Tennis Association, National Tennis Association, National Sporting Goods Association, Illuminating Engineers Society, National Federation of State High School Association, and the U.S. Track & Field Federation. In addition, members participate in industry-wide buying shows, trade shows, conferences, and seminars.

When you join USTC&TBA, you can achieve a higher level of stature and recognition . . .

. . . THE ADVANTAGE IS YOURS!

U.S. TENNIS COURT AND TRACK BUILDERS ASSOCIATION

1800 PICKWICK AVENUE, GLENVIEW, ILLINOIS 60025

YES we want all the advantages of USTC&TBA membership. Please send a membership application so we can join right away.

NAME _____ TITLE _____

FIRM _____

ADDRESS _____

CITY _____ STATE _____ ZIP _____

TELEPHONE _____

Join the Art Institute now and get a month free!

(offer expires June 30, 19   )

Please tear off before mailing.

If you become a Member now, you get a triple bonus:

1 previews and priority access to *The Search for Alexander;*

2 special lectures and free admission to *Master Drawings by Picasso;* and

3 a free month's membership: 13 months for the price of 12.

Yes, I want to become a Member. Enclosed is $_____

Charge to my   ☐ Visa
                 ☐ MasterCard
                 ☐ American Express Card

Account Number _____

Expiration Date _____

MasterCard Interbank No. _____

Signature _____

Daytime phone number _____

New members only please. This is not a renewal notice.
Make checks payable to The Art Institute of Chicago

Membership Categories:

☐ Life $1000
☐ Contributing $100
☐ Family 2 years $65
☐ Family 1 year $35

☐ Individual 2 years $45
☐ Individual 1 year $25
☐ Student 1 year $15
  (Enclose copy of
  student I.D.)

Meet the Challenge! For every $3 you remit in membership dues, the National Endowment for the Humanities will give the Art Institute $1 toward its $1,000,000 challenge grant campaign.

Please send gift memberships to these special people:

Name _____

Address _____

City _____ State ____ Zip ____

Daytime phone _____

Sign gift card _____

☐ Life $1000
☐ Contributing $100
☐ Family $35
☐ Individual $25
☐ Student $15
☐ Send renewal notice
  to me.
☐ Enclosed for gift
  memberships:
$_____

Name _____

Address _____

City _____ State ____ Zip ____

Daytime phone _____

Sign gift card _____

☐ Life $1000
☐ Contributing $100
☐ Family $35
☐ Individual $25
☐ Student $15
☐ Send renewal notice
  to me.
☐ Enclosed for gift
  memberships:
$_____

This Art Institute invitation offers: gift memberships, a $1-for-$3 federal matching program, a free bonus-month of membership, an expiration date for the offer, and much more. Additional inserts describe the benefits in detail and show pictures of some.

148

THE ART INSTITUTE OF CHICAGO

MICHIGAN AVENUE AT ADAMS STREET/CHICAGO, ILLINOIS 60603/TELEPHONE: (312) 443-3600/CABLE: ARTI

March 19

CHAIRMAN
BOARD OF TRUSTEES

Dear Friend of the Art Institute:

I am pleased to announce that two outstanding exhibitions of great
artistic and historical importance will be coming soon to The Art
Institute of Chicago: "The Search for Alexander" and "Master Drawings
by Picasso."

The 2300 year-old legend of Alexander, the charismatic conqueror who
continues to fascinate scholars, historians and artists, will be
revisited at the Art Institute from May 16 to September 7. Highlighting
"The Search for Alexander" exhibition will be objects from the royal
tomb at Vergina, (believed to be that of Alexander's father, Philip
II of Macedonia) and dazzling pieces including a gold wreath of oak
leaves, a diadem, armor and a 22 kilo gold chest. This material
should be fascinating to young and old alike!

"Master Drawings by Picasso," an exhibition celebrating the centennial
of Pablo Picasso's birth in 188 , will represent the first survey of
his drawings to be held in an American museum in more than 70 years.
More than 100 drawings, reflecting all periods of his long career, have
been gathered from Picasso's estate, as well as from private and public
collections and will be on view from April 30 to June 14.

By becoming a Member at this time you will be able to take advantage
of some special benefits that last the whole year -- and more! If
you join now, you will receive AN EXTRA MONTH OF FREE MEMBERSHIP TO
THE ART INSTITUTE! In addition, during "The Search for Alexander,"
Members will be invited to special previews and programs and --
because we expect large audiences for this fine exhibition -- Members
will have preferred access at all times. For more information on the
numerous membership advantages (such as discounts, special invitations
to exclusive programs, free publications, etc.), please refer to the
enclosed brochure.

You will be in good company when you become a Member of the Art Institute.
Alexander and Picasso await you!

Sincerely,

Arthur M. Wood
Chairman

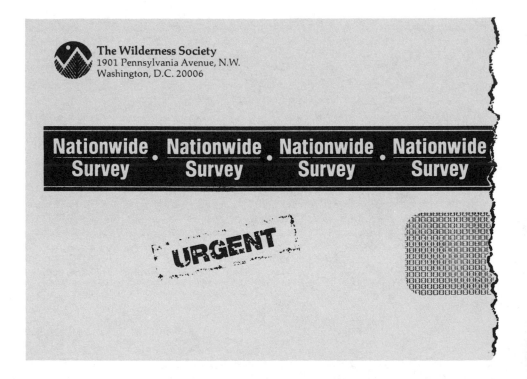

THE WILDERNESS SOCIETY

1901 PENNSYLVANIA AVENUE, N.W., WASHINGTON, D.C. 20006

Dear Friend of Wilderness:

You're being robbed ... robbed of something that can never be replaced.

The Reagan Administration's assault on our natural resources is unprecedented. Interior Department political appointees have sold oil, gas, and coal rights at millions of dollars below their fair market value. They've authorized development which threatens recreation and watershed lands. They've tried to sell off vast portions of the public lands at bargain-basement prices.

But even this looting pales in comparison to the long-term damage of the Reagan Administration's attack on our last remaining wilderness areas.

In addition to huge budget deficits, this Administration has created an enormous environmental deficit which, in some cases, will be impossible to "repay."

Since Ronald Reagan took office, The Wilderness Society has fought to block some of his most destructive public land policies.

If you believe that wilderness areas should be preserved and protected from unnecessary development, then I urge you to join with us in the battle to save our country's last remaining wild lands.

You can help in two important ways.

1. Complete the enclosed NATIONWIDE CONSERVATION SURVEY. This will let the Reagan Administration know that citizens all across the country are concerned about the future of our public land system.

2. By enrolling as a member of The Wilderness Society, you'll be joining one of America's oldest and most respected conservation organizations. Membership is only $15 and brings you our acclaimed WILDERNESS magazine, periodic Action Alerts on crucial issues of the day, as well as invitations to workshops and seminars. You'll also receive a special membership gift for joining now that I'll describe later in this letter.

Here's a brief run-down on the battle so far:

As you know, James Watt was Reagan's point man in the effort to

Conducted by: **The Wilderness Society**
1901 Pennsylvania Avenue, N.W.
Washington, D.C. 20006

To:

NKCB19
CHRISTOPHER W. B. ....
- .... DRIVE
AMBLER, PA   1900^

PLEASE RESPOND IN 10 DAYS!

Nationwide Conservation Survey

Please indicate whether you agree or disagree with these statements:

1. The Reagan Administration must restore the acquisition program for National Parks, refuges and preservation areas that Congress has already authorized and which James Watt illegally blocked.

   ☐ AGREE   ☐ DISAGREE   ☐ NO OPINION

2. The Reagan Administration must restore to "wilderness study" status the more than 1.5 million acres of Bureau of Land Management lands that Watt removed from wilderness protection.

   ☐ AGREE   ☐ DISAGREE   ☐ NO OPINION

3. The Reagan Administration must establish a sound coal leasing policy to assure that taxpayers receive a fair price for publicly-owned coal and that the environment is not compromised.

   ☐ AGREE   ☐ DISAGREE   ☐ NO OPINION

4. The Reagan Administration must stop the giveaway of our natural resources by scaling back Interior Department plans to lease the entire Outer Continental Shelf for oil and gas in just five years.

   ☐ AGREE   ☐ DISAGREE   ☐ NO OPINION

If the prospect has agreed with most of the survey's statements, it is almost a reflex for him or her to go on and check the membership form, too.

5. The Reagan Administration must replace the Watt political appointees who have been carrying out destructive land policies and will continue to do so until they're removed.
   □ AGREE   □ DISAGREE   □ NO OPINION

6. The Reagan Administration must stop the destruction of wildlife refuges by reversing Watt's policy of increased grazing, logging, mining, trapping, and even oil and gas exploration within the wildlife refuges.
   □ AGREE   □ DISAGREE   □ NO OPINION

7. The Reagan Administration must resume the listing of endangered species, a process that Watt brought to a virtual halt.
   □ AGREE   □ DISAGREE   □ NO OPINION

If you agree with most of these statements, then please accept our invitation to join The Wilderness Society.

Membership Acceptance Form

The Wilderness Society, 1901 Pennsylvania Avenue, N.W., Washington, D.C. 20006

YES, I want to help preserve and protect America's endangered wilderness areas and all our public lands as a member of The Wilderness Society.

Please enter my subscription to WILDERNESS magazine and send me—as my welcoming gift—a *free* portfolio of photographs by Ansel Adams and the official results of this Nationwide Survey.

□ $15 Individual Membership
  (regular rate: $25)

□ $20 Family Membership
  (regular rate: $30)

□ I want to add an extra gift:
  My check is for $_____.

□ I'm already a member of
  The Wilderness Society but am
  using this form to make an
  additional contribution of $_____.

□ I do not wish to join The Wilderness Society at this time . . . but please send me results of your official Nationwide Survey.

This ballot is confidential. Results will be tabulated and made public at the discretion of The Wilderness Society.

Make your check payable to The Wilderness Society and return to The Wilderness Society, 1901 Pennsylvania Avenue, N.W., Washington, D.C. 20006. All but $6.00 of your dues and contributions are tax-deductible.

This mailing contains a four-page letter and six-panel folder. But the emphasis is on an "up-front" premium, the decal. Inclusion of such premiums often boosts response dramatically. Decals, allowing the prospect to display his or her support of your cause visibly, work especially well.

PEEL HERE

Sierra Club

530 Bush Street
San Francisco, CA 94108

FREE GIFT
DECAL ENCLOSED!

SIERRA CLUB MEMBERSHIP ENROLLMENT FORM

Enroll me as the newest Member of the Sierra Club.
I am joining because:
☐ I want to enhance my outdoor pleasures
☐ I want to help protect the environment
☐ I want to do both.

I am enclosing my annual membership
dues in the category I have checked. I
understand my membership benefits
and privileges include the bi-monthly
Sierra magazine, special discounts on
books, and the chance to participate
in local and worldwide outings.

Enroll me in the following membership category:

	Individual Dues	Joint Dues
Regular	☐ $29	☐ $33
Supporting	☐ $50	☐ $54
Contributing	☐ $100	☐ $104
Life (per person)	☐ $750	
Student or Senior	☐ $15	☐ $19

Dues include subscription to *Sierra* ($3) and regional newsletter ($1).

Telephone number, please _____
                              (area code)   (number)

To help even more, I am enclosing an extra contribution—over and above my dues—of
☐ $10 ☐ $25 ☐ $50 ☐ $100 ☐ Other _____

FREE DECAL So that you might immediately acknowledge your
Sierra Club membership, we have enclosed our
Sierra Club emblem. Your return of this membership form is your authorization to
display this symbol of your commitment to the Sierra Club and its goals.

SIERRA CLUB

P.O. Box 7959
Rincon Annex
San Francisco, CA 94120

In the previous chapter, one fact probably became obvious: Most of the parts of a membership promotion will have to be printed and then mailed. And somehow you'll be responsible for that job.

So, in this chapter we'll provide a lightning survey of the printing and lettershop industries, along with some tips that may keep you and your projects out of tight situations. One tip is this: If you cannot get your membership promotion printed and mailed on time, it doesn't matter too much how well you designed it, positioned yourself in the market, composed the cover letter, etc. It's also necessary for your promotion to get out in good shape and at the lowest possible cost. Obvious advice, but it's amazing how much money is wasted, even by otherwise sophisticated organizations, because of poor planning and ignorance about the process of production. Even if you farm all your production work out to agencies and suppliers, you'll still have to know something about what's happening. Otherwise, your project will go astray, be overcharged or both. Excellent books on direct mail production are available, and you'll want to read one. By learning even the basics you'll be able to cut your costs to the bone.

Foresight and timing. At least half of the problems in production are caused by rushing and putting unreasonable demands on suppliers. Errors that should have been spotted appear in print, simply because no time was set aside to catch them. Failure to get the proper mailing permits well in advance, to plan envelopes that fit with clearance for machine insertion of the contents, or to provide the lettershop with all details of the mailing — these are examples of oversights that can ruin the profitability of a membership promotion. It takes time to handle all these details. When you give your suppliers plenty of lead time, you'll find that they respond more readily to the unavoidable emergencies that are sure to crop up. Best of all, given sufficient time, the suppliers are apt to pass on to you savings that result when they can plan to do your work during their slow periods.

PRODUCTION AND MAILING

9

Planning with plenty of lead time also gives you the opportunity to ask for bids from several suppliers, a sure way to save regardless of the size of your mailing. Some envelope manufacturers, for example, specialize in small runs that would cost much more from a larger manufacturer (who really doesn't want that kind of business). A small printer you've always used may not be able to compete for your work when your volume rises substantially. The same is true for lettershops. Learn as much as you can about several suppliers in each field, ask for bids on all major jobs, and eventually pick the suppliers who provide the best service at low prices. The key to all of this is your advance planning. When you give a respected supplier time to think about what you are planning to do, the biggest savings of all may come from the free advice he or she gives you.

Ordering envelopes.   If you need more than just a few thousand envelopes, always order directly from an envelope manufacturer rather than from a printer or a lettershop. That way you'll save up to 30 percent just by going to the right source.

- Quantities. Many small organizations plan for a single mailing at a time, and then they order just what they need for that one mailing. If they plan to mail again within a few months and there are no changes in copy, they should think in terms of total needs for six months or even a year. An order of 50,000 envelopes can save as much as 50 percent over 10 orders of 5,000 each. On orders of a million or more, the savings can be as great as 65 percent.

- Sizes and styles. For economy, stick with standard sizes and styles. Every envelope manufacturer can give you a better price on a standard #10 or a 6 × 9″ size than on some custom size. The same rule applies to the size and placement of envelope windows and the covering material for the window. Wallet flap envelopes, combining a postage-paid reply envelope with the membership enrollment form, are more expensive than ordinary reply envelopes. But the advantage of having a form (with room for a brief restatement of the offer) combined with an envelope in which to enclose the check is well worth the small extra cost. In any case, the costs of printing a separate form and paying the mailing house an extra inserting charge may be greater than the extra cost of the wallet flap envelope itself.

- Paper, color and inks. An inexpensive paper stock for envelopes is called "white wove." It is usually used in 24 lb. weight for mailing envelopes and 20 lb. weight for reply envelopes. Very similar but more expensive envelopes are made of a 60 lb. offset stock, which you will probably use if you print photographs on your envelopes. Stocks in colors usually cost a bit more than white paper. Textures, including "laid" stocks, usually add another few dollars per thousand. Using a colored ink instead of the standard black also adds a bit to the cost; two- and three-color printing on envelopes costs much more. But there are some dramatic case studies showing how colored and textured stocks and colored inks can improve response, and you may want to test several combinations for yourself.

- Postage. When you order outer envelopes (mailing envelopes) for large bulk-rate mailings, you have to decide about postage very early in the game. Are you going to print the bulk-rate postal indicia on the envelopes? The only argument in favor of printing indicia is economy. Indicia-printed mail is less likely to *get opened* than bulk-rate metered mail or an envelope with an actual bulk-rate postage stamp pasted on it. And you must remember that you *cannot* use indicia-printed envelopes except by sending them through the U.S. Postal Service. This even includes when you hand a piece to a prospect; legally, it cannot have a postal indicium printed on it.

- Postal regulations and mail classifications. The cardinal rule in planning any major mailing is to check first with the U.S. Postal Service on the latest postal regulations, rulings, and rates. They can and do change often, usually seriously affecting the way you put your mailing package together. And check at a fairly sophisticated post office. If you plan to use computer personalization in any form, for example, you'd better check on the latest ruling governing what you can do and say and still qualify to use third-class, bulk-rate postage.

If an organization qualifies for nonprofit bulk-rate postage and plans to mail at least the minimum number of pieces at a time, there are many reasons to use this highly favorable rate. Surveys indicate that at least 80 percent of bulk-rate mail is opened, dispelling many fears to the contrary. One often overlooked advantage of bulk-rate mailing is that the mailing package is allowed to weigh substantially more than what is permitted in the basic first-class rate for one ounce or less. On the other hand, bulk-rate mail moves slowly, and some of it is never delivered at all. Of course, you'll want to use first-class postage to reach your very high levels of membership on a personal basis. But when you show even your most stubborn board members the increased net profits that can be realized in large mailings by using bulk-rate — or better still, if you qualify, nonprofit bulk-rate — you're likely to get enthusiastic agreement.

In the United States, if your organization doesn't already have the required outgoing third-class, bulk-rate permit, you'll have to file an application for one and pay a small fee. If you plan to mail through a lettershop in another city, you'll have to get another permit there, too, or pay a small annual fee to use theirs. And you'll need a first-class, business-reply-mail permit, which requires still another application and fee and often involves tying up some money in a business-reply or postage-due account.

Ordering printing.   Printing for membership promotion materials may use a variety of processes, depending on quantities, complexity, and creative use of personalization.

The basic printing processes are letterpress (or relief printing), lithography (or offset), gravure (or intaglio ink transfer), ink jet (or squirt printing), electrostatic (or Xerographic printing and in some forms now called "laser" printing), and silk screen reproduction. For some special purposes, you may want to use engraving or thermography (an inexpensive imitation of engraving that gives a raised-letter feeling on letterheads and certificates). Printing can be sheet-fed or (much faster) web/roll-fed, depending on presses, quantities, and other requirements.

However, most printing for membership campaigns is done by lithography (offset). If the quantities are very large, web-fed lithography is usually most economical, and it's always used for continuous forms, including stationery for computer letters. Offset printing is simple. You or your graphic designer give "camera-ready" printing mechanicals to the printer, who simply photographs them to convert them into lithographic plates. It's speedy and relatively inexpensive.

Some elaborate web-fed, offset presses can print up to four colors on both sides, die cut, blind emboss, score, perforate, and perform other sophisticated processes in a single pass through the press. Large web-fed presses are generally used on runs of 200,000 or more and become really economical in runs of a million or more.

If your basic membership letter runs four pages in length, it's a good idea to print it on an 11″×17″ sheet, fold it to 8½″×11″ and then again in thirds, for stuffing in the envelopes with the copy facing out. If you prefer two separate pages instead of a folder, don't print them separately. Print the first page on the right *front* of an 11″×17″ sheet and the second page on the left *back*. Then fold as just described, but afterwards trim off about ¹⁄₁₆″ of the center-fold side, removing the fold and leaving you with two separate pages economically "nested." Most printers have the large paper trimmers and folders needed for this technique. Be sure they make what is called a "regular letterfold," not a "Z" (or "accordion") fold. With the letterfold, the letter can be inserted into the envelope by machine — which is spectacularly less expensive than doing it by hand.

All computer letters printed by impact printers require fan-folded, continuous-form letterheads. Some parts of the letter and the signature may be pre-printed along with the letterhead, leaving room for the computer-printer personalization (which may or may not exactly match the printed copy, but some users claim better results when the match is not perfect). Always get advice from an expert on printing computer letters before attempting it.

Computer, ink jet, and laser printing can personalize the letter with the prospect's name and insert references into the body of the letter — references that apply to him in a way he'll recognize. Personalization, done with taste, is often effective in fund raising. But in *membership*, unless you know a lot about each prospect and have that information in your computer, you're much better off using a printed letter with a printed salutation. Once the prospect becomes a member, however, you'll find that personalization in the renewal series can be well worth the trouble and the expense, especially if you suggest upgrading to a higher classification.

Allow plenty of time for all printing. In fact, when you are asking for bids, specify that the job won't be needed for three months or more. When you do that, a printer who may be busy now but expects a slow time in a month or so can give you a better price and assurance of punctual delivery. Even the most basic lithographed letter and folder will turn out better when you give the printer time to run the job at his or her convenience. You'll also have time to check the proofs more carefully to avoid errors.

Lettershops and mailing. Small organizations that try to stuff the envelopes and put on the postage themselves usually get into a jam as soon as volume increases. Almost without exception, they are far better off working with a lettershop or mailing house — not just for speed but also for economy and efficiency. Small local lettershops are often willing to work with a relatively small mailer. Some of the larger lettershops will be blunt and specify a minimum, such as 25,000 pieces or even much higher. Their automatic equipment requires so much set-up time that they'd rather not handle a small job, but they'll be happy to serve you when you have large mailings, especially when they know you plan to mail regularly on a set schedule. So be frank when discussing your immediate and long-range needs.

All lettershops perform services centered around inserting and mailing letters and enclosures. But some "full service lettershops" can provide many other services necessary for producing some of the most sophisticated mailings. Their services often include the following.

- Copy and art. Assistance in planning the offer, creative copy writing, layout, and finished art work.

- Typesetting. All typography, including headlines, paste up and production of complete camera-ready mechanicals.

- Mailing lists. Arrangements for rental of all types of mailing lists, maintenance of your mailing list, and merge/purge programs (through which two or more lists are "merged" by the computer and then "purged" of duplicates).

- Addressing. Hand addressing, typewriter addressing, and all types of mechanical addressing, including by computer, ink-jet, and laser printing.

- Printing and binding. Ranging from simple, black offset to multi-color and four-color-process printing. Cutting, trimming, folding, stitching, stapling, collating, affixing wafers or response devices or coins or other premiums, spiral binding, and laminating.

- Mail handling. High speed Cheshire label affixing; pressure-sensitive and gum label affixing; mechanical collating, inserting and sealing; bursting, slitting, and folding of computerized forms. Mechanically affixing postage stamps, metering postage. Coding order cards or reply envelopes.

- Electronic data processing. Keypunching, optical scanning, list maintenance, production of mailing labels, production of computer letters, record keeping, and analysis.

- Other services. Storage of envelopes and mailing materials, storage and shipment of merchandise and books, packaging, shrink wrapping, couponing, and premium handling.

All lettershops in the United States must be capable of preparing mail to conform with U.S. Postal Service regulations about ZIP code separation, bundle and mail sack identification, and postal forms necessary for each mailing. When you get involved in high-volume mailings, be sure your lettershop can advise you on, and process, certain types of special handling that earn you substantial postage savings. These usually require special sorting and special endorsements on the mail, the bundles, the bags, etc. And some final tips: Make sure your lettershop sends you a postal receipt with their invoice. The receipt shows the weight per piece, total number of pieces, rate chargeable, and date mailed. That way you know your mailing is not sitting on a loading dock far from any post office.

As in all steps of production, tell your lettershop exactly what you plan to do, where your envelopes and printing are coming from and when, what lists you're using, etc. When the lettershop knows your plans and schedule, it can tell you what parts are missing or even jog the supplier for you.

Most lettershops will require you to prepay your postage, based on an estimate of the number of pieces. You'll get credit for any overpayment or charged for the difference when the estimate is low.

A good lettershop, large or small, is one of your most valuable aids in getting out a membership promotion mailing and, later on, whenever you mail to your membership. The lettershop need not be nearby. Quality is more important than proximity. Many large organizations work with lettershops that are hundreds of miles away or even farther.

No matter how you promote and sell memberships in your organization, whether it's principally by direct mail or by a combination of methods, you are seeking a *measurable* result. Or you should be.

The promotion budgets of nonprofit groups are usually slim. And the only way to get a substantial increase is to show unmistakably that each promotion is profitable or at least promising enough to continue and see how renewals go. When you *code* every response device and keep detailed records of membership sales and renewals, you have the best ammunition possible for continuing and expanding your promotion program.

Testing, the lifeblood of direct marketing, is often a humbling experience. Your "best" ideas don't always turn out to be the best. And you're never done: Very few things, including human motivations, stay the same for long. So an organization must learn to test its membership offer, and the way it is presented, over and over again.

The methodology of testing is simple enough. You code everything that you mail out in such a way that you can identify it when the response comes back. You might code the membership form or the reply envelope itself, or you might code the mailing label if that will be returned with the response. You keep track of how these various codes perform.

Your mailing, in its standard form, is called the "control." And you test against the control; that is, you vary things in an attempt to produce results that are better than those of the control. When you do that, the winning variation becomes the new control, and then you test more variations against that. You test only one variable at a time, otherwise you won't know which variable produced the results. There's a wide range of variables you should test, but here are the major ones.

- Lists. Even when you know a great deal about the profile of your present members and when you select rental lists that match, you may find some that are surprisingly good and others disappointing. Only testing will tell.

- Offers and premiums. By adding a premium, often an inexpensive one, your results can soar by 50 percent or more. Adding a benefit may do the same. A strong sweepstakes offer (such as the IRA payment offered by the American Association of University Women) can make the difference between a resounding success and a modest showing. Other offers flop miserably, but you may learn from them. So test.

- Formats and elements of the package. Next to lists and the offer, the way your package looks and what it says provide the most important targets for testing. This target includes things like the text, enclosures, the use of color and texture, pictures, and the size of the envelopes.

- Timing and seasons. You may think you know the best times for your organization to mail. But you may be surprised when an off-season promotion, featuring an especially attractive benefit such as priority tickets to a very popular event, outpulls the best mailing times of past experience. So test. But how do you test?

TESTING LISTS

If yours is a small organization with limited growth potential, chances are that the lists most likely to work for you will probably be small ones. For example, you may do well with lists of friends of members. The lists may be so small that you'll have to mail to the whole list; you won't be able to extract a valid test sample. (About 5,000 names usually is considered a valid-size test sample.) But that doesn't mean you shouldn't keep accurate records of results. The reason is that you can mail time and again to a successful list and continue to get almost the same results. The reason why it worked so well the first time is that the people on the list were predisposed to consider your offer.

So you simply give them more than one chance to accept. In a sense, you can consider your first use of the full list to be your test.

Before you rent any test sample from a large list, be sure to ask how many total names are available that match your specifications. Then, if the test is successful, you can expand the test (often called a "continuation") one or more times as a further test before investing a fortune in a full "roll-out" of your mailing to the rest of the list. Many times the names you get for the first test of a rental list represent the cream of the list (an unethical but fairly frequent trick in the list business), so continuations fall short of the first results. This is the reason why you want to expand tests slowly.

Some experts maintain that a test producing less than 50 orders won't give you a valid reading. Others say you're okay with 30. But, if you want 50 responses and if you're projecting a response of 1 percent, that means you'll have to test at least 5,000 names. (In fact, if you're renting lists, you'll find it is usually impossible to rent fewer than 5,000 names.)

It's also a good idea to mail to one or more *proven* lists at the same time as you test new lists; this gives you comparative results for the same mailing date.

Even a marginal list may include some profitable segments, and this is where it pays to have an accurate profile of your members. If you know, for example, that 60 percent of your members are women, you might try testing only the women's names on a large marginal list.

You and your suppliers should always be on the alert for new lists to test. If you have a strong and proven membership offer, no other type of test offers as much promise as trying a well-selected new list.

TESTING OTHER VARIABLES

When testing variables other than the list itself — offers, premiums, formats, copy, etc. — remember that the test will be valid only when you mail the control and the variation to virtually the *same* list. You split the list (every other name, one for the control and one for the test) and mail both segments at the same time.

It's usually a good idea to test these other variables by mailing only to lists you've used before and know to be good for your organization. You want to know if the change you're testing substantially outpulls an already successful package when sent to a responsive list.

When testing for timing or seasonal offers, use the best control package you have. Just mail it at a time when you're not in conflict with your usual mailings, and use a list you know or believe will respond well to your offer at the test time you've selected.

CODING AND RECORDING TESTS

Every type of membership form, whether it's mailed or used as a "take-one," should bear a code to tell you the origin of the new membership. This is vital, not only in measuring which promotions work best for you, but also in determining later which lists or sources produce the highest rates of renewal.

One of the simplest and least expensive forms of coding is to riffle a stack of reply envelopes or membership forms so that about ⅛" of the edge of each piece is exposed and then draw a line with a colored felt tip pen so that a colored mark is left on the edge of each one. You can use the same color on continuations by using two or more (one for each new segment) parallel colored lines for your code.

For very large promotions or mailings, you'll want to have someone else do your coding. Codes can be computer printed directly on the Cheshire mailing labels at the same time the list is run. This is called "key-coding." But it only works when the label comes back to you with the check. With key-coding, the label is usually applied to the membership form or membership envelope, in a location that allows it to show through the window of the mailing envelope. A code can also be printed on the reply envelope as the envelopes are manufactured (though this usually means a lot of leftovers) or with a small machine used by many large lettershops. Such codes are often strictly numerical, usually up to three digits, or alpha-numerical, such as "5A." Alpha-numerical coding is an excellent way to record continuations on a list; the continuation becomes "5B." How you do it isn't as important as the fact that you do it, and most important of all, that you keep a detailed master record of codes you use from the beginning. Coded replies sometimes come back years after they were mailed.

The master record.   If you don't maintain test results in your computer, you might want to consider the use of large loose-leaf binders with tabbed sections for each test or group of tests. The first pages are often a running record of codes with a summary of important data with such column headings as these.

MASTER RECORD			Date _____			
Offer _____						
Code	List Name	Mailing Date	Quantity	Number Response	Percent Response	Profit (Loss)

Such a summary is a great stimulator of ideas, even when you have elaborate computer records and reports. Just by browsing through the summary once a month, you're likely to recall some highly successful lists and mailings that are well worth trying again. The section describing each test should include several pieces of information.

- Summary page or pages with all of the key statistics and other details of the mailing: a description of the package used, premium, date mailed, list selections and quantities, numbers of new members by classification, percent of response, cost of promotion, net dollar return, and "half-life" calculation (which we'll describe in just a moment).

- Detailed analysis of results by list. Be sure to include a column to record *two years* of *renewals*, to be filled in when the figures are known.

- Rough daily-record sheets. Keep these for a year or until you're satisfied that you've extracted enough information for the summaries. (You'll see a sample on the next page.)

- Two samples of each piece in the mailing package: outer and reply envelope, letter, enclosures, etc. Move quickly; when you save samples immediately, you avoid the risk of finding there are none.

Daily record sheets.   These are the forms on which you record your receipts day-by-day: number of memberships, number in each membership category, dollar receipts, etc. It's an excellent idea to keep a brief daily summary divided into five-day weeks, starting with the first day mail is received, and giving weekly and cumulative totals.

Day 1 is the first day on which mail is *received* (not necessarily Monday), and each following day is a subsequent day on which mail is received or could be received. By the end of the first 25 days of receiving mail response, you'll be able to observe patterns.

When responses drop to a trickle, you can calculate the "half-life" of the mailing by determining on which day you had received *half* the total responses. Many mailers have determined that for them the half-life is between Day 10 and Day 14. By keeping these records, you'll be able to determine when the half-life point usually comes for you. Knowing this can be invaluable. Let's say you have mailed 10,000 names selected from a total list of 50,000. If you know that a safe half-life for you is Day 12, on that day you can multiply the cumulative receipts by two and

DAILY SUMMARY, BY WEEK

Offer _____ List name _____

Date mailed _____ Quantity mailed _____ Mailing number _____ Code _____ Enclosures _____

	RESPONSE												
WEEK	DAY ONE		DAY TWO		DAY THREE		DAY FOUR		DAY FIVE		WEEK TOTAL		GRAND TOTAL	
#	#	$	#	$	#	$	#	$	#	$	#	$	#	$

come up with a fairly accurate estimate of what the list will pull when all the response is finally in. If the estimated results are very strong, you can order a continuation *immediately* and be back in the mail quickly, without waiting for the total response to arrive, which is often as long as two months later.

Cost analysis.   Another handy form for your master record is a cost analysis. You do one for each variable you test, but only when all the results and costs are known. It's important to analyze costs for each list or other variable tested. The analysis helps you spot the strong and weak variables, regardless of whether the total mailing turns out to be a success or a disaster.

FORMULAS FOR SUCCESS

Whenever an organization (or its board) is reluctant to invest in membership promotion, chances are that no one has grasped how easy it is to test, predict and measure the results realistically. To measure results in membership promotion, you need only two formulas: the Break-Even Formula, and the Allowable-Order-Cost Formula.

The Break-Even Formula.   To recruit a new member, your organization should be willing to break even or even lose a little on the transaction. This is because you probably will be able to renew that membership the next year at a highly profitable rate. To find the percentage of response at which your mailing breaks even — the break-even percentage (BEP) — you first compute the cost per thousand of making your mailing, including printing, envelopes, list rental, lettershop, staff time and all other costs. (The cost per thousand is referred to as CPM in the direct-mail and printing industry. Usually, prices are written in this form: $15/M, meaning $15 per thousand. M is the Roman numeral for 1,000.)

Then you compute all the per-member costs of servicing the order — membership card, reply postage, premium, carton, damaged premiums, overhead, losses of all kinds, costs of membership benefits, etc. When these other costs are sub-

MAILING COST ANALYSIS FORM   Date prepared_____

1) Offer _____

   Name of list_____

   Total size of list_____   Quantity mailed_____

   Variable tested_____

   Code_____   Mailing date_____

2) Costs

   Design, art, photos, mechanicals, etc..............$_____

   Printing: letter, envelopes, folder, etc...........$_____

   Postage   _____..........$_____

                    _____..........$_____

   Addressing, (list rental, list maintenance,
      label run, etc.)................................$_____

   Mailing services (lettershop, etc.)................$_____

   Premiums   _____..........$_____

   Other costs   _____..........$_____

                    _____..........$_____

   General
     overhead   _____..........$_____

   Total costs.......................................$_____

3) Number of memberships............................. _____

4) Percentage of response............................ _____%

5) Total gross income................................$_____

6) Cost per membership...............................$_____

7) Net profit (loss) from mailing....................$_____

8) Renewals: first year.............................. _____

             second year............................. _____

NOTES_____

_____

tracted from the price of your average membership dues you have computed your order margin (OM).

To compute break-even percentage (BEP), the cost per thousand (CPM) is divided by 10 times the order margin (OM).

$$BEP = \frac{CPM}{10 \times OM}$$

Let's assume, for example, that your average membership dues payment is $35, and the order-servicing costs are $4. So your order margin (OM) is $31. And let's assume that your cost-of-mailing per-thousand is $300. Then, applying the formula, we find you'll break even if you get a response of a little under 1 percent — 0.97 percent, to be exact.

$$BEP = \frac{CPM}{10 \times OM}$$

$$BEP = \frac{300}{310}$$

$$BEP = 0.97\%$$

Every list or other type of variable in this mailing that produces at least a 0.97 percent response will break even against the heavy first-year costs of your membership promotion. If a list produces a 2.91 percent response, you'll get back three dollars for every dollar you invested. If your mailing produces a significant number of members in the higher-than-average classifications, your profit will be still greater.

But what if most of your tests fail to break even? Should you discontinue prospecting for new members because of the front-end expense? And if you don't discontinue, just how much can you afford to spend to get a new member? This is where the other formula will help.

The Allowable-Order-Cost Formula. Even the most seasoned professional membership people sometimes overlook the dramatic compounding effect a strong renewal rate can have on the profitability of a membership program. They know in a general way, but lack a good method for proving to themselves and others how renewal figures should affect decisions on membership promotions.

(This apparent lack troubled me so much that I began tinkering with some of the formulas used in magazine-subscription work. By adapting them to membership, I was able to devise this similar and effective formula for membership renewals.)

Here's how the formula works. First, you have to calculate your usual renewal rate as a percentage figure. This should be the renewal rate over the past few years for all of your members, including the first-year members who, as a group, normally have a high cancellation rate. And, when you use one year's membership figure as the base on which to calculate the next year's renewal rate, be sure to use only the *last* year's total *renewable* membership. (If someone dies or moves away or cancels their membership during the year, they can no longer be considered among the renewable members.)

Now, to apply the formula, you use your renewal-rate percentage to compute the average membership-life of each new member. To do this, subtract the renewal rate from 100 and then divide the remainder into 100. For example, if your renewal rate is 80 percent, divide the difference of 20 (100 minus 80) into 100 and arrive at the answer: 5. This means that each new member has an average membership-life of five years.

Now let's assume the same basic $35 membership fee we used in the break-even formula. And assume that from experience, you know that it costs $6 per member per year to service the membership and 75 cents to obtain each renewal. So we plug all these figures into the formula as follows.

Average membership-life in years	5
Average annual income per member	$ 35.00
Average lifetime income per member ($35 × 5 years)	$175.00
Annual cost to service a member	$ 6.00
Annual renewal expense, per member	$ 0.75
Total costs, per member per year	$ 6.75
Lifetime costs ($6.75 x 5 years)	$ 33.75
Maximum net income remaining to acquire a new member: lifetime income, less lifetime costs ($175 minus $33.75)	$141.25

What this computation tells us is that we can afford to spend up to $141.25 to acquire one new member and not take a loss. In fact, even if we spend the entire allowable order cost, we might still be better off financially than if we had never tried. Why? In fund-raising organizations, each new member means much more than just the membership fee. For example, if there is an annual giving program (and there should be), a new member is much more apt to contribute than a cold prospect would be. As cultivation and involvement bring the member still closer to your organization, he or she becomes a prime prospect for a bequest and other types of planned giving.

Naturally, the figures in this formula will change every year, so you must calculate your maximum allowable-order-cost figure annually.

It's unlikely that many organizations will want to spend all of their allowable-order-cost to obtain the "order": the new membership. But a growing trend in many progressive organizations is to set aside a significant percentage, often up to 50 percent, of each year's gross income from *new* memberships to invest immediately in more promotion. They do this with the assurance that they will be much better off than if they stayed with a fixed promotion budget. This practice assures a ready reservoir of promotion funds when sales are good; it also serves as a check on expenditures in slower times.

A page in an unusual book called "You Are Not the Target," by Laura Archera Huxley, transformed the way I thought about memberships. If you think long and often about what Mrs. Huxley says, I'm sure you will search every action of your organization to see how it measures up to her challenge. She writes:

"Most of our human relationships are exchanges, trades. We trade favors, kindnesses, attentions: We also trade unkindnesses, enmities, neglects. The human being is a reactive, responsive organism, and usually his response is of the same quality as the stimulus. The primitive savage within us tends to respond to violence with violence, to friendliness with friendliness.

"In our complex world, our trades are not quite so simple. Most of our giving is to get something in return, although not necessarily of the same kind or from the same person. Often we calculate the return, realistically or not, as the case may be. Often we expect lifelong gratitude or special recognition for what we have given or done. And often we are disappointed and disillusioned. The return is nothing like what we have anticipated."

11

It's all so simple, isn't it? A new member enrolls, and you send him or her a membership card and possibly some other material that seems appropriate. If that's all you do, you lose a one-time opportunity to start a chain of activities that will keep the member close to your organization for years to come. A person's interest in a cause is something that must be cultivated skillfully. But often I find even some of the largest and best organizations passing up this opportunity with mediocre efforts. And I've wondered why.

Could it be that so many of us who have served as staff professionals in membership and development organizations are guilty of a costly oversight? We have become used to doing our best with little need for personal recognition, even for great accomplishments. So we often surmise our new members will also require little in the way of ego massage. Often we are inclined to play by ear, rather than to follow a well thought out, written procedure for reassuring our new members that they have made a sound decision in joining our organization.

A PROMPT, WARM ACKNOWLEDGMENT

A while back my wife accepted a mailed invitation to join a large national organization that she had considered for a long time. She rushed her membership form and check off the next day. Her check cleared promptly — and she waited six weeks before she heard a word from the organization. Her excitement about joining faded very quickly.

One of the big Wisconsin cheese gift companies is so convinced of the importance of prompt acknowledgment that its computer cranks out a personalized post card acknowledging the order and expressing thanks the *same day* as the order is received. A Catholic religious group with a highly successful annual giving program goes a step further and writes a computer letter of thanks within 24 hours after each gift comes in.

The only excuse an organization may have for delaying a warm acknowledgment beyond 72 hours is that it is simply overwhelmed with new members. One major art museum, even though it prepared in advance for a large surge, was stunned by an avalanche of 57,000 new members who joined in anticipation of getting priority tickets for a major exhibition. Even then, some form of acknowledgment was sent within five days.

When the flow of new memberships is normal or moderately heavier after a promotional mailing, you should do your best to acknowledge within 48 hours. Because far too many organizations are lax and slow, you'll win the early affection of new members by surprising them with your promptness. At renewal time they'll still remember your thoughtfulness and courtesy.

The membership card. In membership, we have one of the most valuable cultivation tools of all: the membership card. Look in your on wallet and count the membership cards you carry. If you are typical, you have several. Each is a reminder that you have made a choice and paid dues to belong to a group that was offering you something of value. Make your cause's membership card work for you. It will work splendidly if you give it close attention and thought.

- It should be a convenient size, small enough to slip into a card pocket in a wallet. Most credit cards measure $3\frac{3}{8}'' \times 2\frac{1}{8}''$, a good guide for your sizing.

- It should have attractive graphic design. For the higher, special classes of membership, consider a permanent plastic card or an engraved card with the member's name in calligraphy. Many plastic cards come on carrier strips and can be printed on the computer.

- It should include important information, such as important telephone numbers (motor clubs often list numbers to call for emergency road service). Museums and similar organizations sometimes list museum hours, discounts, etc.

- If possible, it should list the number of years a person has been a member. This helps build a feeling of continuity.

- It should list the *term* of the membership. "For one year from March 1, 19—, to February 28, 19—, (following year)." Or "Valid until February 28, 19—." Never say "Expires on" or "Lapses on" — always assume it will be renewed, and use positive language to suggest that.

Consider sending membership cards, especially for the higher classifications, in a plastic protective case, perhaps with the organization's logo printed or embossed on it.

The letter of welcome.   Even for large memberships, a warm letter of welcome listing some of the major benefits is much better than a printed slip. The letter can be printed with a general salutation: "Dear New Member." But the welcoming letter for your most expensive membership classifications should be a typed, personal letter or a personalized computer or word processing letter. The copy should be as friendly and reassuring as possible — and don't forget to say thanks.

MEMBERSHIP NO.
AA28791 E-21
DUES PAID THRU
01/31/8

MR RICHARD
TRENEETH
EMERGENCY ROAD SERVICE PHONES
GLENVIEW
726-7 00
OTHER AREAS
IL 1-800-5 2-90 1
IN 1-800-62 -521
OTHER CLUB SERVICES PHONE
827-1186

AFFILIATED WITH THE AMERICAN AUTOMOBILE ASSOCIATION

CLUB CODE 20

75th Year

A.I.D. 900020 CDP00020

4 YEARS MEMBER

We are pleased to tell you

that you have received a

GIFT MEMBERSHIP

in the Chicago Motor Club - AAA

from

William F. _____

The Officers and Directors of the Club join me in congratulating you on receiving such a thoughtful and useful gift. Your gift membership in the Chicago Motor Club - AAA is an expression of true friendship and high regard for your safety and convenience.

The enclosed membership card is your passport to maximum service and protection wherever you drive. It identifies you as a Member entitled to all of the unmatched, personalized services offered by your Club.

Your many membership services and privileges are explained in the enclosed booklet. Please read it carefully and plan now to make full use of your membership.

We look forward to serving you for many years of worry-free driving.

Cordially,

Nels L. Pierson

President

members for research and career-related study and branches and
state divisions for public service projects. Last year almost
$2,000,000 was awarded for research and fellowships;

...provides support for our legislative program and our lobbying
efforts, and in particular to our efforts in securing equal opportunities for women in education, industry, government, and the professions;

...provides you with the Graduate Woman magazine six times a year;

...offers you access to other excellent publications, among them
the Job Hunter's Kit, AAUW's Tool Catalog: Techniques and Strategies
for Successful Action Programs, and Action Alert, a biweekly legislative report with suggestions for action;

...gives you access to an annuity plan and to low-cost group life
and supplementary hospital insurance programs, developed exclusively
for AAUW members.

AAUW offices are located in Washington, DC, near the Kennedy
Center, in a beautiful eight-story office building constructed by
the Association in 1958. When in Washington, you are invited to
visit your building and meet the members of the staff. Tin My Thein,
Ph.D., is the director of membership services. Please feel free to

From the American Association of University Women.

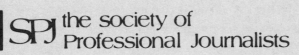

SPJ the society of
Professional Journalists

840 N. LAKE SHORE DRIVE
SUITE 801 WEST
CHICAGO, IL 60611

SPJ the society of
Professional Journalists

    02635   30 12/8
WILLIAM   ALT

AM E   PA   1900

MEMBER, 19

Russell C. Hreben
EXECUTIVE OFFICER

This is your 19   membership card.
National membership entitles you to:
■ a subscription to *The Quill*
■ eligibility for local chapter membership
■ access to the FoI hotline: (202) 466-6312
■ advance notice of the annual convention,
  regional conferences, and a series of
  seminars, internships, and award programs.

Your membership is also a sign of commitment to
freedom of information and high ethical standards
for the profession.

(See reverse side)

Other enclosures.   The card and the letter usually have company in the acknowledgment mailing to a new member. Here are a few of the additional pieces you're apt to find.

- Dues receipt. An official receipt for dues — stating the amount paid and terms of the membership — is important for the member's tax records. Some computerized membership systems print the receipt and membership card on the same form — one with perforations that allow for easy removal of the card.

- Folder describing benefits and privileges. This is the perfect opportunity to provide the new member with full details of the benefits and privileges he or she will be receiving, telephone numbers to call for specific information, and encouragement to make frequent use of the membership. Such a folder can first be used in the selling package and sent again with the new member's other credentials.

- Current newsletter. Let the new member know what you'll soon be offering for his or her enjoyment. Tell new members more about the organization and about some of the people involved. A copy of your most recent newsletter for members may be the easiest medium for this information.

Recognition devices.   For the higher classes of membership, consider sending new members personalized certificates or even plaques, medallions, or paper weights.

Motor clubs probably lead all others in the use of decals, which are usually proudly displayed by the members on their bumpers or windshields — a great form of testimonial advertising. But other groups, such as museums, zoos, theaters, symphonies, etc., also send tasteful decals. Golfing groups find that bag tags are popular. Ski organizations often include shoulder patches as a new-membership benefit. Even pins, neckties, scarves and jewelry bearing the cause's logo are happily worn by new members, anxious to display their new affiliation.

- Certificates. Probably no recognition device is more powerful than a handsome certificate, beautifully designed, embellished with a gold seal, and signed by one or more distinguished officers of the organization. Why? Because the person honored can proudly display a certificate in his or her office or home and look at it often. Because of the difficulty in updating a certificate, it's common to find certificates used only for life memberships and honorary memberships, in which the year of the award is of little importance.

But certificates can be updated. A mylar peel-off label or a dated plastic chip can be used for updating a relatively simple, annual certificate, that marks a basic-level membership. But something more is needed for a certificate recognizing a very high level of renewable membership. One ingenious solution is to present or send the initial certificate *framed* to each recipient. You use a frame with a flat, deep bottom piece that provides room for a series of engraved brass ovals — each showing the current year. The oval for the year in which the membership is started is affixed to the frame at the far left. Then, as the membership is renewed each year, a brass oval (with a pressure-sensitive backing) for each year is sent with the acknowledgment, and the member sticks it in place. Every time the honored member sees the certificate, he or she can look with pride at the string of years. And if the member forgets to renew, the empty space for the current year is a conspicuous reminder.

CARRY OUT YOUR PROMISES

Now, your new member has received a prompt and warm acknowledgment. And your next step in effective cultivation is to carry out all your promises about the benefits that come with membership.

If you offer discounts, for example, tell new members exactly what they are and how they can get them. Many neighborhood organizations arrange attractive membership discounts at local lumber yards and paint stores. And they keep reminding their members of the privilege, so the members will use them enough to convince the merchants they're worth continuing. Museums offer discounts at museum stores, for magazine subscriptions, and for special events. Some cultural centers go a step beyond and arrange discounts at art supply stores and music shops, regularly updating the list of discount bargains they send their members.

If you promise special programs, by all means carry them out. A fine, old but stodgy organization once offered a series of tours to local ethnic neighborhoods as a membership benefit. The officials then failed to produce a single tour for their members. The enthusiastic new members generated by the promised benefit canceled in record numbers.

Organizations with relatively small staffs are often afraid to put some zing into their programs. Why? Because "zing" may involve too much work or may prove to draw too small of a response or an unfavorable response. A technique known as "dry testing" provides a fine remedy for this type of fear. The Chicago Symphony Society, for example, announced to members a series of tours to outstanding music events in the United States and abroad. They asked members to check the ones in which they were interested on a list and return it. The form they used is shown on the next page. When the replies were in, the Society determined that some were not worth pursuing; interest was too low. They so notified those who had checked the least popular events and continued to promote the ones in which there was wide interest.

Just be careful in dry testing to make it clear that the list of offerings is conditional in nature. Call them "proposed" plans. Make no representations to mislead the public. Within four months, notify those who checked unpopular events that there wasn't sufficient interest to continue. By taking these steps you'll comply with guidelines for such things issued by the U.S. Federal Trade Commission and also keep your members happy with you.

Chicago Symphony Society
220 South Michigan Avenue
Chicago, Illinois 60604

Preference Check–List of

PROPOSED MEMBERS' TOURS

I understand that as an Annual Member of the Society I will be eligible to participate in a wide variety of tours planned for Members only. Please send me information on the tours I have checked below as plans develop.

☐ February 22 – March 5

Twelve day tour to Amsterdam, Paris, London. Concerts and special events. Tentative approximate cost: $͵2ͨ per person.

☐ April

Eight days in Torremolinos, Costa del Sol, Spain. An attractive spring holiday at very low cost. Approximately $?͵ per person.

☐ May 11–15

Five days in San Francisco, including the Chicago Symphony concert on May 12. Approximately $ Ÿ͵ per person.

☐ May 26 – June 10

Sixteen day Music Festival Tour to Florence, Milan, Prague, and Vienna. Approximate cost: $ͨ͠ per person.

☐ July

(and)

☐ August

Aspen Music Festival. A double repeat of this year's six–day trip. July tour to include Ballet West. Approximately $͵ͨ͵ per person.

☐ July or August

Munich–Bayreuth–Bregenz–Salzburg "Old World Music Festival", 15 days/14 nights. Tentative cost, if full charter of 141 is enrolled: $ ͨͨ per person.

Member's Name _____

Address _____

City_____ State _____ Zip Code _____

Date of Membership Application _____

KEEP SELLING WITH PUBLICATIONS

You have obtained your new member by communicating to him or her about the benefits offered by membership. Now, you want to keep those benefits in your new member's mind, to excite the new member about them, and to make sure the new member takes full advantage of them.

If you can accomplish all that, it will be easy and inexpensive to renew the membership at the end of the year. In fact, if you forget to send the renewal notice, the member may well call you about it — afraid of missing out on upcoming membership activities.

Effective communication takes skill, thought, time and budget. Much of your communication will continue to be "sales" material of a sort, even if it looks, maybe, like a magazine article. It will be selling your benefits, just as the first membership promotion mailing did. When you communicate with a member, you are doing so for a purpose. Don't forget that purpose. Before you decide on starting a publication or an article, or before you begin to write, ask yourself, "What change in *human behavior* do I want to achieve by doing this?" Then write in such a way that assures the change will happen. Do you want members to send additional gifts? Do you want them to attend a special event and have a good time? Do you want them to know what a fine special event they just missed (or attended)? Do you want them to know of a major good work you have just launched or accomplished? Do you want them to know how prestigious their membership has become? Do you want them to "reenlist"? Ask questions like this before you communicate. And answer yourself truthfully.

Big, rich organizations communicate through lush membership magazines. Little, poor organizations communicate through two-page newsletters. But, as long as the medium is appropriate to the purpose, this difference won't affect the impact of the communication. A two-page newsletter, appropriate to its organization, will change human behavior just as well as the lush magazine — maybe even better.

It's your role to determine what form of communication is most appropriate to your organization, its needs and resources. Here are a few ideas.

Magazines.   When the potential market is broad enough and large enough, the opportunity to publish a regular magazine of the quality of Smithsonian magazine or The National Geographic magazine can open new doors. The American Association of Retired Persons is probably the largest membership organization in the United States. It certainly benefits its members and itself through the publication of Modern Maturity, a fine, broad-spectrum magazine that covers most aspects of life for older people. But many smaller organizations with narrower interests also find that their magazines for members are the principal reason why many people join.

The Mallet, an excellent magazine published by The National Carvers Museum in Colorado, carries how-to articles on wood carving, complete with plans and instructions. To obtain this information is an attractive membership benefit. But the magazine is also the principal link between the Museum and its 25,000 members who live all over the United States and Canada. The Mallet is a principal reason for the rapid growth of the Museum's membership in its early years and the accomplishment of its "burning the mortgage" in a short time. The Mallet is filled with articles about members and is quick to give recognition to them. Members write many of the how-to articles and provide patterns and instructions. Especially well handled are *obituaries*, so often overlooked in membership publications.

One welcome change in many museum magazines in recent times has been the awareness that their principal market is the *members*, not libraries and curators in other museums. Most material relates to membership interests, programs and other benefits and privileges. Even learned material, when it is published, is written and illustrated in such an attractive manner that members will enjoy it too.

Magazines are natural membership benefits for all motor clubs and travel-related organizations. Several AAA clubs jointly publish one excellent magazine, featuring travel information and tips on car maintenance and driving. Then each club tailors the magazine for its own members with a few pages of local news.

Most professional organizations publish competent magazines providing information needed by their members. Even the splinter groups related to some professions, such as the Flying Physicians, publish fine magazines.

Newsletters. The smallest organizations usually publish some type of newsletter. They range from one-sheet publications, mimeographed on both sides, to 4 or 12 pages of attractively printed material. Newsletters are the ideal medium for announcements of new and upcoming events for members, lists of new members, photographs of members enjoying recent events, etc. They can be printed at low cost, easily and very quickly. Some groups use them to carry recent news between issues of a magazine.

Some newsletters reserve a page or two for a continuing series of feature material about the work of the organization or some phase of its focus. For example, the newsletter published by the Evanston (Illinois) Historical Society regularly features short articles on early Evanstonians, how streets got their names, major events in the city's history, etc. Most are written by skilled volunteers who enjoy the involvement and know how to write material that will interest the average member. When an organization runs many activities, some may not appeal to all members. This provides an opportunity to publish several newsletters. Then the general membership can be invited to request one or more newsletters, or some of the newsletters can be a benefit of high levels of membership. For example, many minimum-gift clubs (in which membership is gained by making a gift of a stated minimum size to a nonprofit cause) have their own newsletters, filled with news about the organization and the activities of the club.

Evanston Historical Society
NEWSLETTER

225 Greenwood Street, Evanston, Illinois 60201   Phone: GR 5-3410

VOL. XIII, NO. 1   March-April 19

JOHN EVANS:
A MAN FOR HIS TIMES

DR. JOHN EVANS
(1814-1897)

Most people know Evanston was named after John Evans one of the founders of Northwestern University, but how many know for instance that Dr. John Evans established Chicago's first hospital or organized Chicago's public school system?

Just a brief look at the life of this remarkable man shows a list of accomplishments in many fields that would be noteworthy for a dozen ordinary men. What is more, here is a man who was healthy, wealthy and wise but never lifted his 200 pounds out of bed until 10 or 11 a.m. Perhaps the fact that he was an inveterate whittler gave him more time to apply his great intellect to his many and diverse ventures. He was at once a dreamer and a doer.

John Evans was born in 1814 in Waynesville, Ohio. His father was a successful merchant and farmer who wanted his son to follow in his footsteps. But Evans refused and instead graduated from Lynn Medical College, Cincinnati with financial help from two Waynesville doctors.

WELCOME TO NEW LIFE MEMBER...

Mrs. Lucille B. Crowder   Mr. James S. Siddall

WELCOME TO NEW MEMBERS...

Amundsen High School Sophomores   Evert & Ethel Johnson
Polly Athan   Mr. & Mrs. James D. Mantice
Mr. & Mrs. Wm. E. Cunningham   Mr. & Mrs. John H. Nelson
Richard & Loreen D'Agostino   Mrs. Arthur L. Reincke
Mr. & Mrs. William Debelak   Mr. & Mrs. Robert Rutledge
Mrs. Georgia B. Dominik   Mrs. Raymond R. Scott
Mrs. Robert E. Dorr   Mrs. Walter H. Seidel
Carol Lems-Dworkin   Mr. & Mrs. Marshall S. Shapo
Margaret Gillis   Mr. & Mrs. James U. Snydacker
Mr. & Mrs. James P. Green   Kathryn L. Wilcox
Mrs. F. LeRoy Hess (Jane E.)   Dr. Leland Wilkinson
Mr. & Mrs. Paul F. Huber   Blaine V. Williams
Mr. & Mrs. Arthur C. Jolley   Mr. & Mrs. George H. Williams

SEE THE FABULOUS VATICAN ART COLLECTION--SEPTEMBER 6, 19   ... We depart
from Dawes House around 5:45 p.m. and have a sack-supper on the bus. Upon
our arrival at the Chicago Art Institute, we will see an audio-visual presentation and then view the exhibit. We will be returning to Evanston
around 9 p.m. Sign up sheet will be in the next issue of the Newsletter.

SPLENDORS OF SOUTHERN ITALY...If you are interested in joining our trip to
see the splendors of Southern Italy--October 9-November 3--please sign up
by May 1, 19 . The itinerary was described in the November-December issue
of the Newsletter. Call 475-3410 for details or copy of itinerary.

ABOUT NEW DIRECTIONS FOR HISTORY DISCUSSION GROUP...We are in the process
of reevaluating the present format of the History Discussion Group. On
April 28th at 8 p.m. we plan to have a brainstorming session to discuss new
directions for the group. We value your ideas and hope you will attend the
meeting. Please RSVP 475-3410.

The Evanston Historical Society Newsletter

Editor: Clive Bishop
Assoc. Editor: Patricia Kelly

Newsletter is published six times a year as a benefit of membership
in the Evanston Historical Society, and as a service to the citizens
of Evanston. Contributions of articles and other materials appropriate
to the readership are invited.

SATURDAY ONLY

MEMORIAL SERVICE

A Memorial Service for deceased members will take place at 11:30 a.m. in the Aloha Meeting House. The service will be conducted by The Rev. George Kelsey Dreher. Dr. Roberta Bitgood, distinguished recitalist, composer, director and teacher, will be the organist for the service.

A Dutch Auction

A Dutch Auction will be held in the G. W. Blunt White Library all day Saturday. The Auction is being organized by the Fellows of the Library and

LUNCHEON

MEMBERS' BEER AND CIDER TENT (no charge) AND CASH BAR
Saturday, noon-12:30 P.M.

MEMBERS' PICNIC LUNCHEON

Saturday, 12:30 p.m. Under the tent on the North Green. Chicken salad sandwich, clam chowder, potato salad, pickle, cookie or brownie, fresh fruit, coffee and milk.

For children — Peanut butter and jelly sandwich, cookie or brownie, fresh fruit and milk or a discount lunch at the Galley.

Advance reservations required. See form on

ANNUAL MEETING

The Annual Meeting for all members will take place at 12:45 p.m. Saturday, following the Picnic Luncheon, under the tent on the North Green. Come learn what's happening at your museum!

Cruise with the Starboard Watch

Sabino's 5 p.m. downriver cruise has been chartered for members only and will feature THE STARBOARD WATCH BARBERSHOP QUARTET. Tickets for the cruise (both adults' and children's) are $2.00 and can be purchased at the Sabino booth starting 10 ̶ ̶

to the Mystic River Historical Society, 9 A.M.- 5 P.M. at Seaport Store.

New Year's Eve. 19th-century theme celebration at Seamen's Inne. Reservations required.

Editor: Sheila Murphy

WIND ROSE

ISSN 0049-7657

A Bimonthly Newsletter for the 17,215 Members of
MYSTIC SEAPORT MUSEUM, INC.
MYSTIC, CONNECTICUT 06355

There are still openings in our 19 ̶ ̶ sailing classes, which begin September 11. For more information on adult (beginner, intermediate and racing) or children's (beginner and intermediate) classes, contact Alicia Crossman at (203) 536-2631, ext. 323.

The Spring 19 winner of the Brooks Trophy for Junior Achievement in Sailing was Kurt Jannke of Ledyard, CT. The trophy was given to the Seaport by the late Charles A. Brooks and his wife, Dorothy.

MARY ANNE STETS

Supervisor of Membership: Kate Coakley

Annual reports.   Many membership organizations have learned to tailor their annual reports into effective *membership* cultivation devices. Using photographs showing members enjoying events, these organizations remind members of the benefits available to them and bring back memories of good times related to membership. Financial statements should be condensed and abbreviated as much as possible and presented in a format easily understood by the average member. The emphasis should be on the importance of members' dues and other contributions in making possible the organization's programs and services. This also provides a chance to express warm gratitude for the generous support.

Although it's important to mention names in an annual report, you'll need to establish sensible policies for listing names of members. One major group with a membership in excess of 10,000 fell into the trap of listing the names of all members in its annual report. Each year omissions and errors generated complaints that overshadowed any good accomplished by the listing. When an annual giving program was established, members' names were dropped in favor of the names of *contributors*. As the group's membership continued to grow, there was concern about the costs of sending the complete, elaborate annual report to each member who was not also a contributor. The solution was to send an abbreviated annual report to non-contributing members with an attached post card that enabled them to request a copy of the full report. The abbreviated report also explained that all contributors were listed in the full report and that each contributor would automatically receive the full report. Members who liked to see their name in print got the message, and many became regular annual contributors.

Membership directories.   Most trade and professional organizations publish membership directories — and with good reason. Being in the directory is proof that you're in the profession. Members also find it handy to have the addresses and telephone numbers of fellow professionals easily at hand.

But all kinds of membership groups publish directories. One group even lists the names of deceased members as well as the living in their directory. Each year a copy of the directory is sent to the surviving spouse of each deceased member, and in time many of the survivors establish memorials to the late members through major gifts to the group. A tip: If you list deceased members, don't use the lugubrious heading "Necrology"; use a more upbeat heading, "In Memoriam" or "In Grateful Remembrance."

It's a good idea to preface a membership directory with a brief history of the organization and its accomplishments and also to list all of the past presidents. Even some fairly sophisticated organizations have a way of losing track of their history until it's time to celebrate a significant anniversary. When the history is updated in each year's membership directory, important facts are not lost, and today's leaders have a sense of being current links in a worthy chain of distinguished leadership.

There are businesses that specialize in the publication of directories for alumni groups, fraternities, and honorary societies. Many members willingly pay for copies of the directories, and in some cases, the publishing firms give the organization a percentage of those revenues.

Seminar announcements.   Trade and professional organizations usually offer their members an attractive array of seminars, workshops, conferences, etc., on subjects important to their fields. In large national organizations, many of these sessions are repeated in various cities — usually cities that have tourist attractions and are close to concentrations of members. And the announcements of the seminars are often done in the form of handsome mini-magazines to be kept for reference. The National Restaurant Association, for example, publishes an eight-page listing of seminars every six months. Whether the member attends any or many of the seminars, he or she perceives from the listing that important benefits are offered with the membership.

Research reports.   One major function of trade associations is to act as a clearing house for statistics and other information relating to the trade. Many now have research directors who analyze the data and prepare detailed reports of great value to the membership — and to others in the trade who should be members.

For example, the most comprehensive annual statistical reporting in the field of fund raising is done each year by the American Association of Fund-Raising Counsel. They publish this research in the form of an annual booklet, "Giving USA." The Association and its members (a relatively small but influential group of consulting firms) gain much more publicity and prestige by offering the booklet for sale to the public than they would if it were reserved as a membership-only benefit. The AAFRC and many other trade organizations also compile timely reports on pending legislation affecting their fields and issue "legislative alerts," which urge members to make known their opinions to their elected representatives.

A good many organizations issue valuable reports to their members on typical budgets, salaries, and costs in institutions and companies comparable to those represented by the membership.

When the list of research reports is long, and if some of them are unlikely to be of general interest to the members, it's a good idea to mail out a list of available reports (sometimes stating that a certain number come free with the membership and others are available at a modest charge). When a trade association

SEMINARS BY TOPIC

FOODSERVICE MANAGEMENT COURSES

Banquet Management
2/3   Lexington, KY
2/26 Denver, CO
4/3   Portland, OR
4/5   Seattle, WA
4/14 Boston, MA
6/24 Milwaukee, WI

Beverage Management
2/25-26 Newport Beach, CA
3/3-4   Boston, MA
5/17-18 Chicago, IL

Creative Buffets
3/4   Boston, MA
3/10 Portland, OR
3/11 Seattle, WA
3/27 Rochester, NY
6/9   Denver, CO
6/11 San Francisco, CA

Employee Motivation
3/4 Williamsburg, VA
3/6 Gatlinburg, TN
5/6 Cape Cod, MA

Negotiating for, and Financing, Foodservice Facilities
2/6-7   San Francisco, CA
3/26-27 Fort Worth, TX
5/17-18 Chicago, IL

Off-Premises Catering
2/10-11 Toronto, Ontario, Canada
3/24-25 Vienna, VA
4/14-15 Austin, TX

Planning and Implementing Restaurant Marketing Strategy
1/22-23 Houston, TX
2/25-26 King of Prussia, PA
3/26-27 Portland, OR
4/21-22 Denver, CO
4/30-5/1 Miami, FL
5/17-18 Chicago, IL

Wine and the Bottom Line
4/9   Washington, DC

From the National Restaurant Association.

195

has been in operation a long time and has consistently published "how to" articles in its membership magazine, it often finds a market among newer members for compilations of *reprints.* Useful information, made available free or at low cost, can be one of the most effective cultivation devices available to any membership organization.

Other published information.   Quite a few organizations with high-cost classifications of membership make a practice of mailing advance copies of selected news releases to those top members. This gives the high-level member a sense of being part of the management team, and he or she usually welcomes the opportunity to keep informed. Some groups issue bulletins about their work or about travel and tour opportunities. Others send out recommended reading lists.

Museums and other organizations that publish mail-order catalogs find that those catalogs have a value far beyond the generation of profitable sales. They often show two prices for items: the regular price and a "member's discount" price, reminding members of their benefits.

THE WELCOME INVITATION

Members like to be invited to all types of events sponsored by their organization. They may not attend all of them. They may actually attend very few. But the invitation itself is enough to remind them that they belong to an active organization that thinks of each member as a person several times a year.

The welcome invitation, received *well in advance* of the event, can be one of the strongest cultivation devices available to any organization. Membership events offer some members relief from loneliness and an opportunity to see and mingle with friends — to meet others with similar interests whose company is desirable and worth seeking. Fortunately, there are lots of excuses for sending invitations.

Annual meetings.   Because it's usually required by the bylaws, the annual meeting sometimes is regarded as a dull chore. But it needn't be. Leaders should keep the necessary elections and other official business to a minimum, concentrating instead on an attractive, prestigious program and perhaps a reception following the meeting. The annual meeting also provides opportunities for giving recognition to members who have distinguished themselves during the year, for brief memorial mentions, and for announcing major plans and significant gifts.

Members' previews and receptions.   Arts organizations that sponsor exhibitions and performances usually invite members to an exclusive preview of each event — a privilege that suggests prestige and the convenience of small audiences. At the reception held with the preview, widely known social leaders in the community, identified by tasteful name badges, are often invited to pour tea or punch — giving each member an opportunity to meet and talk with people they recognize as leaders. For many members, this privilege alone is enough to justify belonging and paying dues for years on end.

All cultivation, of course, is aimed at constant improvement of the membership renewal rate.

One of the best cultivation devices is a special reception for new members only. In very large organizations, these are often held twice a year. Ideally, they should fall about midpoint in each new member's first year, providing both a welcome to the group and a reminder of the value of membership. When there is a special room for members and it's large enough to accommodate the new members' reception, that event provides a way of acquainting the member with this facility as another privilege of membership.

Special events.   Invitations to special events — ground breaking ceremonies, dedications of buildings or rooms, mortgage burning ceremonies, etc. — are often coveted by members, especially if they have been involved in achieving the objective being celebrated. With careful planning, these events can be among the most effective of all cultivation devices.

No business can long survive without investing in new customers. But then comes the critical task of tracking their performance, calculating the "value of a customer" through the years and constantly testing new ways to keep those customers as long as possible. It's the heart of the mail-order business, especially in magazine circulation. And it's the heart of the membership process, too.

Lester Wunderman, head of a major direct marketing agency, says that the principal business of direct marketing is not to make sales but to make *customers*. Francis S. "Andy" Andrews, another pioneer in the direct marketing approach to membership and fund raising, contends that retention of the "customer" is always the key factor, the base for true profitability. Peter F. Drucker, the renowned author and philosopher in the field of management, emphasizes that "the customer is the business."

12

Why is it, then, that so many membership organizations pay such scant attention to bringing their members back into the fold, year after year? And why do even more assume that a lapsed member is a lost cause and make no effort to recapture his or her interest and loyalty? Because it's easier to go along old familiar paths and not stop to scrape off the barnacles. In "Managing in Turbulent Times," Mr. Drucker says: "Sloughing off yesterday is particularly important these days for the non-business service institution. Its very success in a great many cases has made its programs, activities, services, obsolete and unproductive." But, nowhere is it more important for a membership organization to take a new look at its practices and operations than in its approach to renewing its present members and recapturing those who have recently fallen by the wayside. If your membership benefits and privileges are sound, and if your cultivation efforts are strong and effective, then there's only one area left where more work may produce more profit: your renewal procedures and your treatment of lapsed members.

REASONABLE RENEWAL EXPECTATIONS

Every group would like to renew 90 to 100 percent of its members every year. But national statistics show that around 20 percent of any group is apt to move to a new address in an average year. And this factor alone will make a big dent in the roster of any membership group. Then, subtract membership loss from deaths, retirement and other conditions that reduce income or change interests, and you'll know how vulnerable even the best organizations are.

A major problem all membership groups have in common is a normal but sometimes shockingly high drop-off rate of first-year members. This is especially true of persons who enroll in response to a premium or free gift offer. The chief reason is the new member's failure to take advantage of the benefits that would weld him or her to the organization. There are two types of membership benefits: passive benefits, which come to the member automatically (your newsletter, for example); and active benefits, which require the member to do something to enjoy them (your cocktail party, for example). When there are relatively few passive benefits, the first-year drop-out rate rises. If a major benefit is free admission to attractive programs, anything you can do to get a new member through the front door in the first year of membership will double your chances of getting the member back again. (Later, we'll touch on some other things you can do to overcome the surprising apathy of the first-year member.)

It's strange that few organizations really know how to compute renewal rates accurately enough to get at the significant facts. For one thing, many never bother to calculate first-year renewals separately, others neglect to find out how many cancellations are caused by such factors as death and moving away. And some make the mistake of calculating renewals on the basis of *present* membership, rather than on the total nember of "renewable" members in the *previous* year.

Renewal rates can vary all over the lot and still be normal. Large, general membership organizations tend to have lower renewal rates than most professional and trade associations, which often have smaller potential markets but also can offer a "seal of approval" type of prestige.

Here's a way to compare your renewal rates with those of other similar groups. Use a standard form like the one shown here in calculating your own rates and then send a copy of your rates and a blank form to those groups you'd like to ask to share their records.

```
                            Date_____

Name of organization_____

Fiscal Year_____(Dates: _____through_____)

Total membership
        Annual (renewable)..............................  _____
        Life.........................................  _____
        Other........................................  _____

                                    TOTAL.....  _____

1. New renewable members acquired in previous fiscal year..  _____

2. First-year members renewing............................  _____

3. Percent first-year renewals (#2 divided by #1)..........  _____ %

4. Total membership, Previous Fiscal Year..................  _____
        Less Life members...................................  _____
        Net renewable members...............................  _____

5. Total renewals this year................................  _____

6. Total renewal percentage (#5 divided by #4).............  _____ %

7. Causes for cancellation
        Death.........................................  _____
        Moved.........................................  _____
        Retired.......................................  _____
        Other.........................................  _____
```

What are reasonable expectations for renewal percentages? Some groups, such as automobile clubs, consistently renew 85 to 90 percent of their members, year after year; but they're exceptional. Most groups are more likely to fall into the following ranges.

	Fair	Good	Excellent
Total renewal percentage	65%	70-75%	75-90%
First-year renewal	50%	65%	70%

Each year, recalculate your total renewal rate and use it to update the Allowable-Order-Cost Formula that was described in the chapter on testing and measuring results. If your results are at least double your actual cost of acquiring a new member, you're on the right track. But remember that even a small improvement can mean substantial income that would have been lost if you hadn't tried some new, successful techniques. When one large organization revised its renewal statement and its series of renewal mailings for the first time in years, it increased renewals by 2.5 percent. This may sound small, but it produced $250,000 in additional income the first year and substantially more compounded.

KEY FACTORS IN RENEWAL

Timing.　For many years, it was normal for most organizations to send their first dues notice 30 days before the membership expiration date. Then some started experimenting with earlier billing and found that it often increased total renewals. In addition, it provided a profitable "float" from dues paid long before the renewal date. Nowadays it's quite common for magazines to start sending renewal notices as long as 120 days before the expiration date.

What's a good billing schedule? For most groups with at least a thousand members, here's one that allows ample time for several billings while the member's interest is still reasonably warm.

First renewal billing ....45 to 60 days before the
                                        membership expires

Second billing ....14 days before expiration
Third billing ....10 days after expiration
Fourth billing ....30 days after expiration

Generally, the best results come with four billings. But, you may want to test a fifth and even a sixth billing at 30-day intervals. Some magazines have found it profitable to try up to 13 times! Too many membership groups stop after two attempts and then wonder why their renewal rates continue to shrink.

Testing.   Applying a little imagination to your renewal procedure can often produce surprising and profitable results. You might try taking a coded sample of members' names in a heavy renewal period, sending their first renewal billing as early as 90 days before expiration and tracking the final results. Or you might test several revisions of the dues statement, making sure that each version meets at least the five basic requirements for dues statements that will be outlined in a moment. Or you could test offering a premium — a free booklet or something else of value — for prompt payment of dues. Just be sure that you're rewarding *promptness.* Give them something extra for moving quickly.

Some organizations have found it extremely effective to send the new membership card with the first renewal billing, especially to *first-year* renewals. You might test such "advance credentialing" and enclose the card in an attractive plastic card case bearing the logo of your organization. There are some obvious potential problems in this technique, but your test might demonstrate that the problems are overshadowed by increased response — and profit. Or, you might plan a special event for new members and enclose the invitation with the first renewal statement.

The renewal is an "offer" just as much as the original sale. So make it as attractive and exciting as possible.

Positivism.   The renewal approach must always be positive, even to the extent of avoiding the word "renewal" on the statement and other enclosures. The emphasis is on "continuing to enjoy" benefits and privileges for a new term of membership. The renewal letter should avoid even suggesting the possibility that the member might consider dropping his or her membership — stressing instead all of the major benefits the member is already receiving and of course will want to continue enjoying. It's a good idea to schedule an especially attractive members-only event to take place just after your new membership year begins — an event that most members would hate to miss. Just as the membership card should avoid the use of such words as "expires" or "lapses," so too must the dues statement and the letter use positive phrases such as "valid until" or "effective through."

Instead of the word "renewal," test using "Your annual dues statement is enclosed" on the outer envelope, and call the renewal statement itself "Annual Dues Statement." If you can, print on the statement the number of years the member has belonged; a sense of continuity can be a strong motivator.

Persistence.   A current member is "a bird in hand," worth at least 10 cold prospects "in the bush." Never assume that the member will definitely receive each renewal notice at a time convenient to him or her. It's easy to overlook mail, especially so for a busy person. So persist. And be polite in your persistence, even suggesting in your later renewal letters that the member may have misplaced the earlier notices. The tardy or wavering member may even feel a little guilt about not having responded and may need only a gentle, polite nudge to act.

This is one of the reasons why telephone follow-up works so well as a final renewal effort, especially for higher level members. You should always make a phone call before you give up. Let members who have not yet renewed know that you have missed them and want them to continue to be part of your organization. This telephone work can be organized exactly as you would organize a fund-raising phonothon.

Acknowledgment.   Promptness is just as important in acknowledging a renewal as it is in acknowledging the original enrollment. If you can't send the card and receipt immediately, consider sending at least a warm form letter of thanks within

48 hours. Explain the reason for the delay and assure the member that his or her membership is in force and that many exciting benefits await. A letter format, even a printed one, is better for this job than a more formal printed slip of acknowledgment.

THE DUES STATEMENT

In most cases, you are not asking for a contribution. You are notifying a member that the term of his or her current membership is about to draw to a close. You are sending a dues bill for another stated term of membership. As you plan your dues statement, make sure it meets these basic requirements.

- It should be easy to understand.

- It should be easy to complete.

- It should look like a bill. It should be simple and uncluttered.

- It should state the term of the membership: "For one year of benefits and privileges from April 1, 19—, through March 31, 19—."

- If yours is a gift-seeking, nonprofit organization, it should provide an easy way of making an additional contribution.

People are accustomed to receiving bills and usually stack them up with others for payment. If your dues statement looks like a bill, it will get prompt treatment. If the statement includes the dues of several family members — as in the case of some motor clubs — it's helpful to show the total to be paid.

If upgrading of the membership level is a possibility, it's a good idea to show the member his or her present classification and the benefits of moving up. Make it easy for the member to indicate a higher classification. The computer-generated dues statement shown on the next page accomplishes this neatly.

ANNUAL

☐ **YES**, *I want*
coming year.

Please check Membership level you prefer.

☐ **Individual* $20
☐ *Participating* $30
☐ *Sustaining* $50
☐ *Supporting* $100
☐ *Donor* $250
☐ *Sponsor* $500
☐ *Guarantor* $1,000
☐ **Junior (12–18)* $10
☐ **Senior-Single (65)* . . . $10
☐ *Senior-Dual (65)* $15
*One Membership card

Mr. Willi₂

Ambler, P/

Current level

Please consider in
return this form
Dues are tax ded₂
authorized by la
Please allow 3–
membership car₂

FLYING PHYSICIANS ASSOCIATION, INC.

Headquarters

801 Green Bay Road

Lake Bluff, Illinois 60044

PHONE (312) 234-6330

Mr. William F. ulth.:
` ::)o:. Drive
Ambler, PA 190J

Amount: $50.00   Date: May 1, 19 .
          Please return top portion with your remittance

ANNUAL MEMBERSHIP DUES
June 1, 19 - May 31, 19 $50.00

(Residents, Fellows, Interns: $20.00)

U.S. FUNDS PLEASE

All orders payable in advance in U.S. funds
FLYING PHYSICIANS ASSOCIATION, INC.

The Flying Physicians Association's statement looks like a doctor's bill and covers all of the basic requirements.

THE DUES RESPONSE ENVELOPE

Most personal checks are at least six inches long, and many business checks are still longer. Make your dues response envelope large enough to accept the check and membership statement without folding either. But make it small enough to fit easily within a standard-size (#10) mailing envelope. That means the dues response envelope should be at least a #7 or a #7¾ size. And here are a few more thoughts on the same subject.

Should you pay the postage?   Enclosing a postage-paid business reply envelope is usually profitable when you're prospecting for new members. But when you're sending your first renewal notice, you should consider testing the postage-paid envelope against a self-addressed reply envelope on which the member must affix a stamp when returning renewal dues. About 80 percent of the members who are going to renew will respond to the first notice, and they are usually the loyal type who don't mind affixing their own stamp. If you have a very large membership, this can save you lots of money.

Generally, it's a good idea to enclose a postage-paid envelope with at least the third and fourth notices, when you're trying to motivate the slower responder who may be wavering about the renewal.

But be sure to test — and keep testing — the effect of providing reply postage against the effect of asking the member to provide his or her own stamp. The increased renewal rate, when postage is paid by you, may more than offset the costs of even substantial reply postage.

Text.   If you use a business reply envelope, you'll have to comply with Postal Service requirements about what gets printed, where and how. But remember that, if you're mailing in the United States, you can take part of the envelope for your own use: your logo, codes, slogan, expressions of thanks, etc.

Don't make the member print his or her own name and address in the upper left corner; it's an unnecessary annoyance.

On the front of response envelopes for which members provide their own stamps, print the name and address of your organization and use an outline box showing where the stamp goes. But, don't print "Place stamp here" in the box. Instead, use text that makes the member feel good about providing his or her own stamp: "Thank you for your stamp" or "Your stamp helps (name of organization)." On the back of the response envelope thank the member for the prompt payment of dues and, if possible, list some special benefits and privileges. Reassure the member that renewal is a sound decision.

THE OUTER ENVELOPE

Many organizations print a headline or "teaser" on the outer (mailing) envelope to attract attention and get it opened.

The AAA-Chicago Motor Club uses a #10 window outer envelope, on the bottom of which is printed: "IMPORTANT: Your MEMBERSHIP DUES Statement Enclosed" (plus a line of copy stressing new benefits.) But on a second-notice mailing, the Club has had success with sticking peel-off labels ("I ACCEPT" or "I DECLINE") on the face of the mailing envelope. It's important to get the member's attention, and sometimes an "involvement device" such as the peel-off label can work well. However, extremely conservative groups probably would be better off limiting the copy on the face of the outer envelope to something as simple as: "Membership Dues Notice."

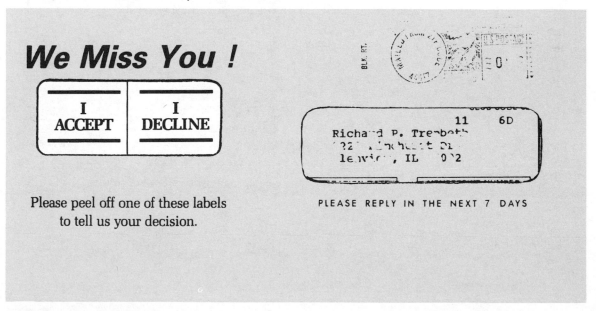

AAA–CHICAGO MOTOR CLUB
66 East South Water Street
Chicago, ILL. 60601

MASTER MEMBERSHIP CARD

CLUB CODE 020

11   6D

Richard ?. Tr?nbet?
2? ?inchur?? ?r.
?l?n?fe , IL ?0.2?

EXPIRATION DATE	MEMBERSHIP NUMBER
3-31-??	O 020?00 03

1. Detach these cards and place in your wallets. Your permanent membership cards and additional materials will be mailed to you.
2. Please make sure you indicate your spouse's first name on the invitation return card. If a name is not indicated, the Free Associate will not be in effect.

AAA–CHICAGO MOTOR CLUB
66 East South Water Street
Chicago, ILL. 60601

FREE ASSOCIATE MEMBERSHIP CARD

CLUB CODE 020

Mr. or Mrs. Tre?beth
?2? ?in?'u?_? ?r.
?lervi? , IL ?00?

EXPIRATION DATE	MEMBERSHIP NUMBER
3-31-??	O 02?0?0? 03

```
*  *  *  *  *  *  *  *  *  *
*    Rejoin AAA today and receive    *
*    a one-year Associate member-
     ship FREE!  A $13.00 value.     *
*    Plus more!
                                     *
*    Please use one of the labels
     on the envelope to tell us      *
*    your decision.
                                     *
*  *  *  *  *  *  *  *  *  *
```

Dear Member:

We miss you! You are very important to the AAA-Chicago Motor
Club, so I was greatly concerned when I discovered that you did
not renew your AAA membership.

I fully realize that you originally joined us because of the
benefits we offered you as a motorist. Now, those benefits have

RENEWAL LETTERS AND SLIPS

At least the first renewal notice should include a warm, friendly letter reassuring the member that membership benefits are better than ever and still more of a bargain. The tone should be optimistic and full of positive references to the principal benefits. Some large groups use attractive renewal reminder slips to carry the message. However, a letter looks much more personal, and the text can be varied more easily through the course of a series of four to six reminders.

If your membership is large and the dues levels justify the expense, you should test using personalized computer letters, especially for the higher levels of membership. Computer personalization, reminding the member of such things as how long he or she has been a member and his or her present level of membership can be powerful motivators. To use such personalization, you'll need to have detailed membership information in your computer. Some large organizations use inexpensive printed letters for the first two reminders; then they turn on the heat (and budget) with computer letters in the final two or three reminders. You'll know what works best for you after a few tests. But keep in mind that the most successful renewal mailing series tend to follow a definite pattern.

- The first letter is a pleasant reminder to pay your dues for another year and to consider upgrading your membership level. The copy mentions recent major events in which the member has shared and warmly lets the member know that he or she is wanted.

- The second letter, close to the end of the membership year, is more urgent in tone and touches on the consequences of losing important benefits, especially when such things as discounts or insurance coverage are involved.

- The third letter, sent just after the membership term has ended, holds the door open but mentions "discontinuation" after a grace period of two weeks.

- The fourth letter or slip announces the discontinuation but still provides a dues statement and reply envelope.

- At least two months after "termination," the fifth approach is a brand new renewal offer, sometimes including the offer of a free booklet or other premium. At this point your records should be in good shape, so there's not much danger of getting backlash from someone receiving this mailing who has already renewed and didn't receive the premium offer.

- One of the best times for a telephone follow-up appears to be about four months after discontinuation, when the former member is likely to feel the loss of benefits. It's a fine opportunity for the caller to ask why the membership was dropped and also to invite comments on services received and on any disappointments.

After two mailings to lapsed members, KCFR, a public radio station in Denver, recaptured 80 lapsed members (and contributions of about $3,000) in the first two days of telephone follow-up. They armed their callers with the effective script shown here, which suggests responses to typical objections that their lapsed members are apt to raise.

Hello, Mr./Mrs. _____!! This is _____ calling from KCFR
Radio...how are you today? Great!!!

Mr./Mrs. _____, I'm a volunteer here at KCFR, and we have you on our
records as being a member up until ____(date)____, and we don't show a
renewal for you since then.

The reason for my call is to invite you to renew your membership because
it's people like you, of course, that make KCFR happen at all.

The basic listener membership is only $30.00 per year, and with your
membership you'll receive "POINT ONE", the bi-monthly KCFR newsletter; and
your membership card which entitles you to one dollar off each record or
tape you purchase at any Sound Warehouse Store, as well as discounts to the
KCFR Botanic Gardens Concert Series. So as you can see, your membership is
a good investment that easily returns its costs.

Other membership categories are 45, 60, 120, 240, and 500 dollars, and
include the same benefits as the basic membership PLUS a variety of fine
premiums, such as KCFR mugs, umbrellas, albums, Botanic Gardens Season
Passes, even a Proton-100 personal FM stereo. Plus of course you'll help
keep KCFR on the air with the fine programming you enjoy.

Mr./Mrs. _____, we show your membership was the the $____ level...
would you like to increase your membership this year?

* * *

Objections...Responses

We Don't Listen Anymore... Why not? (listen...be attentive) What type of
programming do you like? (if they mention something that we do offer,
suggest that they tune KCFR in for a couple days and give us a try.)

We Don't Like The Program Changes...Bob & Ray...Etc... Well, of course, we can't be all things to all people at all times, because we can only air one program at a time. But you do enjoy some of our programming, don't you? (most will say "yes") Then won't you please help support that programming, and we'll pass your comments on to the programming department...

We Don't Have The Money Now... If you like, you can put membership on your Mastercard or Visa, and memberships of $60.00 or more can be paid on the installment plan of just $10.00 per month, to make it easier for you, okay?

You Have Too Many Pledge Drives... Pledge drives are the most effective way to recruit new members and the number of pledge drive days is actually decreasing each year, thanks to renewing members like you...

KCFR Summary Information

The basic listener membership is $30.00 per year. Be sensitive as to how much a person is willing to pledge. Usually if they ask about other categories of membership, they are inclined to move to a higher category than $30.00...encourage those that inquire about higher amount without being pushy. We will, of course, accept donations of any amount, but do encourage small contributions. Use your best judgement in this area.

All memberships are good for one year, after which they must be renewed. Listener support is a subscription to good, non-commercial radio and encourage our listeners to support KCFR every year, not just one time.

ALL MEMBERS AT THE $30.00 (BASIC) LEVEL AND ABOVE RECEIVE:

- **POINT ONE**...The bi-monthly KCFR newsletter, with features on KCFR and NPR staff, A Prairie Home Companion, special programs, KCFR supporters and volunteers, special events, and much more.

- **KCFR MEMBERSHIP CARD**...The membership card entitles you to one dollar off any record or tape at any Sound Warehouse Store. It is also good for 'members-only-discounts' to many KCFR-sponsored events.

- **KCFR BUMPER STICKER**...Metallic silver and blue, with "KCFR 90.1" and logo.

All monies go directly into the KCFR current year budget to pay for basic operating expenses. **TWO THIRDS** of KCFR's annual operating budget depends on listener members.

If you have questions of any kind, or if you handle a call you feel unable to treat correctly (such as somebody wishing to contribute products or services instead of dollars), please refer the call to the phone supervisor.

PREMIUMS:

o $30...Basic membership goodies (listed above.)

o $45...Single KCFR mug...white with repeating KCFR logo and call letters.

- $60...KCFR mug set...2 white mugs with black music staff and KCFR logo and call letters in red.   ...OR...KCFR and Friends Album...Stereo record available ONLY through KCFR with favorite classical selections composed by Gershwin, Mozart, Faure, Barber, Bizet, and Delibes.   ...OR...KCFR umbrella...red and white panels with KCFR logo and call letters on one panel, folds to convenient size.

- $120...KCFR Tote Bag...handsome black and white canvas barrel tote bag with KCFR logo and call letters in small, discreet red letters.   ...OR...KCFR Stadium Blanket, royal blue with KCFR logo and call letters in handy vinyl carrying case.

- $240...KCFR/Botanic Gardens Season Pass...This premium is available ONLY to KCFR members at the $240 level. A great way to insure that you'll avoid the hassles and long lines to get tickets to this year's Botanic Gardens Concert Series.

- $500...Proton-100 FM Stereo Receiving System...a high quality portable FM stereo that is shirt-pocket size and sounds as good as your home stereo. Includes light-weight headphones and leatherette case.

PREMIUMS ARE NOT CUMULATIVE...Please do not offer extra premiums!!!

Premiums will be sent out after KCFR receives your pledge payment. If you are an installment member, premiums will be sent after receipt of your final installment. Please allow 6 to 8 weeks for delivery after KCFR receives payments.

PAYMENTS...

> **CHECKS:** KCFR will send an invoice within a week. Return your check as soon as possible, please.

> **VISA/MASTERCARD:** Get the card number and expiration date. REPEAT ALL INFO BACK TO MEMBER! KCFR will send a voucher to the member for their records.

> **INSTALLMENT PLAN:** Installment levels are:
> - Plan A: $10/month for 6 months ($60.00 pledge)
> - Plan B: $10/month for 12 months ($120 pledge)
> - Plan C: $20/month for 12 months ($240 pledge)

> Installment members will receive a payment booklet with their membership materials, and are required to send payments monthly.

> **ELECTRONIC FUNDS TRANSFER:** An easy way to make installment payments. Funds are transferred automatically each month from member's checking account. Each member will receive a pamphlet explaining how EFT works, and member will sign an EFT agreement.

REMEMBER...COURTESY IS OF THE UTMOST IMPORTANCE!!! If somebody you call indicates that they are having dinner or for any other reason indicates that you called at a bad time, apologize for the inconvenience and tell them that you'll call again another time. Listen with attention to their comments and complaints.

In Washington D.C., the American Medical Association brought in a commercial telemarketing firm to help it renew the memberships of physicians who had ignored three mailings spaced over a five-month period. Using a "live" caller, backed up by a taped message from A.M.A.'s director, the program reached 68 percent of the list and renewed 31 percent of these, generating immediate revenues amounting to seven times the cost of the program. It's likely that in following years renewal income from these recaptured members can more than double the immediate income.

Some organizations have found that a questionnaire, giving the lagging member an opportunity to state reactions to his or her membership experience, works well as part of the third or fourth billing. If you test a questionnaire, be sure to ask the members politely to fill out and return the questionnaire *even* if they are unable to continue their membership. Often, the act of completing a questionnaire is just enough involvement to nudge a hesitant member into paying dues for another year.

Dear Jayne:

(Please check all that apply)

Thanks for letting me know you're thinking about me. I have not renewed because:

☐ I forgot. My check is enclosed.
☐ I moved. My new address is below.
☐ I no longer listen to WKAR Radio. That's because _____
_____
_____

☐ I am not financially able at this time.
☐ I didn't know you missed my friendship. Enclosed is my check made payable to WKAR Radio, or please charge my contribution to my VISA or MasterCard number below.
☐ None of the above. The real reason I haven't stayed in touch is: _____
_____
_____

VISA # _____ MasterCard # _____

Expiration Date _____ Signature _____

Name _____
Address _____
City _____ State _____ Zip _____
Phone (____) _____ (____) _____
              work   home

Please return this questionnaire in the envelope provided. See reverse side for tax advantages

People hate to give up privileges. In some types of mail order sales, one of the most powerful motivators is to stress the uniqueness and limited availability of a product or service. Then you ask the prospect to *release* the product or service *reserved* for him or her by returning a release card if he or she does not care to order. Membership organizations with limited facilities or other evidence of exclusivity could test this "release" tactic in a membership renewal series, probably as part of the second mailing.

The
DAVID ADLER
Cultural Center
Established 1980

1700 NORTH MILWAUKEE AVENUE / LIBERTYVILLE, ILLINOIS 60048   TELEPHONE: 312/367-0707 ■ 312/362-0384

Mr. & Mrs. Richard Trenbeth
2() _ .u ' :ive
Gler ¹€ ', Illinois OC⁻

Dear Mr. & Mrs. Trenbeth,

As a Charter Member who has helped to make this first full year for the Center such a success, you have a very special place in our hearts. We hope you have been able to visit the Center often to see for yourself all of the progress you have helped to make possible.

Most of all, we hope you have enjoyed the many benefits and privileges your membership brings to you. We're adding some new ones, such as an annual Pot Luck Social, the St. Nicholas Party for the whole family, the Libertyville Suzuki Talent Education Program, a slide registry of members' works, an exhibition of works by members, opportunities for other exhibitions of members' works in banks, libraries, and other public places.

As you send in your dues for another year of enjoyment, please accept our thanks for your loyal help and support of the Center.

Sincerely,

Joanne

Mrs. George W. Boehm
President

Home of: The Libertyville Art Center
        The Libertyville School of Folk and Old Time Music

The first letter in a renewal series.

Dear   :

    As you look forward to another year of exciting programs
and the many other privileges you enjoy as a member, we thought
you would appreciate a reminder that your current dues are valid
for just a few more days.

    By sending your check today with your dues statement,
you'll go on enjoying your membership for another year, through
August 1 of next year.

    You'll be interested in the new list of additional
merchants now giving substantial discounts to our members.
Some of our members tell us that their savings from these
discounts more than pay for their annual dues. We hope you've
had many occasions to take advantage of the discounts and
plan to save even more in the coming year.

    Possibly you've been out of town or just mislaid the
first dues notice sent to you a few weeks ago. There's
still time. Just send your dues today and go on enjoying
your privileges for another year. Your loyal interest is
greatly appreciated.

                Sincerely,

*Urgency and the consequences of losing membership benefits
mark this second letter in a renewal series.*

Defenders of Wildlife

1244 19th Street, NW • Washington, DC 20036

Dear Member:

As you round the corner of your first year as a member of Defenders of Wildlife, I'd like to personally thank you for your support during these past months.

With your help, we've made headway in our efforts to block outrages

~~~

As we renew our public alert campaigns, litigation, and lobbying efforts, you might want to consider an upgrade in your membership category.

By increasing the level of your membership now, you'll receive a free bonus gift ... and at the same time, provide vital additional funds for our opposition to biologically short-sighted and inhumane wildlife policies.

Details on your individual upgrade and gift are outlined on the enclosed membership renewal notice. Please read it, then send your check for upgrade or regular renewal rates in the postpaid envelope provided. Coded with your own membership number, your renewal notice will be specially processed as soon as it reaches our office.

By renewing now, you help Defenders of Wildlife avoid costly renewal reminders ... and ensure that our funds will be put to work directly on our fight to save animals exploited by international trade, marine mammals, predators, and endangered species.

I look forward to hearing from you...and welcoming you for your second year of membership in Defenders of Wildlife.

Sincerely,

Allen E. Smith
President

P.S. I've enclosed a personal Defenders of Wildlife membership card for you for the coming year. This is the only membership card I will send. Please detach it from the renewal form and, as soon as you've mailed your check, sign and carry the card with you. Thank you.

First mailing in a series.

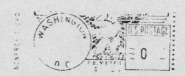

**IMPORTANT Membership Information
Enclosed For:**

Defenders of Wildlife • 1244 19th Street, NW • Washington, DC 20036

MEMBERSHIP RENEWAL NOTICE

— Yes, I would like to renew my support
of Defenders of Wildlife to help save
endangered and threatened American
wildlife species. My check for $25
is enclosed.

19C.? BL.⊡15?C   R1AKAC

— I'd like to increase my membership
support this year. My $35 dues are
enclosed. I understand I will receive
the bonus gift described below ... and
that these additional dues are critical
for wildlife protection in the coming
year.

Christophe⊡ W. Baⱡtha⌐
⌐. ⌐ ⌐⌐ ⌐ D⌐.⌐
Amb⌐e⌐, PA 190⌐

Please return this portion with your check (made payable to Defenders of Wildlife) in the postpaid envelope provided.

By increasing the level of your membership support to $35, you will receive
-- FREE -- a handsome golden eagle poster
... this attractive four-color poster
-- suitable for framing -- measures
21" x 31". It features a diving golden
eagle on one side and illustrations of
six North American soaring hawks on
the reverse side. Ideal for a young
person's room, den, or basement wall.

Detach, sign, and carry

MEMBERSHIP CARD
This certifies that
Christophe⌐ W. Ba⌐tⱡ⌐r⌐
is a current member in good standing
of Defenders of Wildlife, a national
organization dedicated to the preservation of all forms of wildlife.
Expiration Date ____11/⌐⌐____

_____
Signature
Defenders of Wildlife
1244 Nineteenth Street, NW Washington, DC 20036

Defenders of Wildlife • 1244 19th Street, NW • Washington, DC 20036
A copy of our annual report is available upon request from Defenders of Wildlife or the New York Department of State, Office of Charities Registration, Albany, New York, 12231.

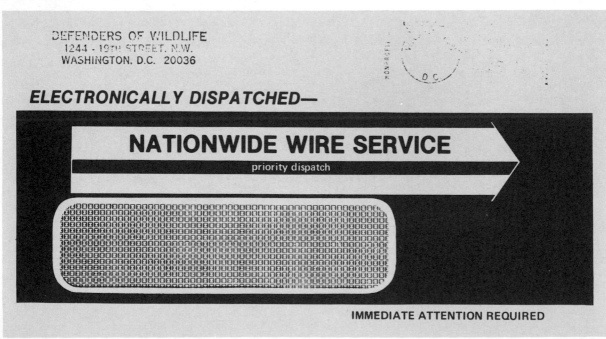

DEFENDERS OF WILDLIFE
1244 - 19TH STREET, N.W.
WASHINGTON, D.C. 20036

ELECTRONICALLY DISPATCHED—

NATIONWIDE WIRE SERVICE

priority dispatch

IMMEDIATE ATTENTION REQUIRED

The more dramatic second mailing.

NATIONWIDE WIRE SERVICE

priority dispatch

From:

ALLEN E. SMITH, PRESIDENT
DEFENDERS OF WILDLIFE
1244 - 19TH STREET, NW
WASHINGTON, DC 20036

Date
DECEMBER 29, 19.

To:

CHRISTOPHE W. P...
. ... DF...
AMBL. PA 1900

Message:

HAVE JUST REVIEWED MEMBERS ROSTER. YOUR MEMBERSHIP IN DEFENDERS OF WILDLIFE IS DUE TO EXPIRE IN A FEW SHORT WEEKS.

IF OVERLOOKED, USE ENCLOSED RENEWAL FORM TO EXTEND MEMBERSHIP IMMEDIATELY FOR COMING YEAR.

SINCE MY LAST LETTER, OUR CAMPAIGN TO PREVENT DES- TRUCTION OF WILDLIFE AND HABITAT MOUNTS.

IN MINNESOTA, ACTIVELY FIGHTING PLANS TO ALLOW KILL- ING OF ENDANGERED GRAY WOLF, EVEN CUBS. IN FLORIDA, FIGHTING PRIVATE CLUB EFFORTS TO GET ACCESS INTO WILDLIFE REFUGE.

DEFENDERS OF WILDLIFE SCIENTIFICALLY ORIENTED ORGANI- ZATION AT HUB OF PUBLIC POLICY DEBATE OVER WILDLIFE.

SLOWDOWNS IN OUR WORK COULD BE DISASTROUS FOR FUTURE GENERATIONS. YOUR CONTINUING SUPPORT ESSENTIAL.

CITIZEN ALERT CAMPAIGNS, WATCHDOG MONITORING OF SPECIES STATUS, LEGISLATIVE LOBBYING, AND LITIGATION WILL CONTINUE. CRUCIAL OUR MEMBERSHIP REMAINS STRONG.

-- RENEW NOW AT ANY MEMBERSHIP LEVEL AND RECEIVE -- FREE -- A HANDSOME GOLDEN EAGLE POSTER. THIS FULL COLOR POSTER MEASURES 21 X 31 INCHES AND IS IDEAL FOR YOUNG PERSON'S ROOM, YOUR DEN OR REC-ROOM WALL.

BECAUSE OF YOUR PAST SUPPORT, WE'VE SCORED VICTORIES IN FIGHT TO PROTECT AMERICAN WILDLIFE. CANNOT STOP NOW.

RETURN ENCLOSED RENEWAL FORM TO ME TODAY. THANK YOU.

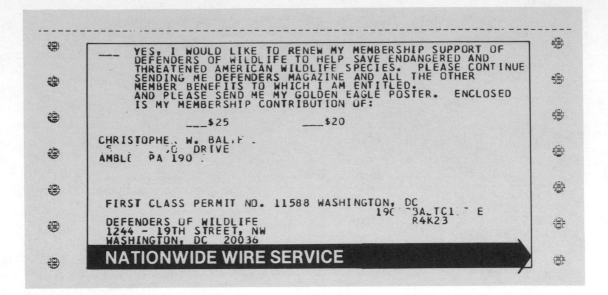

--- YES, I WOULD LIKE TO RENEW MY MEMBERSHIP SUPPORT OF
DEFENDERS OF WILDLIFE TO HELP SAVE ENDANGERED AND
THREATENED AMERICAN WILDLIFE SPECIES. PLEASE CONTINUE
SENDING ME DEFENDERS MAGAZINE AND ALL THE OTHER
MEMBER BENEFITS TO WHICH I AM ENTITLED.
AND PLEASE SEND ME MY GOLDEN EAGLE POSTER. ENCLOSED
IS MY MEMBERSHIP CONTRIBUTION OF:

___$25   ___$20

CHRISTOPHE. W. BAL.F.
5. ,C DRIVE
AMBLE PA 190

FIRST CLASS PERMIT NO. 11588 WASHINGTON, DC
19C BA TC1 E
R4K23

DEFENDERS OF WILDLIFE
1244 - 19TH STREET, NW
WASHINGTON, DC 20036

NATIONWIDE WIRE SERVICE

NATIONWIDE WIRE SERVICE

priority dispatch

BUSINESS REPLY MAIL

POSTAGE WILL BE PAID BY ADDRESSEE

NO POSTAGE
NECESSARY
IF MAILED
IN THE
UNITED STATES

Defenders of Wildlife

1244 19th Street, NW • Washington, DC 20036

FINAL NOTICE

Dear Member:

Time has run out on your Defenders of Wildlife membership.

But I know you care too much for America's animals -- her bald eagles, grizzly bears, bobcats, mountain lions, prairie dogs, whooping cranes, eagles -- to let time run out on their stay here on earth.

That's why I'm truly sorry to see you haven't yet responded to our earlier renewal notices and have let your membership in Defenders of Wildlife expire.

To stop that final count-down clock from ticking (as brutal leghold traps snap shut...government predator control gunners shoot down animals from helicopters...and oil and gas companies drill into wildlife habitats), I've enclosed one FINAL RENEWAL NOTICE with this letter. Please -- send it to me today, along with your check for any desired membership category. I'll see to it that your membership is re-activated immediately.

If you have definitely decided not to renew, for whatever reason, I'd like to know why. Send the enclosed form back to me; write "cancel" on the front, and perhaps a few words of explanation on the back. We've taken care of the return postage.

But first, think hard about your decision. Already, time has run out for the passenger pigeon, the Eastern bison, the Carolina parakeet.

But, for others, it's not too late. The saving of mountain caribou, spotted owl, desert tortoise, bighorn sheep -- the saving of wilderness areas where wild animals can graze, breed, and live -- has, as its final goal, the saving of another important species, man.

The pressing need for our work to block anti-environmental maneuvers of the current Administration has not disappeared, but, in fact, grown.

The minimum membership level -- seems a small price to pay for extending such consequential deadlines. Won't you please send your renewal check today?

Sincerely,

Allen E. Smith
President

P.S. As a special incentive, when you renew now -- at any level -- you will receive, FREE, a handsome wildlife poster. See the enclosed form for details.

The third and final notice in the series.

Defenders of Wildlife • 1244 19th Street, NW • Washington, DC 20036

MEMBERSHIP RENEWAL NOTICE

Yes, I would like to renew my membership support of Defenders of Wildlife
to help save endangered and threatened
American wildlife species. Please
continue sending me DEFENDERS magazine
and all the other member benefits to
which I am entitled. Enclosed is my
membership contribution of:

190BAL   E   R 6K 23X

Christopher W. Balth
 Drv
Amble., PA 190

$25 $20 $15 $10

Please return this portion with your check (**made payable to Defenders of Wildlife**) in the postpaid envelope provided.

This is your LAST OPPORTUNITY to renew your membership in Defenders of Wildlife for the coming
year. Endangered wildlife around the country
depend on your continuing commitment and support.
Please let me hear from you immediately — I'll
mail a handsome golden eagle poster, measuring
21 X 31 inches, as soon as I do.

Allen E. Smith

Defenders of Wildlife • 1244 19th Street, NW • Washington, DC 20036

A copy of our annual report is available upon request from Defenders of Wildlife or the New York Department of State, Office of Charities Registration, Albany, New York, 12231.

We have reserved a
Free Wildlife Gift for you...

BY ACTING TODAY, YOU CAN RETAIN ALL OF YOUR VALUABLE SERVICES
AS A MEMBER OF THE XYZ MOTOR CLUB FOR ANOTHER YEAR. YOU ALSO
SAVE THE $7 ENROLLMENT FEE NOW REQUIRED OF ALL NEW AND LAPSED
MEMBERS.

TECHNICALLY, YOUR MEMBERSHIP HAS ALREADY LAPSED, DEPRIVING
YOU OF THE MANY PRIVILEGES AND SERVICES THAT PROTECT YOUR
SECURITY ON THE ROAD. BUT BECAUSE WE VALUE YOUR LOYALTY
AND YOUR SAFETY, WHEN YOU SAY YES TODAY YOU WILL BE REINSTATED
IMMEDIATELY AND WITHOUT PENALTY.

FOR YOUR SECURITY ANYWHERE, ANY TIME, YOU CAN NOW CALL A
TOLL-FREE 800 NUMBER, LISTED ON YOUR MEMBERSHIP CARD, FOR
EMERGENCY ROAD SERVICE--JUMP STARTS, TIRE CHANGES, AND
EMERGENCY TOWING AT NO EXPENSE. IN FACT, OUR NEW EMERGENCY
TOWING POLICY TAKES YOU WHERE YOU WANT TO GO. OFFICIAL
XYZ STATIONS EVERYWHERE WILL ACCEPT YOUR PERSONAL CHECK
FOR PAYMENT OF EMERGENCY REPAIRS. NO OTHER MOTOR CLUB
GIVES YOU THIS GUARANTEE.

IN THESE DAYS OF INFLATED COSTS--WHEN A NON-XYZ STATION CAN
CHARGE $20 OR MORE FOR A SINGLE BREAKDOWN (IF YOU CAN GET
SERVICE)--THE VALUE OF YOUR XYZ MOTOR CLUB MEMBERSHIP IS
GREATER THAN EVER.

SAY YES TODAY AND ENJOY WORRY-FREE DRIVING. JUST RETURN
THIS LETTER AND YOUR CHECK IN THE ENCLOSED POSTAGE-PAID
ENVELOPE.

- -

☐ YES. I WANT TO RENEW MY MEMBERSHIP TODAY AND SAVE THE
         $7 ENROLLMENT FEE.

    ☐ NO. I DO NOT WANT TO RENEW MY MEMBERSHIP FOR THE
           FOLLOWING REASON:
           _____

*The membership has expired when this third renewal-series letter
goes out — but only "technically."*

```
      H U R R Y !

Your membership benefits and privileges
have just slipped away.  But you can still
rescue them by sending your dues TODAY.
You'll be glad you'll still have your
member's discounts, newsletters, special
events, priority tickets, and the many
things that make your membership a rare
bargain.
```

This printed slip is part of a fourth renewal mailing. A dues statement and reply envelope are enclosed.

HOW TO RECAPTURE THE ONES THAT GOT AWAY

Once, I visited a major institution and toured its membership operation. On the floor of a small room in the basement I spotted a large pile of metal addressing plates and asked what they were. I was told that they represented all of the previous year's annual members who hadn't renewed after two notices and a waiting period of several months. The metal — and the names — had become expensive junk. But far more expensive than the cost of the metal was the cost of the lost *names*.

Here's a surprising fact: A former member who absolutely refused to renew his or her membership, say, two years ago is still an excellent membership prospect! Once the impossible renewals — the deaths and move-away cancellations — have been removed from a file of non-renewed members, the names of the remaining recent members are at least four times more responsive to membership offers than a list of "cold" prospects. Why? Because they have already been customers and need only special wooing to be brought back into the fold. Here's how you do the job.

Quite often a major institution will suffer a horrendous loss of first-year members who enrolled primarily for a one-time special privilege. Too often, generally through inexperience, the institution lacks a strong renewal program and lets far too many members slip away unrenewed when the time for the special privilege is over. Now what?

This is a time to examine the real reason why the fickle new members joined in such large numbers. Was it an especially attractive special gift or bonus? If so, it may be unprofitable for you to come up with a comparable new offer to get over the first-year hump. Many may have just wanted the bonus gift, so they never bothered to get involved in the other benefits. Sometimes even the strongest cultivation program falls short.

But quite often the real reason isn't perceived by the institution itself. Here's a short case history. The American museums that were selected to show the now-definitive King Tut exhibition some years ago realistically expected their memberships to jump dramatically, as they all did. But it wasn't just King Tut that brought the huge increases. The *real* reason was the constant stressing of the membership privilege of getting *priority tickets* to an event everybody knew was going to be jammed and difficult to see.

People like special privileges and time-saving convenience. They also know that another King Tut isn't going to come along for many years. But if the institution constantly reminds its members that they will have priority tickets for *other* attractive major events, many will be reluctant to lose that privilege — with or without King Tut.

For example, the Museum Society, a membership group for the three major fine arts museums in San Francisco, continued to lose many of its first-year members who joined for King Tut priority tickets. So it launched a carefully planned "recapture" series of mailings. Best of all, it took aggressive action in scheduling more major exhibitions that were likely to become blockbusters. A series of recapture letters, beginning about nine months after the crest of the major losses, brought back many who wanted to be part of the "in" crowd with priority tickets when the new major exhibitions came around. The results of the first letter were so good that a series of two more recapture letters was sent with equally strong results.

The second letter in the series, incidentally, wound up with a request for a "release" on priority ticket privileges to someone else. Here are the last two paragraphs of that letter.

> Once again, you can decide to go on enjoying the best things life has to offer. If your decision has to be "No," we'd appreciate it if you would let us know so we can assign your priority ticket privileges to someone else.
>
> We sincerely hope your decision is "Yes." As you mail your check in the convenient reply envelope, let me thank you again for your loyal interest in our San Francisco art museums.

THE MUSEUM SOCIETY

M. H. de YOUNG	Golden Gate Park
MEMORIAL	San Francisco, Ca 94118
MUSEUM	(415) 752-2800

CALIFORNIA
PALACE OF THE
LEGION OF HONOR

ASIAN ART
MUSEUM OF
SAN FRANCISCO

Dear Once and Future Member:

For one brief, shining moment, San Francisco became Camelot-on-the-Bay.

When the spell of King Tut and the charm of Dresden lured you and hundreds of thousands of others through our doors, you became one of more than 57,000 new Members of your Museum Society who helped to establish here a record for the largest growth in museum membership in the United States in a single year. For several shining months, San Francisco had the largest art museum membership in the world!

It's no mystery why so many new Members joined in anticipation of the coming of Tut. Stories of long lines and thousands of disappointed would-be viewers in other cities drifted back

The same priority admission privileges you enjoyed for King Tut and Dresden will now be carried over to such popular future exhibitions as The Search for Alexander and another major event just confirmed (but still in the confidential stages).

You may recall that when all of the priority tickets for Tut were allocated back in January, we reluctantly had to stop taking in new Members until after the exhibition was over, many months later. Many of our recent new Members who missed the cut have no intention of missing out again on priority tickets for Alexander and other great exhibitions.

We have missed you this year. Possibly you have mislaid our earlier notices for your annual dues and need only this special reminder to continue to enjoy your many privileges.

Send us your membership check today and come soon and often to your three museums. You'll be reminded again and again that belonging to your Museum Society is an open door to the best things life has to offer.

Sincerely,

Test a few recapture letters on your own first-year drop-outs. Stress the benefits and privileges that most people find hard to give up. Then, after another six months or so, put the names back in the hopper for another new membership offer. You've done your best.

Membership comes in three steps. Step number one is to recruit a dues-paying member. Step two is to induce that new member to renew his or her membership when the time comes.

But, for gift-seeking organizations, step number three is to get the renewed member to begin increasing the size of his or her dues.

One way to do this is simply to ask. Ask for an additional gift, or ask for an increased gift. Another way is to offer better benefits for bigger dues. But perhaps one of the most effective ways to get an increased gift is through the medium of what is called a "minimum-gift club." Only by giving at a specified, higher-dues level can the member join such a club. You can have several such clubs within your overall membership organization. There may be benefits attached, such as social events, but the prime benefit usually seems to be prestige — which is a very convincing benefit. For an additional, say, $50 per year, your ordinary "member" can become a member of the prestigious-sounding "President's Associates." People take such things seriously; you often see minimum-gift club memberships listed in obituaries.

13

How do you go about starting one or more miminum-gift clubs within your organization? And what do you have to gain? In the "FRI Annual Giving Book," M. Jane Williams sets forth advantages of such clubs. Here are her thoughts, with a few additional ideas tacked on.

- You'll have a better reason to ask people to increase their giving to a specific higher level — and many will do as you ask.

- You will be offering prestige. Your prospects will recognize the prestigious names of your club members and will want *their* names to appear on the same list. They may also want to join those people at the social functions you offer as privileges of membership.

- You have a logical way to give special recognition to your major donors.

- By offering personal recognition and small social events, you'll cultivate the interest of your major donors, and you'll be able to get to know them individually.

- You'll have established higher goals for the rest of your constituency to aspire to and consider.

- By including bequests and other forms of planned giving among the ways a donor can meet the minimum-gift requirement, you'll motivate many to think about their wills and estates for the first time — and in relation to a pleasant, attainable goal.

The minimum-gift club technique is an ideal way to focus your gift solicitation and renewal effort on that very important 10 to 20 percent of your constituents who always give most of the money. In many cases, substantial annual giving in the form of prescribed dues is required to maintain membership in a minimum-gift club. But, a few such clubs have cumulative lifetime-total-giving requirements with no specified annual increments.

It's especially important to define clearly the qualifications for club membership. For example, do corporate matching gifts qualify? Do corporate gifts from a company the donor owns count? Can only individuals be members? Or can corporations and foundations become members? What about restricted and capital gifts? Do deferred gifts count and, if so, how? Are spouses automatically included in the membership at the basic minimum level? Usually it's a good idea to be as liberal as possible in favor of the member. Just be sure the member understands the deal from your clearly stated description. Here are some more tips from the "FRI Annual Giving Book" and other sources to guide you in setting up your club or clubs.

- Gauge your donors' gift-potential carefully when establishing gift qualifications. It's a good idea to have one lofty top club, but you should also consider having others with lower and different qualifications.

- Give meaningful names to your gift clubs and don't change them. Look for names linked with individuals closely associated with your organization (founders, respected presidents or deans, etc.), historic events, places, projects, activities, or interests.

- Build carefully researched prospect lists and assign close friends of your cause or prestigious persons to make the initial membership invitation and, if possible, the renewal solicitation.

- Design attractive and appropriate stationery, brochures, certificates, gift acknowledgment forms, and recognition devices. Those who qualify will feel they deserve the best your institution can bestow.

- Plan attractive and varied social events appropriate to the purposes of the club. Remember, some lonely people will want to join just for these events.

- Make certain that the total list of benefits is frequently and attractively presented to logical prospects. Describe your clubs on materials that are widely distributed to your *general* constituency.

- Make it clear that deceased members will have their names published in a special, "In-Memoriam" section of the membership directory, if you have one — and you should. Send a copy of the directory each year to any surviving spouse who is not a member.

- Publish a special newsletter for club members at least twice a year reporting on club activities, new members, and significant programs and services of the institution.

Sometimes it's worth starting a club just to be able to send a targeted newsletter to its members to acquaint them with "inside" news and details of unusual philanthropic opportunities. One museum found individual donors for four different major projects in a single year, simply by describing the projects and what they would accomplish. The descriptions appeared in the newsletter written expressly for a special club with a membership of about 400! Now, let's look at a model minimum-gift club.

The John Evans Club.　John Evans, M.D., started his career in the mid-19th century as a young physician in Indiana. He invented surgical instruments, helped open the state's first mental hospital and first school for the deaf and the first hospital in Chicago. He became a community leader, and this took him into the railroad-building business, which took him into the city-building business (Evanston, Ill., among others). He was a church leader and a political leader. He left the former Northwest Territory area in 1862, going farther west to become territorial governor of Colorado at the request of President Abraham Lincoln.

But before he left for that post, he had also helped found a university: Northwestern University. Dr. Evans gave $1,000 as the first payment on the University's campus in Evanston. He gave $100,000 to create the University's first two endowed professorships. He was president of the University's Board of Trustees until 1894.

In short, Dr. John Evans was a spectacular, broadly focused, tremendously effective leader — one of the best of his time. Almost a century after his death, his mark remains strong on the area in which he served. And he is an inspiring model to name a minimum-gift club after — something that Northwestern University realized in 1954.

Here are some of the printed pieces used by Northwestern to promote membership in The John Evans Club. If you read them over, you'll get a good idea of how such a club is structured and promoted.

Purposes of The John Evans Club

The purposes of The John Evans Club are:

1. To establish an exemplary pattern of substantial financial support to the University by its alumni and friends who have a sustained interest in Northwestern.

2. To offer the assistance and counsel of its members to the general programs and activities of the University, including fund-raising.

3. To hold meetings to which University representatives will be Invited to discuss the plans and objectives of Northwestern.

4. To sponsor programs and events for the benefit of members, their families, and friends.

Meetings and Events

The John Evans Club holds several meetings each year at which University administrative officers and faculty members acquaint John Evans Club members with the plans and needs of the University. Throughout the year, the Club schedules regular events, including the Night at Ravinia. a Football Luncheon, the Anniversary Dinner, the Waa-Mu Dinner and Show, the Ladies Luncheon, and the Annual Meeting and Brunch, as well as special programs as the occasions may arise.

Organization

The membership of the Board of Directors, which governs the activities of The John Evans Club, is approved annually by the University Trustees. The Board consists of twenty-one members (at least fifteen of whom shall be alumni of the University) with terms of three years, staggered so that seven terms expire each year. The President and Vice-President for Development of the University, the President of the Northwestern University Alumni Association, and the University's Director of Alumni Relations serve ex-officio.

Membership

Membership in The John Evans Club is open to all alumni and special friends of Northwestern University who have demonstrated concern for and loyalty to the University and who signify by a pledge that it is their intention to contribute $15,000 or more to the University over a period of fifteen years, or who signify their hope and intention to provide $25,000 or more through their estate.

Membership in The John Evans Club can be of three types:

Class I   Active Members

All living members and their spouses who have met the membership requirements shall be active members of The John Evans Club. A husband or wife of any member, deceased or living, shall be an active member of The John Evans Club.

Class II   Honorary Members

The Board of Directors may elect to honorary membership individuals who have demonstrated extraordinary loyalty to the University through continuous service and support and who have brought prestige and esteem to Northwestern. Honorary members shall be entitled to all the rights and privileges of The John Evans Club.

Class III   In Memoriam Members

Deceased John Evans Club members are carried as members In Memoriam. The Board of Directors may also elect deceased persons and/or their spouses who have contributed $15,000 or more to Northwestern in earlier years as members In Memoriam.

Use of Gifts

In perpetuating the memory and work of John Evans, members may choose any one of the following options regarding disposition of their gifts:

1. Unrestricted—such gifts shall be used to support projects selected by the Trustees of the University as deserving priority.

2. Restricted—such gifts shall be used for whatever fund or purpose the donor desires, provided such use is acceptable to the Trustees of the University.

3. Deferred gifts in the form of bequests, annuities, or any other deferred giving program may be unrestricted or restricted as the donor designates. If designation is not made prior to the donor's death, the principal shall become available for use of the University at the discretion of the Trustees.

4. Trust Fund—donors may request that their gifts be placed in special funds to be known as The John Evans Pioneer Trust Funds. Income realized from such funds may be added to the fund or may be used to support current projects designated by the Trustees of the University. The donor may at any time designate the use of all or any part of the principal or income of his trust fund for any project meeting the approval of the Trustees. If designation is not made prior to death, the principal shall become available for use of the University at the discretion of the Trustees.

Forfeiture of Membership

Failure to show good faith in honoring a pledge to The John Evans Club may, upon action of the Board of Directors of The John Evans Club, terminate membership.

Disloyalty to the country or to the accepted standards of educated men and women may, upon action of the Board of Directors, terminate membership.

The John Evans Club Membership Pledge

I acknowledge my election to membership in The John Evans Club of Northwestern University and hereby indicate my acceptance. In so doing I am joining with a group of Northwestern alumni and friends to maintain the tradition John Evans established in the first century of Northwestern University's growth.

As an expression of cooperation with other Northwestern alumni and friends similarly elected to membership in The John Evans Club,

☐ I hereby signify my hope and intention to subscribe the sum of $15,000 or more to Northwestern University over a period of fifteen years, at the rate of $1,000 or more annually, or,

☐ I hereby signify my hope and intention to provide $25,000 or more by bequest, or,

☐ I am joining with a paid-in-full membership.

It is my intention that my gift be used:

☐ as an unrestricted gift to the University, or,

☐ as a gift designated for_____, or,

☐ for the establishment of a Pioneer Trust Fund.

Donors may request that their gifts be placed in special funds to be known as The John Evans Pioneer Trust Funds. Income realized from such funds may be added to the fund or may be used to support current projects designated by the Trustees of the University. The donor may at any time designate the use of all or any part of the principal or income of his trust fund for any project meeting the approval of the Trustees. If designation is not made prior to death, the principal shall become available for the use of the University at the discretion of the Trustees.

☐ Income from the fund to be added to the fund.

☐ Income from the fund to be used to support current projects designated by the Trustees of the University.

Name_____

Date_____

240

The John Evans Club newsletter

John Evans 1814-1897
A founder of
Northwestern University
and of Evanston, Illinois

Northwestern University   **Evanston, Illinois**   **Fall 198**

Class of '32: $1 million to Northwestern

Half a century ago, Northwestern's graduating seniors of 1932 pledged $1 million over 25 years as their class gift to the University. It was a bold I.O.U. from the Depression-era students, a commitment made when jobs were scarce and the nation's economy was at it lowest ebb. The million dollar promise was kept, providing funds for scholarships and loans for students.

Now, 50 years later, the Class of '32 has done it again. During

COMING EVENTS

John Evans Club events are being scheduled for the coming year. Plan to attend. Your guests are always welcome; just make reservations for them with the Club secretary at the Department of Alumni Relations, 1800 Sheridan Road, Evanston, Ill. 60201; phone 312/492-7200.

JEC welcomes Trustee William William Smithburg

JEC is proud to announce that Northwestern Trustee William D. Smithburg and his wife, Alberta (Happ), have accepted membership in The John Evans Club.

A leader in the business community, Smithburg is president and chief executive officer of The Quaker Oats Company, Chicago. After completing his bachelor of science degree in economics and marketing at DePaul University, Smithburg earned the MBA at Northwestern's J.L. Kellogg Graduate School of Management in 1961. That year, he joined Leo Burnett Company, Inc., as a research analyst and assistant account executive, leaving two years later to take a position as account executive at McCann Erickson, Inc., Chicago. In 1966, he became brand manager for frozen foods at Quaker Oats, and began his rise to the top of the company's leadership.

After serving as product group manager/cereals and general manager of the Cereals Division, Smithburg became vice-president and general manager of Quaker Oats' Cereals Division in 1971. Subsequently, he served as vice-president and general manager/Cereals and Mixes Division, president of the Foods Division, and executive vice-president (U.S.) for grocery products. In 1978, he became a member of the company's executive committee and board of directors, and was promoted to president and chief operating officer the following year. He took his present post as president and CEO in 1981.

Throughout his impressive business career, Smithburg has continued to devote his time and talents to a number of Northwestern activities (see New

William D. Smithburg

Members, page 15), and was elected to the University's Board of Trustees in 1979. We welcome him to membership in JEC—his latest expression of commitment to Northwestern.

NEW MEMBERS AND GUESTS AT JOHN EVANS CLUB EVENTS

Mr. and Mrs. William W. Brady
332 Vincent Place
Elgin, Illinois 60120

Brady *EB 36, L 40* is a partner in the Elgin law firm of Brady, McQueen, Martin, Collins & Jensen. He was a member of Northwestern's School of Law faculty for 40 years,

Mr. and Mrs. Edward Buker
1640 Mellody Road
Lake Forest, Illinois 60045

Buker is president of Coach and Car Equipment Corporation, Elk Grove Village, Ill. As an undergraduate at Northwestern, he joined Sigma Nu and received his degree in 1932 from the University's School of Commerce. He is married to the

Kelm *CAS 51, L 54* is president and chief executive officer of Sahara Coal Company, Chicago. A member of Lambda Chi Alpha as a Northwestern undergraduate, he has remained a dedicated alumnus, acting as a Class Representative, 1968-78, and now serving as chairman of the National Foundations Division of the School of Law fund-raising campaign for

John Evans Club members in the spotlight

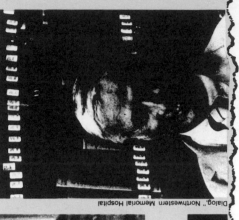

"Dialog," Northwestern Memorial Hospital

Following June 19 Commencement exercises at McGaw Memorial Hall, Dr. Martin J. Aliker *D 58* of Nairobi, Kenya, spoke to graduates at the Dental School Convocation in Alice Millar Chapel.

In Memoriam

In gratitude for many years of loyalty and devotion to Northwestern, The John Evans Club pays tribute to these deceased members:

P. Goff Beach *CB 40*
Northwestern Trustee
August 14, 1982

C. Laury Botthof *GSM 40*
May 30, 1982

Charles C. Jarchow *CB 16*
June 30, 1982

Gertrude Dana Kestnbaum
May 28, 1982

L. Shirley Tark *L 16*
August 5, 1982

JEC leads kickoff for athletic facilities

Northwestern's Sports programs have entered a "NU era"—officially heralded June 8 with a kickoff dinner to announce the University's $16 million Athletic Facilities Campaign. Plans include the construction of a centrally located sports center and adjacent aquatics center on the Evanston campus, and the renovation of McGaw Memorial Hall.

For the drive's formal announcement, Campaign leaders joined Northwestern officials and friends for dinner and a program in a tent near Dyche Stadium. "The Board of Trustees and your University administration are enthusiastically committed to this project," President Robert H. Strotz told the audience.

"Traditionally, Northwestern has offered its students a rich and challenging educational experience. Through the Athletic Facilities facilities has now come—and these new facilities will be tops in quality, suitable for a university of our character and of our pride."

Master of ceremonies at the kickoff was Trustee and National Campaign Chairman Patrick G. Ryan, president and chief executive officer of Combined International, insurance firm. Ryan, a member of The John Evans Club and an alumnus of Northwestern's School of Business, presented an overview of the plans to revitalize intercollegiate and recreational sports programs at the University.

Heading the list of Campaign priorities is the construction of a sports center that will more than double interior recreational floor space, offering students a superior facility for intercollegiate, intramural and self-directed sports activities. The center will include three regulation-size multipurpose

Patrick G. Ryan, National Campaign Chairman and Northwestern Trustee

lounge/pro shop, spectator viewing areas, and administrative and service space.

The aquatics center will replace

245

In addition to its top John Evans Club, Northwestern offers at least 15 other minimum-gift societies based on specific interests and on the various schools of the university. Some are shown here. Gifts toward membership in any or all of the societies count toward the much higher John Evans Club requirements. (The listing of the N Fund for athletics provides a "scoreboard" of specific benefits and privileges at each level of giving within the Fund.) If you're looking for ideas for starting minimum-gift clubs of your own, here is an inspiring check list.

NORTHWESTERN UNIVERSITY

SPECIAL GIFT SOCIETIES

1. The JOHN EVANS CLUB is a group of Northwestern alumni who have provided contributions totaling $15,000 or more over a 15 year period or a bequest of at least $25,000. All gifts, restricted or unrestricted, count towards membership. Once the pledge is made, the donor is a member for life and is able to participate in the 4-8 annual events. Members have provided more than $88 million since the John Evans Club was founded in 1954.

2. The FRIENDS OF ART society was founded in 1972 to provide financial support for the University's Department of Art History. It now supports the Mary and Leigh Block Gallery.

   Levels of Membership

$1,000 or more	Benefactor
$ 500-$999	Associate Member
$ 300-$499	Subscriber
$ 100-$299	Patron
$ 50-$ 99	Contributor
$ 25	Friend

3. The LIBRARY COUNCIL is an association of friends of the Library created in 1973. The contributions, regardless of level, enrich the collections of Northwestern University's research library.

   Levels of Membership

$1,000 or more	Benefactor
$ 750	Sponsor
$ 400	Patron
$ 150	Donor

   Contributing Members:
   $75 per couple
   $50 per individual
   $40 per faculty/staff couple
   $25 per faculty/staff individual
   $ 5 per student

4. The MUSIC SOCIETY is composed of generous patrons of the performing arts, allowing the University to bring premier musical performers to campus.

   Levels of Membership

$5,000 or more	Guarantor
$1,000-$4,999	Benefactor
$ 500-$ 999	Sustainer
$ 100-$ 499	Patron

5. The N FUND supports Northwestern's Big 10, intercollegiate and intramural athletic programs, providing grants-in-aid, sports equipment and recreational facilites.

Levels of Membership

$8,085	Living Scholarship
$3,000-$8,084	Coaches Bench
$1,000-$2,999	Benchwarmer
$ 500-$ 999	Big Ten Bench
$ 100-$ 499	Wildcat Bench
$ 25-$ 99	Benchbackers

SCHOOL RECOGNITION AND SPECIAL GIFT SOCIETIES

1. ### COLLEGE OF ARTS AND SCIENCES

All alumni and friends are encouraged to support the College.

Levels of Giving

$1,000 or more	Dean's Fund
$ 500-$999	CAS Century Fund (Benefactor)
$ 250-$499	CAS Century Fund (Sponsor)
$ 100-$249	CAS Century Fund (Member)

2. ### DENTAL SCHOOL

Membership in the G.V. BLACK SOCIETY provides recognition for gifts to the Dental School.

Levels of Giving

$5,000 or more (cumulative)	Life Fellow
$2,000 (cumulative)	Life Member
$ 500	Fellow
$ 200	Member
$ 50	Associate Member (alums of 4 yrs.)

3. ### SCHOOL OF EDUCATION

Membership in the JOHN E. STOUT SOCIETY is given to those alumni contributing $100 or more to the School each year.

The N Fund

*"Northwestern offers the best combination – a great athletic program and an outstanding education. By providing scholarships through **The N Fund**, we offer these young student-athletes a tremendous opportunity.*

Sandy Stap Clifton
Tennis Coach

Eric Mogentale

Kathleen Kochmansky

*"The support of our alumni and friends across the country is vital to our commitment to academic and athletic excellence. We must identify and attract the nation's finest student-athletes if we expect to enjoy athletic success. **The N Fund** helps tremendously in our recruiting efforts."*

Rich Falk
Basketball Coach

Pattijean McCahill

Andre Goode

The N Fund Benefits	Scholarship Bench $8,895 +	Director's Bench $5000 to $8894	Coaches' Bench $3000 to $4999	Bench-warmer $1000 to $2999	Big Ten Bench $500 to $999	Wildcat Bench $100 to $499	Bench-backer $35 to $99
Named Scholarship	YES						
Director's Club	Member	Member					
Special Social Events	YES	YES	YES	YES			
VIP Parking	VIP	VIP	Special	Special			
Benchwarmer Icebucket	YES	YES	YES	YES			
Recognition Plaque	YES	YES	YES	YES			
Football and Basketball Media Guides	YES	YES	YES	YES	YES		
N Club Member Decal	YES	YES	YES	YES	YES	YES	
NU Direction Newsletter	YES	YES	YES	YES	YES	YES	YES
Listed in various Northwestern publications	YES	YES	YES	YES	YES	YES	YES
Ticket Priority for Football and Basketball	1st	2nd	3rd	4th	5th	6th	7th
Tax Deduction	YES	YES	YES	YES	YES	YES	YES
N Club Membership	YES	YES	YES	YES	YES	YES	YES

Keeper's Club. Most successful minimum-gift clubs are used as upgrading tools to elevate the sights of people who are already members at a basic rate.

An excellent example of this was created by the Zoological Society of San Diego. Some of their membership material, done a few years ago, is shown here. When this material was in use, people who had been members of the Zoological Society for three or more consecutive years were invited to join a group called the Keeper's Club by contributing a higher membership fee, which, at the time, was $100. Prospects were allowed to credit their currently paid membership dues against the higher contribution required for the Club. They were offered a multi-payment pledge option that about half the respondents chose. Among the incentives included in the invitation to join were special Club functions and tours, a personalized membership card, and an animal print lithograph. But the strongest appeal to people willing to give at this higher level seems to have been the Zoo's recognition of their long-standing support and the opportunity to help out more significantly.

Judging from written responses that came in at the time, many donors considered the invitation an honor. The initial cost-per-dollar to enroll a new member in the Keeper's Club was under 50 cents. And as time went by, about 85 percent of those new members renewed their memberships in subsequent years, resulting in an eventual overall cost of three cents-per-dollar-raised.

But the Zoological Society of San Diego had still another membership category. And at renewal time, Keeper's Club members first received an invitation to join the Curator's Club by making what was then a $250 cash contribution. The Curator's Club invitation stressed membership in an elite group of community leaders and offered many special membership benefits. Nearly 10 percent of the Keepers chose to become Curators. Those who did not were then asked to renew their expiring membership in the Keeper's Club.

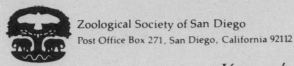

Zoological Society of San Diego
Post Office Box 271, San Diego, California 92112

Keeper's Club

August 12, 19

Mr. John D. Sample
24 New England Executive Park
Burlington, Massachusetts 01803

Dear Mr. Sample:

On behalf of the Board of Trustees, I am pleased to
extend to you this special invitation to participate in
the Keeper's Club of the Zoological Society of San Diego.

You have been selected to receive this special
invitation because of your support as a loyal Member of the
Zoological Society since 1977. Participation in the
Keeper's Club reaffirms that support and helps to provide
the funds that are vital to the continued excellence of the
San Diego Zoo and the Wild Animal Park.

If you accept our invitation, you will receive many
valuable and prestigious benefits such as your own
Keeper's Club Card, invitations to special Keeper's Club
events, an evening with the Zoological Society Keepers, a
yearly preview, and exciting "behind-the-scenes" tours.
A beautiful 8" X 10" lithographed animal drawing will also
be yours, as well as all of the benefits of regular membership which you now enjoy.

An annual contribution or pledge of $100 or more is
necessary for Keeper's Club participation, but since your
Single Membership is current, we will apply the $20 renewal
fee you paid in March to the cost of your Keeper's Club
support. Therefore, your actual additional payment
required is only $80.

If you decide to pay this amount in full, please return
the enclosed white "Full Payment" Acceptance Form with your
check for $80.

Or if you would like to pledge your Keeper's Club
contribution, you may do so by paying $25 today and sending
the balance of $55 over the next few months. (You will
receive pledge reminders.) Just return the enclosed

Page Two

yellow "Pledge Option" Acceptance Form with your check
for $25.

Either way, as soon as we receive your Keeper's Club
Acceptance Form, you will be eligible for all Keeper's
Club benefits and privileges for one full year from the
date of your acceptance.

The Keeper's Club was established to recognize
loyal Members who have helped the San Diego Zoo and the
Wild Animal Park achieve their world-renowned status.
I know you will enjoy the events we have planned, and I
look forward to welcoming you to the Keeper's Club.

Sincerely,

George L. Gildred
President

GG/msm

Zoological Society of San Diego
Post Office Box 271, San Diego, California 92112

September 8, 19

Mr. John A. Sample
123 Main Street
Anywhere, USA   00000

Dear Mr. Sample:

The enclosed special invitation is limited to a very select group of friends.

It comes to you because of your wonderful support through the Keeper's Club and other important projects of the Zoological Society of San Diego. I hope you will accept this personal invitation to join our newly formed Curator's Club.

The Curator's Club is not for everyone. Annual support of $250 is required for your participation in this distinguished group. You will find your fellow members are leaders in the San Diego community.

Naturally, there are many benefits and privileges associated with the Curator's Club. In addition to those you already enjoy -- ZOONOOZ and free guest passes -- you will receive personal invitations to previews of new exhibits, fascinating "behind-the-scenes" tours, and special events hosted by our own Zoological Society Curators. These respected professionals will share with you the real inside story of your Zoo and Wild Animal Park. And they'll be interested in your feedback about our future plans.

You will also receive an embossed Curator's Club Card. This unique card will gain you instant recognition and unlimited entrance to both the Zoo and the Wild Animal Park.

But perhaps even more important than these benefits is the feeling you will have by knowing your special support allows us to maintain our world-renowned excellence. This contributes so greatly to the quality of life we enjoy in San Diego.

I want you to know that the Board of Trustees and I extend you this very special invitation with our sincere desire for your acceptance. I look forward to the opportunity of personally welcoming you to the Curator's Club.

Sincerely,

George L. Gildred, President

P.S. Join us now to take advantage of the special events currently planned for you as a supporter of the Curator's Club.

Curator's Club
Acceptance Form

To: George L. Gildred, President, Zoological Society of San Diego

From: Mr. John A. Sample
      123 Main Street
      Anywhere, USA   00000

☐ **Yes,** I would like to accept your invitation to become a supporter of the Curator's Club of the Zoological Society of San Diego. Enclosed is my full contribution of $250. I understand this will entitle me to the benefits below:

Membership Benefits

- One year's unlimited ENTRANCE to the San Diego Zoo and the Wild Animal Park
- 12 Colorful and informative issues of ZOONOOZ Magazine
- 4 Free GUEST PASSES for friends and family
- QUARTERLY NEWSLETTER with calendar of events
- Personal Invitations to PREVIEWS of new exhibits

- Unique embossed CURATOR'S CLUB CARD
- Fascinating "behind-the-scenes" TOURS of the Zoo and the Wild Animal Park
- Special EVENTS hosted by Zoological Society Curators
- Special matted ANIMAL DRAWING of a San Diego Zoo or Wild Animal Park animal

123456A 2111 XX K1

(Please return this Acceptance Form with your gift made payable to the Zoological Society of San Diego in the envelope provided today. Thank you!)

Zoological Society of San Diego • Post Office Box 271 • San Diego, California 92112

The club name. The name of the minimum-gift club should have a certain cachet that appeals to those most likely to join. Some of the more popular names include such logical choices as President's Club, Founders Club, Life Patrons, etc. One of the most appealing names was coined by the legendary Dorothy Buffum Chandler when she led the movement to establish the Los Angeles Performing Arts Center (where Dorothy Chandler Pavilion is familiar to viewers of the Academy Awards). Mrs. Chandler said she wanted a name that suggested top level giving and also a flavor of exclusivity. She came up with a real winner: The Blue Ribbon 400. At first only 400 persons were permitted to join, but such a long waiting list developed that the "400" was expanded and the number designation was dropped. But it's still one of the most attractive names around.

Complete and flexible records are the food that sustains every membership group. Without them, even the best organization will slowly die. They can be as simple as $3 \times 5''$ file cards or metal addressing plates or as elaborate as today's computer technology permits. They must be appropriate to your organization and inexpensive to use (in relation to the profit they bring back). They must allow you to use the marketing and fund-raising techniques that will produce maximum profits.

And you've got to keep an eye on them. In older organizations, records systems tend to become top-heavy with traditional procedures of little current value. (One very hardworking records crew complained that with the heavy influx of new members brought in by expert promotion, they had little time to do their "regular work." And what was the regular work? Their explanation, expressed with pride, was that much of what they were doing enabled them to detect five or six cheaters each year in a membership of more than 20,000. The labor cost of carrying out the detection steps in the records was probably several hundred times greater than any possible loss through cheating.)

It's important to know just what kinds of information you'll need to obtain from your records, now and in the future. Many membership records systems are unable to produce potentially valuable information simply because it wasn't recorded in usable form from the outset — things as basic as the sex of the member, date and source of the first sale, etc.

On the other hand, it costs money to maintain records, and the more you maintain, the more it costs. So avoid collecting costly data that you'll never be able to use.

Whether you're starting from scratch or bringing an old system up to date, you may find that employing a records management consultant is a sound investment. But you, personally, must get to know the system in detail so you can manage the people who will be running it and so you can be assured that the system doesn't hamper your ability to raise income.

14

WHAT GOES INTO A MEMBERSHIP RECORD

Even a basic card-file membership record must include certain data about each member. And it should be maintained in a uniform format and a uniform style. Most membership records contain a minimum of the following information.

Sex.

First name and initial.

Last name.

Suffix. This includes such suffixes as Junior, III, MD, DDS, Ph.D.; other advanced degrees; certifications such as CFRE, CPA, and CLU; military affiliations such as USN, USA, USAF, USMC; and others. Complete compilations of standardized suffix abbreviations may be found in "Acronyms and Initialisms Dictionary" published by Gale Research Company, and also in "Address Abbreviations, Publication 59," January 1976, of the United States Postal Service.

Title. Prefix titles include Mr., Mrs., Ms., Miss, Dr., military titles, academic titles, religious and governmental titles, and royal and noble titles. Most of these have been standardized for computer formats.

Street address.

City or town.

State or county.

ZIP code. (If in the United States)

Country. (If yours is an international group)

Original source. It's important to know whether the member joined in response to direct mail (which list and which offer), counter sale, convention booth, telephone sale, etc. Start early to develop coding that takes up little room on the record and still gives you this important information.

Occupation.

Date of original entry.

Financial transactions.   This includes dates and dollar amounts and nature of transaction. The usual transaction will be payment of membership fees. If the membership record is combined with a contribution record, say for annual giving, the difference between those transactions should be made clear.

Salutations.   Some organizations that use computer letters and other highly personalized communications go a step further and include in their membership records the personal salutations used by the chief executive officer and other potential letter-signers: "Dear Sam," etc.

Optional data.   Some membership records may include much more detailed data needed to serve the member or to run the membership program efficiently. Such optional data could include:

- 10-digit telephone number (home and/or office);
- "Non-mail" code, in case you don't want all members to receive all mailings;
- Affiliation with the organization (board, officer, minimum-gift clubs, volunteer, etc.);
- VIP codes, usually identifying major-gift prospects;
- Social Security number;
- Birth date;
- Credit card information, if you accept payment that way.

Now, on the next page you'll see what all this information might look like when entered on a 5×8″ record card in your office. Many offices code these cards by printing them on different color stocks, indicating different classifications of membership.

From the information in your records, you can now produce a profile sheet for an individual prospect. Such sheets are extremely helpful when fund-raising volunteers are considering members who have potential major-gift status. The profile gives the needed information in easily-read form. If your records are maintained by computer, generation of such profiles is easy.

To the right is a membership-donor-record-profile format developed by DataMation, a firm that pioneered in computer-based systems for membership organizations. This format is for individual members (as opposed to corporate members, which many trade and professional associations have. Additional data for corporate members would include such things as: name of the corporation or its foundation, dollar volume of sales, contact person, names of officers, etc.)

```
NAME:   SMITH, Mr. and Mrs. William, Jr.              SOURCE: WN83
        1234 Bay Avenue, Apartment 314
        Seattle Washington 98002                   SALUTATIONS
                                                       CEO: Bill, Marianne
                                                       MO: Bill, Mrs.

          PHONE:  (206) 555-4279 (home), 555-3802 (office)
                                                    NON-MAIL
  TYPE & NO.:  Governing Annual 012-12345-67          CODES: B, D
  OCCUPATION:  Attorney (Partner, Stocks & Bond, Inc.)

ORIGINAL DATE:  October 198      AFFILIATION: Trustee (Mr.), Woman's Board (Mrs.)
RENEWAL DATE:   February
```

Date	Receipt No.	Amount	Remarks	Date	Receipt No.	Amount	Remarks
11 Feb 84	4-4002	$65.00	regular				
5 Feb 85	5-3269	$65.00	regular				
14 Feb 86	6-5073	$100.00	President's Club				

258

MEMBER PROFILE

NAME:	Mr. and Mrs. William J. Smith, Jr.
ADDRESS:	1234 Bay Avenue, Apartment 314
CITY/STATE/ZIP:	Seattle, Washington 98002
PHONE:	(206) 555-4279
FIRST NAME:	Marianne - Bill
SEX:	M & F
AGE:	40 - 50
NUMBER OF CHILDREN:	Four - grown
HOME:	Condominium
OCCUPATION:	Attorney
MEMBERSHIP NUMBER:	012-12345-67
TYPE OF MEMBERSHIP:	Governing Annual
ORIGINAL DATE:	October 1984
ORIGINAL SOURCE:	WN83
RENEWAL DATE:	February
AMOUNT OF DOLLARS:	$100.00
DATE OF LAST PAYMENT:	February 1986

```
OTHER NAME:                    Marwill Foundation

   ADDRESS:                    One First Bank Plaza
                               Seattle, Washington 98214

TYPE OF DONOR:
     ANNUAL                    December
     CAPITAL                   1986 - 1987 - 1988 Pledge
     PLANNED/DEFERRED          --

     MAILINGS:                 --
     CALLS:                    --
     VISITS:                   --
     BEQUEST:                  Yes
     TRUST:                    No
     ANNUITY:                  No
     ATTORNEY:                 Joseph Stocks, Stocks & Bond
     TRUST OFFICER:            Robert L. Quill, First Bank

HISTORY OF GIVING:

                          ACCT                            SOURCE CODE
     12-10-84             1126    Securities $ 1,000         DN42
      1-6-85              9312    Check      $   500         GF84
      3-10-86             9122    Check      $10,000         GF85


PLEDGE:    Total $ pledge.................: $30,000
           Payment cycle..................: annual
           $ per cycle/installment........: $10,000
           Total $ received...............: $10,000

TYPES OF GRANTS:

PROPOSAL DEADLINE:     June 30, December 30
```

WHAT HELP SHOULD YOUR RECORDS SYSTEM PROVIDE?

Analysis. The real gold in your records system is found when you use it to analyze the profile of your membership. With the right kind of profile data in hand, you can spot the rental lists that most closely match the profile of your own current members. Then you test those lists, observe the results, retest the best ZIP codes and use the response to upgrade your prospecting for new members. This technique works best for large organizations with lots of potential markets. But even on a smaller scale it can be helpful. Here are some pointers. In the United States, list compilers and marketers have broken down many ZIP codes into census tracts and even into blocks of houses. Knowing precisely where your present members live is a very strong clue to finding other prospects much like them. Although it's possible to make ZIP codes analyses manually, the computer gives the ultimate assistance. So make sure that your records system provides the best ZIP code information possible.

- Sex. Why is it important to know the sex of your members? Let's say you have determined that 72 percent of your members are women. If you get marginal results from testing a large and promising list, you might test mailing only to the women on the list and find a responsive, profitable market. In addition, offers of interest to women probably will be best received if you direct them just to the women on your own membership list. Usually the sex of a member is apparent by the title (Ms., Miss, etc.) they give in the application or by the first name. If the title is missing, there are computer programs that analyze first names and assign a sex and title (probably stumbling over the Shirleys, Leslies, and other unisexual names).

- Occupation. Finding out the occupations of your members is no problem for professional and trade associations, but it can be difficult for many others. Some groups have uncovered the information by asking a member to check a list or fill in a line on an annual dues statement. Many will cooperate if you give a logical reason for wanting to know (to help in planning programs, tours, etc.) But why do you really want to know the occupation? Here's why: If you find strong occupational patterns among your members, you can test compiled lists of people in such occupations or lists of subscribers to trade magazines serving those occupational fields.

- Age. Schools and colleges can guess at ages by knowing the year of graduation. But many other groups must discreetly ask members to identify which of several age brackets they fall into, as an aid in planning programs and activities. You don't usually need to know a person's exact age, just the bracket: 50-55, 55-60, etc.

- Source. Knowing how your member was enrolled (direct mail, list, counter sale, take-one, etc.) and the date of enrollment can help pinpoint the techniques that produce the most members and those members who renew for the longest periods. You can analyze your recruitment techniques and spot the ones that give the best return per dollar spent. It can be done manually, but it's much easier on a computer. If your member enrolled in response to a direct-mail promotion, be sure to identify the list in your source code. Knowing the enrollment date and list then allows you to rate lists by their renewal strength. As important as it is to know which lists made the most initial sales, it's the renewal record that is probably most important to you.

- Tenure. Once the original enrollment date is recorded, it's fairly easy to track the number of years a members has belonged. And the records systems should have ways of flagging members who reach the 5-, 10-, 20-, 25-year marks (overlooking occasional lapses). If you remind a member on the renewal statement that he or she has been a member for 10 years, and possibly award a small certificate for that, you can't miss boosting your renewal rate. Some auto clubs print your tenure on your membership card (''4 years member'') as a constant reminder of your loyalty. An organization can even plan special occasions to honor members when they reach significant anniversaries, just as college alumni groups hold special ceremonies to induct alumni into Half Century Clubs.

- Recency/frequency/monetary value. Your records system, of course, should record each dues transaction — the date, the amount of the dues, additional contributions, upgrading, etc. This is the equivalent of the "recency/frequency/monetary-value" record so dear to mail-order merchandisers. Remember, you're apt to get at least 80 percent of your money from 20 percent or less of your constituency. Your membership-records system should be able to tell you quickly who those major prospects are. If yours is a gift-supported organization with annual, capital, or planned gift opportunities, it's important to have a link between the membership records and the giving records.

Mailing and billing. The two main functional operations of a membership records system are addressing mail to the members and letting them know when it's time to pay their dues again. Both are easily accomplished on a computer system, but they can also be done efficiently manually.

Postage savings. Using bulk-rate, nonprofit and other discount postage rates can save thousands of dollars in even a small mailing. But to qualify for these rates, your records system must permit addressing according to Postal Service requirements. In the United States, the main requirement is that your labels emerge in ZIP-code order. It's relatively easy to do this on most computer systems and not too difficult with addressing systems using metal or paper plates.

WHEN SHOULD YOU GO ON COMPUTER?

It's necessary to have a records system with the needed information capacity, that's flexible, and that allows you to use the techniques described in this book. But these major objectives may or may not require a computer. If your membership program is relatively simple and there's no giving program connected with it, you may not need all of the sophistication a computer can give you. Some of the many questions you'll have to ask yourself before getting an in-house computer include these.

- Can you afford the cost of complex data collection? Can you staff such a system?

- Is the right software available for the computer system you plan to use? Or would you have to create your own programs?

- Can your proposed computer system expand to accommodate larger and more complex database information?

- Will the system give you ready access to the information you need? How quickly can you get the segmentation you need for analysis and renewal? Can it generate the reports you need?

- Will the system let you produce mailing labels, dues statements, receipts, and other types of acknowledgments? Will it be able to personalize your communications to your members?

- If you intend to test large mailing lists, can the proposed computer system use a merge/purge program to eliminate duplicates?

- Is the proposed computer system compatible with word processing equipment you may already own?

How long should you run parallel? Will you be switching from a manual system to a computer system? Anyone who has been through a "computer conversion" knows the danger of dropping the manual system too soon. Generally, it's a good idea to run the two systems parallel for at least a year, just to make sure that important information and historical data aren't lost.

Some large organizations have been known to keep metal plate addressing systems indefinitely for quick addressing of small special lists — boards of trustees, high classifications of members, etc.

" 'Will you walk a little faster?' said a whiting to a snail.
" 'There's a porpoise close behind us, and he's treading on my tail.' "
— SONG OF THE MOCK TURTLE
"ALICE'S ADVENTURES IN WONDERLAND"
BY LEWIS CARROLL

In the "Wonderland" of membership, there are often more snails than whiting or porpoises. Even in some of the largest and most progressive organizations, work on the membership program proceeds at a snail's pace until hard times require faster action. Just ask membership executives what holds them back, and you're likely to get two persistent complaints.

√ Boards and chief executive officers tend to have unrealistic expectations about immediate results and big dollars.

√ Membership promotion budgets are far too low to get the best and most profitable results.

15

These complaints are real and yet hard to comprehend in relation to what's at stake. The best way to counteract unreasonable expectations is to educate your leadership about the realities of membership acquisition. Get their attention by showing them what will happen to even the most profitable membership program if little is done to acquire and keep new members. Here are some tested ways to demonstrate this, step by step.

• Prepare a simple analysis of each prospecting effort based on the Allowable-Order-Cost Formula. This should impress those who are numbers-oriented, especially when the renewal pattern is strong.

• If your organization is gift-supported, at least twice a year do the following: Prepare a detailed accounting of additional annual giving, capital gifts, and planned gifts from your members. Often this income will be substantially greater than the dues income.

- Analyze all other types of the organization's income and total the amount attributable to your *members*. These may include such items as: store and catalog sales, convention and seminar fees, theater and other admissions, tour income, exhibitor fees, gifts in kind, etc.

When the dollar value of all of these income items from *members* is compared with your cause's total income, there will be few doubters (though there will always be someone with "a friend in direct mail" who still expects unreasonable response rates).

What is an adequate budget? With so many complaints from staff about inadequate budgets, there should be a simple answer about what is adequate. But the question is complicated by the wide variety of organizations that engage in membership solicitation. The only simple answer is that the membership promotion budget should be large enough to accomplish carefully planned membership growth goals realistically, while producing a significant long-term net income.

One guide is what others spend on membership promotion, and one source of this information is a publication called the Association Operating Ratio Report, which is published regularly by the American Society of Association Executives. This report shows that membership promotion costs can range from as low as less than 1 percent of the total budget to as high as 10 percent, with an average about 7 percent. This doesn't mean that anything within those ranges is optimum. It just means that organizations are surviving and possibly even growing by spending up to 10 percent of their total budget for membership promotion. In some cases, that may even be far too little to produce the optimum net profits.

The size of your membership promotion budget should be governed by a realistic appraisal of what must be done to meet your membership growth goals. What's a realistic goal? Well, in even the best and strongest organizations, normal attrition (deaths, address changes, etc.) will wipe out more than 20 percent of the membership in a year if nothing is done to replace lapsed members with new ones. So it's essential to keep moving forward, even in routine years, just to stay in the same place. When there's an annual growth goal of 10 percent, you're apt to hold your own and gain a little each year. Having such a goal assures you, at the minimum, the budget and sanction necessary to counter the effects of normal attrition and inflation. And attempting to increase total membership gives your group the subtle forward momentum that's necessary to keep it aggressive and vital. Now, here's how to translate all this into a budget.

Let's analyze the membership promotion budget requirements of an organization with a total membership of, say, 20,000 persons and a strong renewal rate of 80 percent. If it does nothing to acquire new members, it will lose 4,000 members the first year it stops promotion. If we assume that it wants to grow at the rate of 10 percent a year, it will have to acquire 4,000 new members to replace the lapsed members and 2,000 additional ones to meet the 10 percent growth goal: 6,000 new members in all.

Because of its strong appeal to a broad constituency, it has experienced a 1.6 percent response to previous promotion efforts. It uses direct mail and other forms of promotion, paying an average of $300 to reach each 1,000 prospects. With several classifications of memberships offered, it receives average dues of $25.

Here's what its promotion budget will look like.

Estimated expenses

New members to be acquired 6,000

Necessary total market to be reached
(6,000 divided by .016) 375,000

Promotion cost @ $300 per thousand .. $112,500

Estimated income

Dues income from 6,000 @ $25 each ... $150,000

Net profit, first-year dues ....$ 37,500

If the total budget of the organization is $750,000, the promotion budget of $112,500 is exactly 15 percent of the total budget, somewhat high by ASAE averages but necessary and entirely financially sound. When projected renewals are calculated in the Allowable Order-Cost Formula, the organization could afford to spend considerably more than 15 percent and still come out far ahead. If the response rate from the promotion drops below the usual 1.6 percent, there may even be a first-year loss (more common than a profit). But chances are the first-year loss will be relatively small and entirely recoverable and more than recovered in the first year of renewal.

When the prospect market is small and the dues are high, the cost-per-thousand of reaching the prospects may be more than double the example above — and the profits much larger.

In short, an organization must be prepared to budget enough for membership promotion to replace lapsed members and to grow at a realistic rate. If it doesn't, it will die swiftly of attrition.

PROFITABLE TRENDS, PRESENT AND FUTURE

Current trends can have very profitable effects on your membership program. But you've got to observe what's happening, plan accordingly, and test new offers constantly. Some trends will strengthen your current programs but cause other programs to wither. You've got to stay alert to keep growing — or more significantly to avoid waking up one morning to discover you've lost your constituency.

Here are some of the most important trends as I see them.

Older people are an expanding market.   By the year 2030, fully one-fifth of the American population will consist of men and women of the age 65 and older, according to the Census Bureau. Some prophets are estimating even higher: at least one-third by the end of this century. The biggest gains of all have been made in the 85-and-over group, up 165 percent in 22 years and likely to get much larger.

Although there are economic differences within the older groups, all have wants and needs that can be met through membership benefits and privileges — especially benefits that offer savings and convenience and relief from loneliness. There's a very strong "for me at last" attitude among many older people who've postponed their own gratifications until their nests are empty. In many cases, a sense of "entitlement" leads to expenditures far above past levels, even when retirement income is substantially lower.

If your membership attracts large numbers of older people, you may find outside organizations — businesses, for example — anxious to offer privileges to your members at no cost to your organization. Banks, hotels and insurance companies, eager to reach the older market, are glad to offer special discounts and other privileges to members of groups with predominantly older members. And these opportunities will grow, along with the percentage of active people over 65. Be alert and do some thinking about how your organization can take advantage of this truly significant trend.

At the same time, keep the needs of an aging population in mind. Be sure that all of your printed material is set in fairly large type (12 point or larger). Reverse printing (white type on a dark background) should be used sparingly and only for headlines and other large type. Keep these same guidelines in mind when you're preparing signs, descriptive labels for exhibits, and directions. If yours is the kind of institution that members will visit frequently, be sure you provide easy access for wheelchairs, motorized carts, and the slightly disabled persons who use walkers. Remember, too, that many older people are frightened by escalators and much prefer to use elevators. They are also frightened by lack of security, dangerous neighborhoods, isolated parking lots, etc. They often feel uneasy about leaving the safety of their homes at night. So do everything you can to make your events safe and easy to get to, preferably in daylight or via group transportation. Many people are reluctant to acknowledge this fear but will welcome everything you can do to eliminate it or at least minimize it by clearly having their safety in mind. True marketing means responding to all of the wants and needs of your customers or members. When you anticipate and provide for both their physical and psychological needs, you're apt to keep them close to you for many years.

More market research is being done. There will be more surveys and questionnaires of members' needs and wants, and better use will be made of the findings. Commercial market research techniques apply well to membership organizations. You can quickly find out what your members and prospects want by sending them carefully prepared questionnaires. One very complete survey is the Members' Needs Assessment Survey conducted by the Ceilings & Interior Systems Contractors Association. This eight-page questionnaire regularly generates a high rate of response (64 percent for one recent survey) and provides many insights to guide the Association's planned offerings to members. Through the survey, CISCA members have asked for more information and training in office automation, computerization, word processing, new products and techniques. Officials of CISCA use this information to plan future programs, publications, and conventions. Here's what the questionnaire looks like.

5. Would you like to serve as a committee chairman, committee member, CISCA officer, or CISCA board member?

    Yes [ ]   No [ ]

6. Have you or any of your firm's personnel attended any of the last five CISCA conventions? The last five conventions were in Toronto (1982), San Diego (1981), Miami Beach (1980), San Francisco (1979) and Dallas (1978).

    Yes [ ]   No [ ]

7. What was your company's total gross sales for the last full fiscal year?

    a. [ ] Up to $1,000,000
    b. [ ] $1,000,000 to $3,500,000
    c. [ ] Over $3,500,000

8. What is the total average number of employees in your firm for the last year?

    A - Salaried   B - Hourly (inlcude field personnel)

    a. 5 and under _____   a. 10 and under _____
    b. 5 - 10   _____   b. 10 - 20   _____
    c. 10 - 20   _____   c. 20 - 40   _____
    d. over 20   _____   d. over 40   _____

In the first section of the CISCA questionnaire, questions like these help classify the member firm by its size and the nature of its business. And question five helps spot future volunteer leadership.

PART A. BASIC IMPORTANCE OF CISCA PROGRAMS AND SERVICES

The items listed below describe some of the major services and benefits related to being a CISCA member. State your estimate of the value of each item, please circle any number between "5" and "1" (if you have "No Opinion", cirlce "0"). The HIGHER numbers should be used if a CISCA program or service is HIGHLY VALUABLE to you. The LOWER numbers should be used if a CISCA program or service is of LESS VALUE to you.

CISCA PROGRAMS & SERVICES	VALUABLE			LESS VALUABLE		NO OPINION
1. PUBLICATIONS						
a. Soundings Newsletter	5	4	3	2	1	0
b. INSIDE CONTRACTING Trade Journal	5	4	3	2	1	0
c. Membership Directory	5	4	3	2	1	0
d. Acoustical Ceilings - Use & Practice . . .	5	4	3	2	1	0
2. FINANCIAL STUDIES						
a. Cost-of-Doing-Business Study	5	4	3	2	1	0
b. Executive Compensation Study	5	4	3	2	1	0
					1	

PART B: GENERAL CHARACTERISTICS OF CISCA

DIRECTIONS: Please indicate the degree of your agreement or disagreement with each of the following statements about CISCA by circling any number between "5" and "1". The HIGHER numbers indicate stronger agreement. The LOWER numbers indiacte stronger disagreement. (If you have "No Opinion", circle "0".)

GENERAL CHARACTERISTICS	AGREE STRONGLY		DISAGREE STRONGLY			NO OPINION
1. Overall, CISCA's services and programs are worth the cost of my firm's dues to the association.	5	4	3	2	1	0
2. CISCA committees are effective in recommending programs and projects that fulfill the needs of most members.	5	4	3	2	1	0
3. CISCA is effective in helping to build business management expertise in my firm.	5	4	3	2	1	0
4. CISCA's meetings and seminar subjects are effective in fulfilling the educational needs of my company and its personnel.	5	4	3	2	1	0
5. In the future, training seminars and publications offered by other sources are likely to reduce my reliance on CISCA for those services.	5	4	3	2	1	0
6. The CISCA Board of Directors effectively represent the interests						

In section two, the questions in Part A pin down what the member sees to be the most significant membership benefits. And in Part B, the survey gauges the member's attitudes toward the organization, its benefits and its way of doing business.

PART C. APPLICABILITY OF VARIOUS POSSIBLE BUSINESS MANAGEMENT SUBJECTS

As you know, one of CISCA's major interests since the early 1970's is focused in the continuing education needs of its member companies and their personnel. Please read the list of business management subjects given below, and then evaluate each in terms of its applicability to the educational needs of the personnel in your company by circling the appropriate number. You may circle more than one number.

BUSINESS MANAGEMENT SUBJECTS	APPLICABLE TO:				
	SENIOR MANAGEMENT	MIDDLE MANAGEMENT	SALES PERSONNEL	SUPERINTENDENTS	NOT APPLICABLE TO ANY
1. Short-term financial analysis and planning	5	4	3	2	1
2. Long-term financial analysis and planning	5	4	3	2	1
3. Financial control	5	4	3	2	1
4. Accounting analyses	5	4	3	2	1
5. Budget techniques	5	4	3	2	1
6. Collection techniques	5	4	3	2	1

Here, the CISCA membership executives prospect to uncover what subjects will "sell" best as future benefits and to whom.

SECTION III - INDUSTRY ISSUES

As you assess the next three to five years, what major issues will confront CISCA member firms? Please evaluate the following issues by reading each potential industry issue carefully and please indicate if you agree or disagree with the statement by circling the appropriate number. Also indicate if you are uncertain or whether you have no opinion.

POTENTIAL INDUSTRY ISSUES	STRONGLY AGREE	AGREE	DISAGREE	STRONGLY DISAGREE	UNCERTAIN	NO OPINION
1. Many potential customers still do not recognize the value of the interior systems contractor and its services.	5	4	3	2	1	0
2. Segments of the general business and construction community consider interior systems contractors to be relatively unimportant parts of the subcontracting industry.	5	4	3	2	1	0

Section three is aimed at spotting major areas in which CISCA may help members in the future. Eighteen issues are surveyed in this section.

The final section, on page eight of the questionnaire, asks general questions requiring essay answers — just in case the multiple-choice questions have missed anything important. Other questions not shown are: why did you join CISCA, why do you retain your membership, and CISCA's worst shortcoming (or your biggest gripe) is...?

SECTION IV

The first three sections of this questionnaire were for statistical purposes limited in your ability to express your opinions more fully and in detail. Please use the following questions to express any other ideas not covered above.

The thing I like best about CISCA is _____
_____
_____
_____
_____

What should CISCA do that it is not presently doing? _____
_____
_____
_____

Membership market research done by the Friends of the Zoo at Audubon Park in New Orleans has determined that free admission and a members-only special admission gate on weekends and holidays rank at the top of their membership benefits and privileges. So, on the membership card itself and in all related publications and publicity, these two privileges are mentioned first. Friends of the Zoo has several thrusts to its market research program. It regularly surveys visitors as they exit. In addition, telephone surveys of members are directed to: persons who have been current members for at least six months, new members of six months or less, lapsed members, former members, etc.

Travel benefits will boom in popularity.   Tours for older people are growing fastest of all. In the United States, more than a third of the airline passengers are over age 60, and after the summer holidays, the highways are crowded with tour buses filled with older people. Many people join imaginative organizations just for the privilege of taking part in the group tours. So take a look at your opportunities to give your members travel that's tailored to their wants and needs.

Upscale memberships will increase.   If the benefits are attractive enough, price seems to be no problem. Test expensive benefits without fear. But also remember that you still have to offer plenty of choices at lower dues levels. One institution that received the largest gift in its history discovered that the donor was first attracted by a bargain membership offer. The very wealthy are often the thriftiest buyers.

Direct marketing will grow in importance.   Some of the largest and most effective membership organizations got that way through astute use of direct marketing techniques and the building of databases. Many started small but soon learned how to apply direct-marketing techniques to reach their goals for growth. In the future, you'll be increasingly concerned with such things as segmented lists, computer mail, telemarketing and credit cards. The AAA-Chicago Motor Club offers its members free credit cards and automatic payment of dues (they just show up on your credit card statement).

AAA CHICAGO MOTOR CLUB

ILLINOIS·INDIANA

* *

GREAT NEWS FOR AAA MEMBERS!

Your FREE AAA/VISA card and MasterCard are already approved

with a package of 10 BIG BENEFITS you
won't find with any other credit cards!

Even if you already have a VISA or MasterCard,
you'll want to have these, too. Read on to
find out why!!

* *

Dear Member,

I have reserved in your name a new kind of VISA and MasterCard. Like other
cards, they're good at hundreds of thousands of shops, restaurants, hotels,
airlines, banks, etc., in the U.S. and around the world. In fact, they are good
wherever a regular VISA and MasterCard are accepted.

But the AAA/VISA card and MasterCard are better. And they're FREE.

YOU GET 10 IMPORTANT BENEFITS!!!

1. They're free! There is no cost to get them, no annual fee and no
transaction charge. Did you know that many banks are now charging
up to $20.00 a year for VISA and MasterCard?

2. Your card is already approved. As a AAA member in good standing a
AAA/VISA card and MasterCard are reserved and waiting for you. No
long application and no credit investigation.

Sincerely,
CHICAGO MOTOR CLUB

C. G. Keller

C. G. Keller
Membership Enrollment

P.S. I'll be surprised if you decide not to take us up on this offer. But if
you don't want your cards and the additional line of credit, please return
the Reservation Certificate anyway, with the "NO" sticker on it, so I can
take your name off the reserved list.

Your prompt response will be very helpful and appreciated. If you have any
questions about AAA/VISA please call us at 1-800-THE-CLUB or (312) 372-1818
or your local office.

Purdue National Bank, Lafayette, IN, is the owner and issuer of the AAA/VISA Card and MasterCard.

Computerization will leap ahead.   For all of its explosive growth in the past several decades, the computer and its new, easier uses will continue to have profound effects on membership organizations. As your membership expands, the computer will ease your problems and open new opportunities for stronger and better cultivation of your prospects and members. You owe it to yourself and your organization to stay posted.

More catalogs and merchandise will be offered.   Museums once were the leaders among membership organizations offering catalogs and special merchandise to their members. But then public television stations and even colleges and universities started sending out catalogs offering tote bags, T-shirts, and other items bearing the cause's insignia. What's especially wonderful about the right kind of merchandise offers is that they enable you to reach interested markets that are far away and have no earlier relationship with your cause. Mystic Seaport, for example, has a line of attractive and often expensive merchandise related to the sea and of interest to everyone who sails or owns a boat.

If you take a good look at your opportunities and potential markets, you may find that a catalog and special merchandise could represent important future profit centers for you, especially if you can offer substantial discounts to your members.

More insurance and investment opportunities.   One famous fortune was based on the observation of an astute insurance man that medical doctors (of all people) then had no group hospital insurance available to them. Possibly some of your members have similar, unmet needs that you can offer as membership benefits — at no cost to your organization. As investment opportunities have become more sophisticated, some organizations even have offered their members a variety of funds they can invest in by mail. The whole financial services universe is changing rapidly and offers increasing potential benefits to membership organizations.

More newsletters and technical publications.   People are hungry for information. And you can readily collect and deliver it to them. Members of trade associations want to know how much it costs other members to do business, how much they pay their executives, how to estimate jobs, etc. They're even willing to pay extra for technical studies you publish and will readily send you orders for professional books you recommend.

Social events for members will increase.   As older members lose friends who move away or die, they welcome opportunities to go to social events and meet other people like themselves. The foresighted organization that provides such events (after careful studies of the members' wants and convenience) will attract many new friends. Once again, be aware always that loneliness is a major motivation for membership. As Irish novelist Edna O'Brien observes: "I think people join clubs and go to parties to keep at bay the beasts of loneliness. . . I think it is a longing for absolutes, for God, a spiritual loneliness."

Adult education will grow as a benefit.   The Chicago Council on Foreign Relations built a whole new market for its membership. It tested new adult education classes designed to attract the attention of those who had originally joined for travel benefits. These people had begun to lose interest when tour privileges became less unique. Professional membership organizations usually offer many different seminars, often holding them in several cities near concentrations of membership. A smashing success in the United States called Elderhostel offers a wide variety of adult education courses on college campuses during the summer and other academic slow times. The courses provide older people with an interesting low-cost vacation as well as the opportunity to learn, and the colleges are delighted to have the extra income.

In another variation, an arts center found that enrollment in some of its most popular classes far exceeded its physical facilities. Officials approached a nearby junior college that made light use of its facilities in the evenings. The college gladly rented classrooms at low cost and eventually asked the arts center to provide classes for its own students. Interest in the crafts provides many opportunities. The National Carvers Museum, through excellent marketing techniques, has built a strong national membership by offering instruction and equipment. Another form of adult education is the preparation of instructional videocassettes for distribution to members.

Test classes, seminars, and other types of educational benefits of your own. Not all of them will succeed, but that's what testing is all about.

People want recognition.   Plaques, published honor rolls, certificates, and other recognition devices will become more important as competition increases. Many suppliers of recognition devices now exhibit at fund-raising and marketing conventions. Make it your business to find out what they have to offer.

Accountability will be stressed.   Major donors and foundations are increasingly concerned with how well your organization is being run. The alert organization executive must be prepared to offer documented evidence showing how well he or she is promoting membership, often the source of 75 percent or more of a group's total income. Good managers take calculated risks and move quickly to test new offers and ideas. They reject perfectionism in the interests of good timing and aggressive action. They always have time for thorough planning, they have clear goals, and they reject complacency.

THE MEMBERSHIP MYSTIQUE

Membership is much more than a group of people banded together to accomplish some goal or to meet some need. Yes, there's order and sociability, but there's also a kind of binding spirit that transcends the matter-of-fact mechanics of forming an organization and carrying out objectives.

Some have said that membership is a fine example of synergism — that action in which the total effect is greater than the sum of the parts taken separately. Yes, it's that, but it's still more. It's difficult to explain the bond of membership and its ability to work what often seem to be miracles. What's important is to know that it does work, and that it richly deserves all of the attention and investment needed to bring about its miracles.

Those who would forecast the future in business and in culture would do well to study what new organizations are being formed and in what magnitude. The quiet rise of such oddities as foreign car clubs long preceded a strong trend toward foreign cars as an important segment of the American automobile market. And how about computer clubs? Many were formed long before the impact of the personal computer hit many households or offices.

Find new clubs being formed, and you'll have advance notice of major cultural changes and new demands in the consumer market.

IT'S UP TO YOU

By now you're armed with everything you need to know about making your membership program the best and strongest it can possibly be.

You know what you want your organization to be, now and (in progressive steps) for the next five years, ten years, and beyond. You know how to develop membership benefits and privileges that meet the wants and needs of the key segments in the broad market you plan to approach. And best of all, you know how to frame an offer and put it before each person in every segment of your market. You can measure the results of each promotion and plan your budget accordingly.

When your plans are ready for action, consider hiring an experienced consultant to review them and to help you fine-tune your program. It's also a good idea to bring the consultant back at least once a year to audit your results and to make recommendations for improving your performance. Successful businesses do just that — and you're in a very competitive business.

You have so many things going for you. There's an amazing amount of latent interest. It needs only your professional ability to strike a spark and fan it into flame. As John Updike observes, we welcome almost any interruption of dullness. Make your interruption the one that *commands* attention. Then make your attention-getter attractive and easy to order. At every step, say *thank you* as warmly and frequently as you can. Listen to what your members are saying, by word and deed, about your programs and services. See how your benefits meet your members' needs — or fall short.

How well your organization moves forward is up to you. Some of the most successful membership groups begin as a vision of a determined man or woman who sees in the membership mystique a way of accomplishing hopes and dreams and then moves mountains to make that membership bloom. *You* can be that person. You may never get the recognition you deserve for your efforts, but when it's all over, you'll have the warm glow that comes from knowing how much good you helped to bring about.

As said in the famous eulogy to the British architect Sir Christopher Wren, if you would see your memorial, look about you.